Look Forward®
Beyond Lean and Six Sigma

A Self-Perpetuating Enterprise Improvement Method

by Robert Dirgo

CO-PUBLISHED WITH THE
INSTITUTE OF AEROSPACE EXCELLENCE®

Copyright ©2006 by Aircraft Braking Systems Corporation

ISBN 1-932159-46-0

Printed and bound in the U.S.A. Printed on acid-free paper
10 9 8 7 6 5 4 3 2 1

Library of Congress Cataloging-in-Publication Data

Dirgo, Robert.
  Look forward beyond lean and Six Sigma / by Robert Dirgo.
    p. cm.
  Includes bibliographical references and index.
  ISBN 1-932159-46-0 (hardback : alk. paper)
  1. Total quality management. 2. Six sigma (Quality control standard). 3.
Theory of constraints (Management). 4. Total quality control. 5.
Leadership. 6. Industrial management. I. Title.
  HD62.15.D57 2005
  658.4′013—dc22   2005011210

    Direct all inquiries to J. Ross Publishing, Inc., 5765 North Andrews Way, Fort Lauderdale, Florida 33309.

Phone: (954) 727-9333
Fax: (561) 892-0700
Web: www.jrosspub.com

TABLE OF CONTENTS

FOREWORD

TQM, quality circles, kaizen, SPC, PDCA, Lean, Six Sigma…the list goes on and on. Quality improvement tools and methodologies have been around for a long time. Their roots go back to the early days of Shewhart, Deming, Juran, and others during World War II. Further, as quality systems have evolved over the years, these tools, and quality improvement in general, are no longer limited to product quality alone. Today, most business leaders are at least familiar with these tools. They have a basic understanding that these tools are applicable to the broader scope of process improvement. Some companies have had great success using these and other tools. Many others have used some of them with a certain level of success, but have found that they failed or became "flavor of the month" despite top management support. Why? Many of the tools and methodologies have common elements and themes in their approaches. Are the tools bad or the methodologies flawed? No. On the contrary, when any of these tools is applied properly in an appropriate application, great benefits can be realized. In fact, a few chapters in this book are dedicated to some of these tools and methodologies, including Lean, Six Sigma, and Theory of Constraints.

This book describes why some initiatives fail or become "flavor of the month." It describes a home-grown continuous improvement approach used by an aerospace wheel and brake manufacturer. It is an approach that recognizes that Lean and Six Sigma are valuable assets in a continuous improvement tool belt, but using "too big" a tool can be a mistake. It is an approach that believes that for an organization to label itself as strictly a Lean or Six Sigma company is a mistake. Being a company that is dedicated to continuous improvement and employs the best tool available for a given application is better. It is an approach that emphasizes the measurable improvement gained, not how many black belts you have. It is an approach that at its core is based on instilling a shared ownership of important business metrics at the individual employee level. It is an approach that believes that employees should have allegiance to the process in which they work first and their department second. It is an approach that recognizes that management must support and coach the team and individuals involved in the process, but also knows that much of the time management just needs to get out of the way. It is an approach that our company has used in the manufacturing environment for years and is now expanding into other business processes. It is an approach that we feel is key to us strategically. It is an approach called Look Forward®.

Our company is not perfect. We realize that the continuous improvement road is just that — continuous. We recognize that there is always an opportunity for improvement just around the corner. We feel that Look Forward® is key to our future success. It is our hope that a piece of it might work for you as well.

J. Mark Graham, Director
Quality Assurance & Manufacturing Engineering
Aircraft Braking Systems Corporation

PREFACE

For those who are interested in achieving excellence in business and continuously improving their processes, it is tough to even imagine doing so without the Lean, Six Sigma, and Theory of Constraints tools, although it really has not been very long that these tools have been available to us. Lean manufacturing was popularized in the United States by Jim Womack, Daniel Jones, and Daniel Roos in the book entitled *The Machine That Changed the World,* which was based on their study of the Toyota Production System. That was 1990 — a mere 15 years ago.

Six Sigma was the brainchild of Bill Smith, an engineer at Motorola. In 1986, he introduced it as a way to standardize how defects were counted. Over the past 19 years, Six Sigma has been adopted by many companies as an essential element to their business strategy. Motorola won the Malcolm Baldrige Award largely due to its Six Sigma corporate philosophy, and General Electric became one of Six Sigma's strongest proponents under the leadership of Jack Welch.

Theory of Constraints, although perhaps not as popular as Lean or Six Sigma, is no less beneficial to a company embracing continuous improvement. It was first introduced to the world by physicist and author Dr. Eliyahu M. Goldratt in his novel entitled *The Goal.* Initially published in 1986, *The Goal* is a nontraditional continuous improvement book that communicates the method through the descriptive operations of a fictional company. This novel has been extremely popular, selling over three million copies, and has been the thrust behind many a company's decision to adopt Theory of Constraints in its operations strategy.

Choosing from this menu of continuous improvement methods is similar to going to a fine restaurant and having to decide between the filet mignon, fettuccine Alfredo, and grilled salmon. All of these dishes are delicious, and each has its unique flair. The meat eater who likes a good steak and has no issues with red meat may select the filet mignon. The vegetarian who passes on meat and fish may select the fettuccini Alfredo. Finally, there are those who are neither vegetarians nor red meat eaters. The grilled salmon is probably the meal of choice for this group. All of the meals are excellent in their own right, but seem to be most appropriate for a particular clientele. Someone who is a red meat eater today, however, could become a vegetarian a year from now, because people are dynamic, ever-changing, and adapting to the environment around them.

So it is with a business. A business is not static, but rather a living entity that should be ever-evolving, and changing as appropriate, to maximize its potential in an ever-changing market. The challenge for any business is to have a clear understanding of the health of the organization and be able to apply those preemptive measures that will ensure continued vitality. In some areas of the organization, Six Sigma is the best choice and in others Lean is. Also, similar to the diet analogy, applying Six Sigma today in a particular area of the business may not be appropriate tomorrow. Maybe Lean will be more appropriate. The key is to know what will optimize the health of the organization.

That is where this book comes in. It describes a management approach that has been successful in keeping its pulse on the health of the organization and infusing appropriate doses of continuous improvement methodology in order to thrive in a challenging environment.

This book introduces the Look Forward® approach to continual improvement. Its objective is to ensure that continual improvement is self-perpetuating, ever-evolving, and — continuous — without the need for intervention.

Look Forward® is a management approach to continual improvement which fosters an environment that infuses continuous improvement into the very fabric of the business operations. As a result, improvement is not an initiative or a project, but rather a naturally occurring event that is anticipated, expected, and prevalent.

The Look Forward® method was developed in the aerospace industry at Aircraft Braking Systems Corporation, an aircraft wheel and brake supplier headquartered in Akron, Ohio. Its beginnings date back to 1996, and the impact it has had on its founding company's improvement has been impressive.

Look Forward® is not a substitute for Six Sigma, Lean, or Theory of Constraints, but rather a necessary complement to each of these in order to ensure self-perpetuating improvement that is ingrained in the corporate culture. Look Forward® in turn needs Six Sigma, Lean, and Theory of Constraints to be the fuel for the continual improvement engine that drives a company forward.

Any business serious about improvement will consider Six Sigma, Lean, and Theory of Constraints in the overall scope of its operations and the unique benefits each brings to the table. The uniqueness of each of these methods will be addressed in Chapters 3 through 5. Since so much already has been written about these methods, I will not delve deeply into any of them, but rather will provide a general introduction.

The reader will be introduced to various aspects of the Look Forward® management approach in Chapters 6 through 10. Since Look Forward® was developed in an aerospace environment, this book has an aerospace flavor to its presentation. However, Look Forward® is not an "aerospace" management approach, but rather a business management approach that has been proven successful in aerospace and can be effective in any industry.

This book proposes that for sustained improvement, Six Sigma, Lean, and Theory of Constraints need to be intertwined with Look Forward®. On their own, each of these is strong, but a business that successfully integrates them together becomes unbeatable.

Robert T. Dirgo

DEDICATION

This book is dedicated to the Aircraft Braking Systems Corporation (ABSC) "past, present, and future" Look Forward® team members. The success of the Look Forward® approach at ABSC is a tribute to their talent, initiative, and creative abilities.

ACKNOWLEDGMENTS

I want to give special acknowledgment to Todd Figard, Bruce Feeney, Gary Svoboda, Aaron Bradford, and Terry Bilas of the Institute of Aerospace Excellence®. Their talent, initiative, and hard work have contributed significantly to making this book possible.

ABOUT THE AUTHOR

 **Robert T. Dirgo** has 25 years of experience working in industry. His career began in the steel industry and as a supplier to the automotive, commercial manufacturing, and oil industries. He worked in machine design and was responsible for project management of the design, build, and installation of new machines.

During the past 22 years, he has held a variety of positions in the aerospace industry, the last 14 in a managerial role. He has been responsible for the management of quality systems, quality audits, quality projects, customer-focused quality, and supplier management.

In his current position as manager of process quality assurance, he is responsible for the management of the continuous improvement cross-functional teams from a middle management perspective. As one of the overseers of the continuous improvement effort, he was also one of the original management members that developed the Look Forward® management method in 1996. He was also the quality project lead for the corporation's implementation of the enterprise resource planning business process solution, SAP.

Mr. Dirgo has fostered a discipline for research and analysis over the years through his academic pursuits. He holds a bachelor's degree in mechanical engineering, a master's degree in statistics, and completed additional graduate course work toward a Ph.D. in operations research and a second master's degree in community counseling.

His demonstrated proficiency in the quality sciences resulted in his being recognized as certified by the American Society of Quality as a Certified Six Sigma Black Belt, a Certified Quality Engineer, and a Certified Quality Auditor. In addition, he successfully completed the Lean Office Certificate Program at the University of Michigan.

An established author who published his first book in 2001, he is also president and founder of the all-volunteer nonprofit corporation Gennesaret, Inc., headquartered in Akron, Ohio. For his efforts with this nonprofit corporation, he was named Ohio Outstanding Volunteer Administrator for Public or Private Non Profit Organizations in 1996, received the JC Penney Golden Rule Award in 1994, was nominated for the President of the United States Service Award in 1995, and was nominated for the National Ernst & Young Entrepreneur of the Year Award in 1996.

The author resides in a suburb of Cleveland, Ohio with his wife, Mary. He can be contacted at rtdirgo@aircraftbraking.com.

Web Added Value

Free value-added materials available from
the Download Resource Center at www.jrosspub.com

At J. Ross Publishing we are committed to providing today's professional with practical, hands-on tools that enhance the learning experience and give readers an opportunity to apply what they have learned. That is why we offer free ancillary materials available for download on this book and all participating Web Added Value™ publications. These online resources may include interactive versions of material that appears in the book or supplemental templates, worksheets, models, plans, case studies, proposals, spreadsheets and assessment tools, among other things. Whenever you see the WAV™ symbol in any of our publications, it means bonus materials accompany the book and are available from the Web Added Value Download Resource Center at www.jrosspub.com.

Downloads available for _Look Forward® Beyond Lean and Six Sigma: A Self-Perpetuating Enterprise Improvement Method_ consist of slides that provide a valuable overview of Lean, Six Sigma, Theory of Constraints, and the Look Forward® continuous improvement method, as well as a glossary of important terms.

Look Forward®

An approach used for the management of a corporation's continuous improvement program, with the objective of fostering an improvement culture that is self-perpetuating, ever-evolving, and continuously improving without the need for intervention.

Look Forward® facilitates the integration of existing continuous improvement tools like Lean, Six Sigma, and Theory of Constraints within a process-driven cross-functional team environment. These permanent teams are accountable for all activities of their commodity or process across the supply and demand chains. This accountability is evaluated through performance to metrics that are key to the business objectives.

PART 1.
CHARACTERISTICS THAT
AFFECT IMPROVEMENT

HOW TO MANAGE THE BUSINESS OF IMPROVEMENT

As one of the leaders in your company, you are charged with the responsibility and accountability for establishing how the company will be better this time next year. Now, you may be thinking to yourself, "He's wrong there. That's not my responsibility; that's the quality director's role, along with the quality assurance managers." Or maybe your company has a designated focal point for improvement initiatives in the form of a vice president of Lean or a change management director. Maybe you are thinking that person is obviously responsible and accountable for establishing how the company will be better next year.

If that is what you are thinking, then you need to change your thinking fast. Anyone in a leadership role in any company should be constantly looking for ways to do things faster, cheaper, better, and smarter. You do not have the luxury of delegating the responsibility for improvement to someone else who may have a title that seems to be associated with improvement.

So how much better will your company be next year? If your company has a mature continuous improvement program in place, you are going to evaluate where you are and what improvement projects are planned and come up with a pretty good forecast of how much better you will be next year. You are in the driver's seat, and you have an updated map that will guide you to your destination.

If you have picked up this book to read, chances are you have had some association with the business of continuous improvement. It has been around forever and is part of any industry. How it is packaged may be slightly different depending on the industry you are in, but the core of what is inside is basically the same. The objectives are obviously the same — to do what you do better, cheaper, and faster.

This book begins by taking a look at the packaging of various continuous improvement initiatives within a few different industries. Once we have peeled away the packaging, we can take a peek at what is inside and how those initiatives compare from industry to industry.

The industries we will examine are automotive, aerospace, and electronic equipment (i.e., computers, cell phones, etc.). They will provide a diverse representation of approaches and allow us to evaluate the strengths of each. Much of the information in this chapter is based on my personal visits to and/or interviews conducted with leading management within the organizations presented. Let's start with the automotive industry.

AUTOMOTIVE

Probably one of the most predominant implementers of the continuous improvement tools is the automotive industry. It has accelerated its utilization of Lean and/or Six Sigma due to the aggressive nature of the competition in the automotive business sector. The Toyota Production System is a model example of Lean implementation. However, some of the techniques that are at the heart of it were first used at the Ford Motor Company's Highland Park facility way back in 1913. Henry Ford documented these techniques in his 1926 book entitled *Today and Tomorrow*[2] (recently rereleased by Productivity Press).

Let's take a closer look at some of the characteristics of the Toyota Production System as well as some of the other leading automakers, to see what they are doing in regard to continuous improvement.

Toyota

The Toyota Production System Is a Lifestyle

On November 5, 2004, I and several of my associates had the pleasure of visiting Toyota Motor Manufacturing, Kentucky, Inc. (TMMK). The purpose of the visit was to gain some insight into the Toyota Production System (TPS) and what the current state of improvement was at this facility. The driving force behind improvement at Toyota is TPS and not just the application of some of the improvement tools. Granted, the Lean tools are most certainly used abundantly, but the formal application of Six Sigma and Theory of Constraints is not a part of the improvement focus.

By the end of our visit to this facility, it became clear to all of us that TPS is much more than the application of Lean tools. *"TPS is a lifestyle,"* as we were told by Wil James, vice president of manufacturing at TMMK. It is not a quantitative entity that is easily described and understood by those trying to model TPS in their own facilities. It is ingrained into every aspect of the organization, from janitorial services to executive management. It truly is part of the DNA of Toyota. From my perspective, it was apparent that everyone was in concert in regard to how improvement was to be pursued. There are no competing interests in how improvement should be pursued. Operations does not have one mind-set and engineering another. The team members working on the line do not think that things should be done one way and administration another. Everyone is singing the same tune in a harmonious fashion. Improvement is spoken daily by engineering, management, janitorial services, etc. Improvement is an expected way of life. The performance metrics achieved by this company make it the envy of a majority of other businesses. One might think that this success would breed a certain amount of smugness and cockiness toward Toyota outsiders. Our experience was entirely the opposite. Instead of meeting with one of the world leaders in its industry, you would think that we were meeting with a young start-up company scratching and clawing to get ahead. A quiet humility and respectful spirit emanated from everyone we encountered. Clearly, it is this spirit of humility that permits them not to get too caught up in yesterday's success but rather seek out today's improvement.

Oftentimes, our human nature instills within us a desire to be recognized for our successes, and we should be. Humility enables us to receive this recognition without getting too big a head. In addition, it plays an additional key function in the human interaction dynamic. It allows us to receive suggestions on how our successful accomplishments could be improved upon, without becoming defensive or angry. It is this aspect of humility that seems to permeate the culture of Toyota and supports an ongoing evaluation and improvement of every aspect of the organization. This type of philosophy, combined with a knowledge of the Lean tools throughout the company, provides the necessary support mechanisms to sustain improvement.

TPS is not management driven. It depends upon an empowered workforce that is motivated to make changes that will benefit the company. Those who are closest to the process are in the best position to understand and develop improvement ideas. Therefore, management encourages all team members to participate in quality circles and the company suggestion program. Every employee is allocated one hour a week for participation within a quality circle. Oftentimes, a quality circle topic will be cross-process oriented, where one or more members from one team will meet with one or more members of another team to solve a mutually shared problem.

All employees are encouraged to share in the company's suggestion program, and many do. The incentive for participation is a financial reward that is determined by the benefit realized from the suggestion. Suggestion rewards can range from $20 to $25,000. We saw a $25,000 suggestion in action while we were there: an automated parts mover that was guided by a magnetic strip in the floor. An electric eye in the front detected anything in its way, and it played a catchy musical tune to let you know it was coming.

Problem solving at Toyota is not limited to quality circles and the suggestion program. Kaizen blitzes are focused on intense activities that address a known problem and may or may not be organized by management. In the Operational Development Group, members from management are assigned to TPS training for a two-year period, during which they are constantly working on problems and issues using the Lean tools within the TPS context.

These employee involvement activities illustrate the empowerment that exists at TMMK, which happens to be a nonunion facility. I was curious about how the TPS principles were applied at a union facility, so I asked Gary Convis, president of TMMK, what his experience at New United Motor Manufacturing, Inc. (NUMMI) was. NUMMI is a collaborative effort between Toyota and General Motors that was initiated in 1984. Mr. Convis joined NUMMI in 1984 as the plant general manager, responsible for manufacturing operations and personnel. In 1987, he assumed the responsibilities of vice president of manufacturing, in 1994 became a senior vice president, and in 1997 was made executive vice president. He said: "When implemented properly, TPS always makes the team members' job simpler, easier, and ergonomically safer. It also makes the work more productive by exposing and reducing nonvalue-added work. All team members, including union, must understand and proactively participate in the process. Nobody is isolated from global competition, so survival requires such cooperation. Management must share facts and related information openly and act in an ongoing team-building way whenever possible."

TPS at TMMK is a journey. It is the endless pursuit of the elimination of waste, constantly striving to come up with new ways to identify waste and improve the *level of the eye*. In essence, it is the inbred desire to continuously strive to be smarter about the business so that your ability to "see" wasteful activities improves. Things that may have been unrecognizable a year ago may now be glaringly obvious. This ability to "see" waste is affected by multiple factors: knowledge of the process, knowledge of the Lean tools, knowledge of motion and people. In an attempt to ensure that all team members have 20/20 vision when it comes to "seeing" waste, Toyota has a dedication to continuous learning and fostering a learning environment. One example of this is the Operational Development Group. Another is the on-site training center, which prepares team members for job advancement and enables them to take college courses offered on-site by several colleges and universities. Typically, an assembly line team member will go through a 13-week training program before being released to work on a particular job on his or her own. What is interesting is that in addition to this training, team members assigned to line positions also benefit from two weeks of physical training given at Toyota's on-site fitness facility. Working on the line is a physically demanding activity, and Toyota views these members as "industrial athletes." All athletes want to optimize their conditioning in order to perform to their maximum capability. At Toyota, they can and they do.

The underlying philosophy of TPS is fairly static. It provides the support structure within which the improvement activities are executed. It is these activities that are dynamic and may change to some degree as a greater awareness of the processes is gained. At Toyota, these activities surely will involve the application of various Lean tools. It was my impression that the "big-bang" type of improvements that make a good headline were not predominant within Toyota (i.e., company X saves millions of dollars applying continuous improvement tool Z throughout its operations). Rather, it is the incremental daily changes which provide ongoing benefits that are viewed as having the most effective impact on improving corporate performance. This is not to say that "big-bang" improvements are nonexistent, but just that they are not viewed as the most significant aspect of TPS.

One issue most companies that are mature in their improvement efforts seem to run into is the challenge of sustaining that effort once the low-hanging fruit is gone. I was curious to hear what Mr. James thought about this challenge at Toyota, so I asked him how improvement is sustained at TMMK. I found his answer quite interesting. He said that the low-hanging fruit never goes away. It is always there. The problem is that sometimes it becomes harder to see it. Hence the emphasis on empowering all the team members with the ability to "see" waste or the low-hanging fruit. He said that some of the issues being addressed today are no different than those dealt with 16 years ago. Many are forms of waste of motion. It is how the motion is viewed that has changed. They have become smarter about how the motion can be changed and are able to "see" wasteful activity previously undetected. Some of this could be due to forms of automation that are now available or perhaps even ergonomic considerations previously unrecognized.

Clearly, the core of the TPS success at TMMK is the 10,000 people who execute its philosophy day in and day out. The team members who have bought into the Toyota philosophy are directly responsible for its success. More than 600,000 suggestions from team members have been implemented since production began a short 16 years ago. The perfect attendance rate of team members is 60%.

Those with perfect attendance are eligible for various raffles throughout the year. Prizes include gift certificates to various merchants, and each and every year 15 people with perfect attendance win a brand new Camry. Now that is an incentive to show up each day! In addition, once a year the company throws a bash for everyone with perfect attendance, and the star of the show is a big-name performer like David Copperfield, Bill Cosby, or the band Alabama.

People seem to enjoy working at TMMK. Certainly the raffles and various activities have something to do with it, as do receiving a fair wage and the empowerment each team member has in his or her job. At each workstation, there is an andon cord that team members can pull if for some reason they are unable to perform their job function in the designated takt time. When we visited, the takt time at TMMK was 55 seconds. Every 55 seconds a new car rolled off the line. Therefore, the various tasks for assembling an automobile along the assembly line are segmented into 55-second activities. At each of these stations, team members have 55 seconds to perform their job function. If someone does not feel they can perform their function, for whatever reason, they pull the andon cord. This lights up a visible sign to indicate that the team member has a problem. The team leader is thus alerted of the problem and goes to the workstation to see if it can be resolved in the 55-second window available for performing the task. If it cannot, the team leader stops the line. The andon cords are pulled an average of 5000 times a day at TMMK, and the line is stopped an average of 200 times a day. This illustrates the point that the team members feel empowered to stop the line because something is not right. While 5000 times a day seems astronomical and my initial thought was that everything should be done to lower this number, that is not the case at TMMK. With the continuous learning environment and empowered workforce, pulling the andon cord is encouraged, and the number of times it is pulled is not an issue. In fact, the view is that the more the cord is pulled, the better off TMMK will be because a quality issue is being addressed at the point of discovery. What seems crazy is wanting to let something go by and not bring attention to an issue that needs to be addressed.

Since employees enjoy working there so much, they tend to want to stay longer. This longevity provides a stable workforce that promotes a sense of continuity in any continuous improvement effort, thereby improving overall effectiveness.

I asked Mr. James to identify three primary ways that TMMK promoted longevity in the tenure of its team members. He said that, first and foremost, all employees are treated with respect. This respect is manifested in the personal relations between people and in the job assignments that are given. TMMK tries to use the team members' brains and not their brawn. In addition, there is a constant effort to tax each team member with TPS problem solving. This is a welcome challenge to the employees that enables them to stretch beyond what they thought themselves capable of. It is a sign of respect and results in inspiring the team members to excel.

Second, the expected quality of the product being produced is something that all team members are proud of. People feel good about making one of the best products in the world.

Third, people feel good about being associated with a winner. Beyond the quality level of the product, the company has proven excellence in multiple fronts. Everyone likes to be associated with a winner.

The benefit of an empowered workforce that sticks around is the continuous pursuit of perfection and a continuous improvement in the ability to "see" opportunities for improvement.

TPS is clearly a holistic management system that fosters an environment within which improvement activities are expected and flourish. It draws upon the improvement tools of Lean as the instrument for executing the reduction of waste. It provides a framework to work within and depends upon the creativity and inspiration of all team members for its success. It promotes the "just do it" mentality and not getting bogged down with unnecessary encumbrances. That is exactly what is being done at TMMK, and the state of improvement at this facility is continuous.

Next let's look at some of the improvement activities that are taking place at the DaimlerChrysler Corporation.

DaimlerChrysler

An Energized Workforce Is a Powerful Improvement Tool

The objective of any continuous improvement program or production system is to foster a climate that promotes the empowerment of the workforce. This is the Holy Grail of continuous improvement. How it is achieved is not necessarily the same from company to company, due to all of the unique factors that need to be considered when trying to create this climate. These factors include the corporate culture, the regional culture, the corporate personality, the host of personalities represented in the workforce, whether or not there is a union in the facility, the company's history...the list goes on and on. With all the factors that impact successful empowerment of the workforce, it's a wonder it is even possible. One thing that is clear is that there is not a cookie-cutter solution that can be easily applied to any factory. Truly achieving empowerment requires a clear understanding of all the unique factors that impact the facility and a common vision by all of those in leadership. But when it is achieved, it is as if you have reached utopia compared to functioning in a nonempowered work environment. This is true from both a labor and management viewpoint.

Management is happy because employees own the work within their world and are proactively engaged in problem resolution. The workforce is happy because people are in control of their own destiny and can take more pride in their work because they have been given control.

This is the culture I found to exist during my visit to the Chrysler Group's North Assembly Plant in Toledo, Ohio. It is a state-of-the-art facility where Lean manufacturing, Six Sigma, and Theory of Constraints are used throughout to achieve improvement. Improvement initiatives seem to have been successfully integrated into the culture such that they appear to be a part of the natural rhythm of the factory. A significant amount of effort has been invested in developing people in a manner that supports the corporate culture. The Toledo plant operates under DaimlerChrysler's overriding operating principles and customizes its management system to its unique culture.

The DaimlerChrysler operating principles represent the way the company does business and maintains its Lean Extended Enterprise system. It begins with core values and beliefs, the philosophical principles from which decisions are made. From there, the system analyzes the "how," identifying the enablers and subsystems needed to execute the work (such as workforce levels, balanced schedules, value-added activities, and robust processes). It then identifies ways to support those processes, tools for implementation, and standardized measurements to gauge effectiveness.

The operating principles give employees at the plant the "big picture" framework from which to operate, while at the same time providing standardized methods and repeatable processes. The end result can be tracked and improved by focusing on safety, quality, delivery, cost, and morale — internal gauges to which each employee contributes. Because continuous improvement is one of the core beliefs, the process never stops.

This was clear to me when I had the pleasure of talking with Tom Hall, team leader at the Toledo North Assembly Plant. He shared with me a little about what his role as a team leader consisted of and what drove his behavior. Our discussion took place in front of a large movable board that was full of sheets of paper that represented all of the metrics his team was accountable for. What was interesting was that many of the global corporate metrics were listed on this board and updated daily. The corporate objectives were being reinforced at the factory floor level, where they are impacted the most.

Mr. Hall has a meeting with all of his team members every morning, and they review their performance metrics. Quality, for example, had a team goal of 95%, but team members' efforts have enabled them to consistently beat that goal. The goal now is 100%. Beyond just meeting prescribed objectives, the most impressive aspect of my interview with Mr. Hall was Mr. Hall himself. He exhibited a level of passion and excitement about his team members and his role as a team leader that was inspiring. Did I mention that he is an hourly union employee? From the ownership he displayed, you would have thought that he runs the company. This is true workforce empowerment.

This empowerment did not just happen at this facility; it was part of the overall strategic plan of the company. The leadership at the Toledo plant will be the first to tell you that they are not yet where they want to be in terms of empowerment. They attribute much of their success to the work team environment they have implemented. The DaimlerChrysler plant in Mexico is recognized as the company's model plant for effective team performance, and the folks in Toledo believe that they are next in line. There are 112 teams in the Toledo North Assembly Plant that are dedicated to owning every aspect of a particular process. Communication and training have been key to the Toledo plant's rollout of the team concept. Week-long off-site training classes were given to all team members to explain what their roles and responsibilities were. In addition, soft skills training was given to help the team members learn how to work well in a team environment. Senior management and union leadership were in concert with one another from the beginning regarding the rollout of the team concept. In order to enable this partnership between senior management and union leadership, the two groups get together weekly to discuss any continuous improvement issues pertaining to the plant. The objective of this meeting is to ensure that everyone is aligned and marching down the same path. If management wants to apply a particular improvement tool in the plant, the business case is presented to the union leadership in order to obtain their buy-in. The union leadership was taken to the Mexico plant to see its "best practices" and be a part of bringing some of those ideas back to Toledo. It is all about the mutually shared goal of sustaining jobs.

This was a key factor in the future plans for the Toledo plant's involvement in an innovative manufacturing project that will feature the most advanced use yet of supplier co-location in North America. Part of a $2.1 billion total program investment, the project will be located on the company's existing manufacturing complex and will produce a family of future vehicles for sale worldwide.

In the Chrysler Group's co-location project, three suppliers will build and manage key manufacturing process facilities for body, paint, and chassis operations that are totally within the plant "footprint." The companies chosen for this supplier co-location project, pending final negotiation of purchase agreements, are The Kuka Group (body shop operations), Haden (paint shop operations), and Hyundai Mobis (chassis assembly).

Tom LaSorda, Chrysler Group chief operating officer, called the concept an alternative to the traditional "greenfield site" approach to new manufacturing facilities employed by many automakers. "At the Chrysler Group, we love to defy conventional wisdom," said Mr. LaSorda. "That's why, today, 23 of our

24 major manufacturing facilities are still in urban locations…and are still part of the economic lifeblood of their communities."

Chrysler Group is able to achieve savings similar to "greenfield" concepts because supplier investment in the project will equate to an approximate $300 million savings, "enough to pay for one additional derivative product," said Mr. LaSorda. Total capital investment for the Toledo project is projected to be $900 million.

The uniqueness of the project does not stop there, however, noted Frank Ewasyshyn, executive vice president manufacturing. "This is a true collaborative partnership with the UAW as well," he said. "We had to look long and hard at what kind of innovative work practices would allow an investment like this to happen in an operation like Toledo, the oldest manufacturing facility in America."

Chrysler Group and the UAW signed an unprecedented eight-year agreement in December 2004 for Toledo Jeep employees that paved the way for this partnership. "The UAW recognized that having suppliers based in our facility could open new opportunities…it just meant looking at it from a different direction," said Mr. Ewasyshyn. In the case of chassis-builder Hyundai Mobis, for example, it meant attracting a new supplier to the Midwest. Hyundai Mobis has plans to open a facility in Alabama and currently operates primarily in China and Korea.

"This project keeps approximately 3800 jobs right here in Toledo, and it enables us to implement new ways to become competitive in a rapidly changing time for our industry," said Lloyd Mahaffey, UAW regional director, Toledo Region.

Mr. Ewasyshyn also recognized the current Toledo workforce for its efforts to improve quality, productivity, and safety in the plant operations. In the 2004 Harbour Report,[3] the Toledo North Assembly Plant achieved 9.5% improvement over the previous year's performance. The complex was also recognized by the National Safety Council with the "Green Cross for Excellence" and "Significant Improvement" awards for making outstanding strides in plant safety. Those achievements directly contributed to making the new manufacturing project a reality.

There are a number of reasons for the recognized improvement over the previous year as cited by the Harbour Report. The plant has a holistic management system that utilizes Lean, Six Sigma, and Theory of Constraints as appropriate to achieve continuous improvement. The plant that manufactures the Jeep Liberty is a state-of-the-art facility with all the bells and whistles. A message is electronically broadcast to all of the plant's suppliers every 72 seconds to identify the current needs. It is a complete pull system that is driven from orders placed by dealers. When a supplier receives a broadcast that one of its components is required, it delivers the component to the assembly plant within a two-hour period. The only exception is the seat supplier, which takes six hours to deliver its product. Having all the suppliers located in the general region works well to facilitate this type of lead time.

As you ride through the plant, you see numerous automated guided vehicles (AGVs) transporting material from point A to point B; 85% of the bulk material is transported using AGVs.

The software used to guide the AGVs is nothing like the software used to design the assembly plant and its tooling. Manufacturing simulation software was used to design the plant and its tooling. It enables the Toledo plant to make tooling and equipment updates in a virtual environment rather than having to do so first on the actual tooling. This simulation allows the tooling process within the manufacturing facility to be much more precise, resulting in assembly operations being brought up to speed faster and with fewer issues. With this application, the company can create a seamless union between product development and manufacturing by using compatible systems to design the vehicles and simulate build processes in the plant.

The vision is to allow the integrated system to cover all aspects of manufacturing, from part design to plant design, which helps to get new products to market faster. With this system, DaimlerChrysler was able to simulate the manufacturing environment long before construction of the plant began. As the new Jeep Liberty evolved through its development, the manufacturing processes evolved with it, enabling simultaneous engineering to take place.

The system uses a single-language database across the entire product development and manufacturing process, from product development to plant design. This increases communication, efficiency, and supply chain integration. The goal is to use the system to simulate and visualize the entire manufacturing process and plant before any hardware is installed.

This will be an asset for the supplier co-location project slated to be operational in 2006. However, the greatest asset that I recognized during my visit to the Toledo plant was its people. They are clearly energized and effective in perpetuating ongoing improvement.

Ford

Ford is not wasting any time in doing what it has to do in order to become the world's best auto manufacturer. The revitalization of its Rouge facility in Dearborn, Michigan represents the best that Ford has to offer. It is the model of how Ford believes manufacturing should be executed now and in the future.

It is an impressive undertaking that has energized people at Ford with the vision of being the best automaker in the world. The Rouge plant reopened in April 2004 to rave reviews. Let's take a closer look at the Rouge.

The Factory of the Future Is Here Today at the Ford Motor Company

The Ford Motor Company has set the standard for an automotive manufacturing facility at the newly revitalized Ford Rouge Center. Ford touts it as the way automotive manufacturing will be performed in the 21st century. After having had the opportunity to walk through the facility, I heartily concur. In some ways, visiting the Rouge is like a "back to the future" experience. Many of the Lean manufacturing concepts envisioned by Henry Ford in the 1920s for the Rouge are part of the very lifeblood of the revitalized facility.

Streamlining the entire value chain was important to Henry Ford when the Rouge complex was envisioned. In the early days of the Ford Motor Company, the Highland Park manufacturing site was the flagship facility that manufactured the Model Ts. One of the opportunities for improvement identified from the Model T experience was the lead time associated with supplier components. To address this opportunity, Henry Ford envisioned a vertically integrated facility that would be able to minimize the lead time across the entire value stream. This was the vision for the Rouge. When the Rouge was cranking out Model As in the 1920s, the facility was able to take iron ore and transfer it into a completed automobile in 72 hours. The Rouge had its own blast furnaces and other vertically integrated manufacturing functions that enabled it to achieve this aggressive lead time. At the time, the Rouge employed 100,000 people, and all of its facilities were spread out over 2000 acres.

Some of the Lean concepts practiced at the Rouge to help achieve this 72-hour lead time were error proofing, synchronous flow, and continuous flow. These same concepts still thrive at the Rouge.

If you visit the Rouge today, you will witness how these tools are being integrated in the manufacturing processes of the Dearborn Truck Plant. The Dearborn Truck Plant is an all-new state-of-the-art, 2.3-million-square-foot facility that resides on the grounds of the Rouge. It is where the new Ford F-150 truck is manufactured and is the focal point of the $2 billion Rouge renovation. Within this facility you will witness some of the most innovative approaches available today in automobile manufacturing and environmental science. This marriage of industry and science is one of the most fascinating aspects of the Rouge.

Many of the environmental overtures that permeate every aspect of the Ford Rouge Center and the Dearborn Truck Plant can be attributed to the influence of the world-renowned architect William McDonough. The focus of McDonough + Partners is to achieve a design that establishes a balance between the business, ecosystems, and the culture. They have done that at the Ford Rouge Center.

How they achieved this objective is fascinating and exciting. This excitement is apparent in the employees I had the pleasure of interviewing during my visit to the Rouge, especially James L. Richardson II, who was the project manager for the Rouge revitalization. Mr. Richardson has a long history with Ford and is a virtual treasure chest of information, especially information pertaining to the Rouge. He told me that the Rouge is the best example of the application of the Ford Production System (FPS). FPS is a holistic management system that governs all improvement initiatives. Within FPS, Ford utilizes all three of the primary continuous improvement tools: Six Sigma, Theory of Constraints, and Lean. Based on my visit to the truck plant, I would describe it as a model of an ergonomically friendly workplace that is driven by the Lean desire to eliminate wasted motion.

Three key words come to mind when thinking of the Rouge's Dearborn Truck Plant: Lean, flexible, and sustainable. These are the three tiers upon which the foundation of this facility is built. The Dearborn Truck Plant's new, next-generation flexible manufacturing system is capable of producing nine different models off three platforms. It is Ford's most flexible assembly plant globally, with the ability to quickly change plant production to meet customer demand.

Dearborn Truck has implemented world-class Lean manufacturing standards that include synchronous material flow, in-line vehicle sequencing, waste reduction, and team-based processes for problem solving and strict quality control. Dearborn Truck's synchronous material flow is based on a weekly predictive scheduling system, which coordinates with suppliers to provide just-in-time component inventory for vehicle production, minimizing on-site inventories. Using the same schedule, in-line vehicle sequencing produces vehicles in a particular order, so that vehicle bodies match the proper components and arrive at the operator at precisely the right time and place. Both processes help Ford to reduce waste, minimize vehicle and parts storage space, and optimize production efficiency.

Team-based Lean processes include measures to improve quality and standardize work routines. Key elements include in-station process control that gives the line operators responsibility for producing products that leave their work areas with no quality issues. Operators are empowered to identify and resolve issues in their areas.

To create a Lean and high-quality facility, Dearborn Truck's hourly employees assume roles of responsibility and decision making. Typically in a plant, supervisors manage operators. In Ford's inverted pyramid system, operators work in small teams, with a team leader. Supervisors are manufacturing advisers, supporting the team.

The culture of improvement is an ever-evolving entity, and such is the case at the truck plant. The organization's ability to further this culture is totally dependent upon the people within it and how they relate to one another. Clearly, a working partnership between Ford and the UAW enables a furthering of this culture at the truck plant. The employees welcome the Lean improvement techniques, as well as Six Sigma and Theory of Constraints. Every team leader in the plant is trained as a Six Sigma green belt, and within the teams there is tactical use of Theory of Constraints for constraint analysis.

Any partnership is a two-way street, and Ford has demonstrated its commitment to its employees by creating an innovative workplace environment that is second to none. All employees have access to a fitness center and a medical center at the Rouge facility and, most importantly, have a safe and comfortable workplace. Mezzanine levels and overhead walkways minimize the amount of pedestrian traffic on the factory floor. No forklifts are permitted in the production areas. The thought behind this is that many accidents that occur in the factory are related to the interaction of a person with a machine, with the machine normally winning. Minimizing the opportunities for these interactions improves safety.

Many ergonomic considerations have been adopted in the design of the factory and provide for a pleasant working environment, including:

- **Skillet conveyors** — These conveyors look like an accordion-type support that the frame of a car rests upon as it travels through the factory. This accordion goes up and down automatically to accommodate the desired height for performing a particular task, so that the operator does not have to reach or stoop to perform a task.
- **Doors off process** — This process is the removal of the doors while the car frame travels through the factory to enable easy access for the assembly of components. Once the assembly is completed, the doors are matched back up with the respective car frame.
- **Floating chair** — This chair is attached to an arm that enables the worker to float in and out of a car as it travels along the assembly line. This makes the car more accessible and the task easier.
- **Flooring** — Most of the flooring along the assembly line is made of birch. It was chosen because studies have shown that birch is most friendly to the body when standing for extended periods of time.
- **Electrical tools** — The overhead tools that the operators use to perform their tasks as a vehicle travels through the shop are electric instead of

pneumatic. As a result, the sound level is considerably lower than in a typical factory. It was very easy to carry on a conversation. In addition, the tools are much lighter and easier to handle.

These are just a few of the ergonomic initiatives implemented at the truck plant, and they all work to eliminate wasted motion. These Lean activities and the efforts of the improvement teams enable the plant to support a takt time of 54 seconds. While quite impressive, this is only half of the story at the truck plant. The other half is the innovative, environmentally friendly characteristics of the facility.

Project planners implemented a sustainable system that uses ecologically advanced methods for storm-water management, energy usage, air quality, and soil restoration. Ford worked with internationally renowned environmental architect William McDonough, who led the design team for the environmental innovations and test beds at the site. "What's happening at the Rouge will once again influence the whole world of industrial production," Mr. McDonough said. "Ford's redevelopment of the Rouge Center is revolutionary and will produce fantastic shareholder value. The management's environmental foresight has resulted in a sustaining system that will pay economic, social, and environmental dividends immediately and into the long-term future."

Among the initiatives are:

■ The world's largest living roof, composed of a perennial ground cover called sedum, which helps insulate the building and reduces storm-water runoff

■ The test use of a biological process called phytoremediation, which uses specific plants to remove polyaromatic hydrocarbons, a by-product of steel manufacturing

■ Special ditches called swales that mimic the cleaning action of natural wetlands

■ The nation's largest porous parking lot on 16 acres at the vehicle shipping yard, which helps control and cleanse storm-water runoff

■ Ten huge window boxes called monitors and 60 overhead skylights, which will bring daylight into Dearborn Truck's body shop and final assembly buildings, creating a more pleasant work environment while reducing lighting costs

■ Restoration of natural areas, including the installation of three beehives with 20,000 bees

■ A patent-pending "Fumes-to-Fuel" pilot system that transforms the volatile organic compounds found in paint fumes into a fuel source for electricity

Ford's progressive environmental initiatives already have been recognized by the Wildlife Habitat Council, which has designated the Ford Rouge Center site as a wildlife habitat, a significant honor for a brownfield industrial site.

Of all the environmentally inspired innovations at the Rouge, the 10.4-acre living roof shown in Figure 1-1 is the most fascinating. It looks like a huge grassy field on top of the roof. It is actually composed of a drought-resistant perennial ground cover, called sedum, which is planted in a specially layered bed. On hot summer days, the sedum growing on the roof reflects the heat from the sun that otherwise would be soaked up by the roof. It provides natural overhead insulation for the final assembly building, thereby reducing energy costs. It is also expected to last twice as long as a traditionally constructed roof.

Virtually maintenance free, it can absorb up to four million gallons of rainwater annually and is part of a broader storm-water management system installed at the Rouge. Instead of a chemically based storm-water treatment plant, Ford designed a system that mimics nature. The sedum on the roof absorbs most of the rain and snow that falls on the surface, which is filtered through the plant roots and soil bed. Excess runoff then is directed into an intricate storm-water management system composed of filtering rock beds and ground-level plantings, ditches filled with greenery called swales, porous pavement installations, retention ponds, and underground storage basins. All of these work in harmony to eliminate the need for a conventional storm-water treatment system that would cost tens of millions of dollars for a facility the size of the truck plant. In addition, such a facility would cost hundreds of thousands of dollars annually to operate. The natural system at the truck plant cost a third the amount of a conventional system and has virtually no operating costs.

Sustainability is a consistent theme throughout the facility, including the paint shop. Ford developed a creative partnership with DTE Energy, Fuel Cell Technologies, Ltd., and the State of Michigan to create a patent-pending "Fumes-to-Fuel" system at the truck plant. The system works in three stages. The first stage concentrates paint fumes. The second stage, called a reformer, converts concentrated fumes into a hydrogen-rich mixture. The third stage feeds hydrogen gas into fuel cells, where hydrogen reacts chemically with air to create electricity, hot water, and only a tiny bit of carbon dioxide. Unlike power generators, fuel cells produce no harmful emissions. They cost less to install and maintain and run more efficiently and quietly. Fuel cells provide "clean" power and stable voltage. When fully developed, the potential savings from the "Fumes-to-Fuel" system are in the millions. It is also estimated that carbon dioxide emissions from the Rouge paint shop could be reduced by 1600 tons annually.

This is the future of manufacturing. It is the future and it is here today — at the Ford Rouge Center and in the new Dearborn Truck Plant.

Figure 1-1. The living roof at the Rouge's Dearborn Truck Plant. (Reprinted with permission from the Ford Motor Company.)

General Motors

General Motors holds the distinction of being the world's largest manufacturer of automobiles as measured by the number of cars produced. Toyota has grown to secure the number two slot behind GM.[1] These two companies partnered on a venture in 1984 known as New United Motor Manufacturing, Inc. (NUMMI).

GM's Global Manufacturing System (GMS) is an important building block of an integrated strategy to develop and build great cars and trucks.

GMS is a system built around people. The system stresses the value of teamwork and is based on an underlying philosophy that everyone, in every position, adds value. At the heart of the system is the operator in the plant — the person who builds GM's great products. Plants and processes are designed around providing support for the operators and teams on the plant floor, so they can build great vehicles that provide our customers with higher quality, value, and responsiveness.

Several factors played a role in the evolution of GMS. The experience gained through NUMMI, a joint venture with Toyota, provided GM the introduction of the Toyota Production System.

GM's newest plants in Eisenach, Germany; Shanghai, China; and Rosario, Argentina also helped lay the foundation for today's GMS. These new plants take the experiences from NUMMI to the next level. These plants embody best-in-class manufacturing techniques and serve as models for all of our plants. In addition, GM's new plant in Brazil, which extensively uses concepts of co-design and a systems approach, is a key building block of GMS.

Manufacturing performance is improved through the consistent adoption of five principles — people involvement, standardization, built-in quality, short lead time, and continuous improvement. The principles are interrelated and implemented as a complete system.

The GMS principles maximize performance in the areas of people systems, safety, quality, customer responsiveness, and cost.

People — Products, plants, and processes are designed to allow GM's people to use their skills and abilities as efficiently as possible. Workers are organized into small teams and trained and empowered to run their areas.

GM is working with the UAW and its other unions on many aspects of GM's people systems strategy. This includes maintaining a high level of communication and cooperation with the UAW, IUE, and other unions. The communications process and environment are dedicated to helping employees understand their work and allowing them to have input into improving their jobs.

Improved people systems, with a focus on the operator, and improved material handling help to attain world-class competitiveness. The system allows more efficient delivery and presentation of material to the assembly line operator, eliminating the need for costly inventory while providing a safety benefit through the reduction of forklift traffic in the plant.

Figure 1-2. General Motors' Global Manufacturing System. (Reprinted with permission from General Motors Corporation.)

Through this collaborative effort, GM was introduced to the Toyota Production System. Over the last 20 years, GM has infused much of the Toyota Production System into its corporate-wide manufacturing system and made enhancements to it as appropriate. This has evolved into what is referred to today as GM's Global Manufacturing System. An explanation of GM's Global Manufacturing System provided by General Motors appears in Figure 1-2.

Safety — GM is the industry benchmark in safety, a goal achieved through a strong partnership between GM and its unions. Because GMS is built around people, safety is a top priority. Providing a safe working environment is an essential part of creating an organization where each person is important and critical to the overall success.

Quality — Developing vehicles that are simpler to build and use fewer parts enhances quality. The team concept is a critical part of managing quality by making each team responsible for managing quality in its area. Team members receive extensive training in identifying and solving problems and in quality systems such as Andon to request assistance and even stop production in their area if necessary to remedy problems. Error-proofing strategies and implementing standardized work also enhance first-time product quality.

Responsiveness — GM's manufacturing strategy maximizes customer responsiveness, by responding fast to customer and market trends. GM is shifting from a "make-and-sell" to a "sense-and-respond" organization. A make-and-sell organization predicts what the market will want, makes it, and then tries to sell it. It is a system based on high-volume manufacturing.

Sense-and-respond is all about moving with speed in a market that is evolving to fragmented, niche products with less volume per entry and being flexible enough to deal with uncertainty and generate options for the product and the customer.

Another fundamental of the system is an emphasis on responding fast to customer and market trends. This flexibility begins with developing vehicles that are simpler to build. Flexible global vehicle architectures allow GM to more easily build cars, trucks, and crossovers off the same architecture in one or more plants.

Cost — GM's manufacturing system concentrates on cost savings by eliminating all forms of waste that detract from our ability to be competitive and support the assembly line operator.

Machinery and equipment are purchased as integrated systems, not as bits and pieces. A lean, more efficient plant structure requires lower capital investment and allows GM to run its business more competitively.

Computer technology is also helping GM reduce costs. Virtual reality technology is being used to reduce development costs and improve overall efficiency. To help ensure that equipment and processes support the assembly line operators, GM uses 3-D math modeling to create a "virtual factory" that helps planners integrate equipment, tools, fixtures, and machinery that will be used in the plant.

GM's Global Manufacturing System — a system to build great cars and trucks.

Summary

The continuous improvement efforts outlined at these automotive companies provide some insight into how their worlds are changing for the better. It is fair to say that in the future we can expect to see more enterprise-wide improvement in the automotive industry, as well as a continuation of factory floor improvement initiatives.

AEROSPACE

The aerospace industry is in the midst of a revitalization of its approach to continuous improvement. The industry has always been driven to perform at high levels of quality due to the nature of the commodity. However, in the past decade, transformation activities have permeated aerospace organizations with a broader orientation. Market demands, global competition, 9/11, and a host of other factors have contributed to this new focus. The International Aerospace Quality Group, which consists of the Americas Aerospace Quality Group, the European Aerospace Quality Group, and the Asia-Pacific Aerospace Quality Group, was instrumental in the development and implementation of the current governing specification for the aerospace industry, AS9100. AS9100 required the aerospace industry to take a fresh look at how it evaluated the effectiveness of the way it does business, including the approach to continuous improvement. The effect of industry specifications will be discussed in detail in the next chapter.

The Lean Aerospace Initiative (LAI) was established in 1993 with the objective of transforming the aerospace industry at the enterprise level. The Massachusetts Institute of Technology is one of the key players in LAI and has served as an incubator for promoting the Lean transformation of the aerospace industry. LAI is an impressive consortium of industry, government, and academia working together to facilitate this transformation.

These are some of the broader initiatives that are having an impact on the direction in which continuous improvement is heading in the aerospace industry. Let's look at some aerospace companies to get a feel for what each company is uniquely doing.

Boeing

Boeing Revolutionizes Commercial Airplane Manufacturing

With a heritage that mirrors the first 100 years of flight, the Boeing Company provides products and services to customers in 145 countries. Boeing has been the premier manufacturer of commercial jetliners for more than 40 years and is a global market leader in military aircraft, satellites, missile defense, human space flight, and launch systems and services. Total company revenues for 2004 were $52.5 billion.

Boeing continues to expand its product line and develop new technologies to meet customer needs. By creating new models for its family of commercial airplanes; developing, producing, supporting, and modifying aircraft for the U.S. military; building launch vehicles capable of lifting more than 14 tons into orbit; and improving communications for people around the world through an advanced network of satellites, Boeing is carrying forward a long tradition of technical excellence and innovation.

Boeing employs nearly 156,000 people in 70 countries and 48 states in the United States, with major operations in the Puget Sound area of Washington State, southern California, Wichita, and St. Louis.

With the McDonnell Douglas merger in 1997, Boeing's legacy of leadership in commercial jets now is joined with the lineage of Douglas airplanes, giving the combined company a 70-year heritage of leadership in commercial aviation. Today, the main commercial products consist of the 717, 737, 747, 767, and 777 families of airplanes and the Boeing Business Jet.

Our discussion will focus on the improvement activity for the 717, which is manufactured in the Long Beach, California facility, and the 737, which is manufactured in the Renton, Washington facility. That is because with these two airplanes, Boeing is doing what has never been done before in the history of commercial airplane manufacturing. It is using a moving assembly line in conjunction with Lean manufacturing techniques to manufacture the airplanes.

Both the Renton and Long Beach facilities will be discussed throughout this section, but let's start with some of the insights into the business of improvement at the Renton facility. I had the pleasure of speaking at length with Steve Westby, vice president manufacturing for Boeing Commercial Airplanes, and Mike Herscher, director of the Lean Enterprise Office for Commercial Airplanes, about the exciting things that are taking place at Renton.

The moving assembly line is at the top of the list because it is literally revolutionizing the way commercial aircraft will be made in the future. Boeing is in a position to take this bold step into the future because of its long history of creating a corporate culture of improvement. This culture of ongoing continuous improvement did not just happen, but rather is a direct by-product of the Boeing Production System.

It was back in the 1978–1980 time frame when Boeing first began educating itself on the principles of Lean manufacturing and putting quality circles into practice. Boeing now has approximately 25 years under its belt along its process improvement journey. The intensity of the education and the application of Lean have progressed as well from those early years. Looking back at the high points over the years, it is hard to imagine what a more robust journey would look like. Not every company can list Dr. Juran and Dr. Deming as improvement consultants in the mid-1980s. But Boeing can. This commitment to seek out the best the world has to offer, and learn as much as possible from the best, is what has enabled Boeing to remain the world's leading manufacturer of commercial aircraft. A strong competitive threat from Airbus has for the first time in many years puts its world-leader position in jeopardy, but Boeing is confidently up for the challenge. It is meeting this challenge by trying to squeeze every bit of nonvalue-added activity out of all of its processes across the enterprise. It already has reaped tremendous benefits from its long history of Lean transformation and is committed to aggressively continue to improve. Boeing looks at continuous improvement as a race without a finish line. As a marathon runner, I understand that to continue going forward without a finish line in sight requires a tremendous amount of focus on the process of running. Such is the focus at Boeing on continuous improvement.

One of the by-products of this focus is the moving assembly line. Adapted from automotive Lean manufacturing methods in Japan, a continuously moving assembly line slowly moves products from one assembly team to the next. This technique keeps production moving at a steady pace, allowing employees to gauge production status at a glance and reduce the amount of work-in-process inventory.

The moving assembly lines, and the accompanying Lean techniques, enable a smooth, continuous production flow, which enhances the quality and efficiency of production processes. In addition to reducing flow time and production costs, moving assembly lines also create an environment that makes it easier for employees to do their jobs. All the tools, parts, plans, and work instructions are delivered to employees so that they have everything they need where and when they need it. Boeing considers the people working on the planes analogous to surgeons. A surgeon does not have to walk down the hall to get a scalpel in the middle of surgery. Neither should these airplane surgeons on the assembly line have to try to find something to perform their operation. Just as the surgeon has a tray within arm's reach, full of the instruments needed to perform surgery, so too does the airplane surgeon. "Kitting carts" contain everything needed for a particular task and are placed within arm's reach of the airplane surgeon. These "kitting carts" are stocked with what is required and put in place by a kitting group. Boeing provides a two-hour buffer time between shifts to permit the kitting groups to prepare and put the kits in place. This helps the people who build the airplanes to work more efficiently, eliminating the need to search for and gather materials to complete work.

The airplanes are pulled on their landing gear by a self-guided tug, which follows a thin magnetic strip attached to the factory floor. The length of the line for the 737 is 700 feet, and the speed at which the airplane rolls along is two inches per minute. The moving line for the 737 at Renton became fully operational in January 2002. The 717 in Long Beach preceded the 737 by becoming fully operational in 1999.

The moving line itself is the impetus for a number of other activities. It requires the establishment of standard work for the various assembly activities. Once the activities have been standardized, they can be optimized by continuous improvement. Since specific segmented work activities have been designated for particular points along the line, it becomes apparent within minutes if some work is falling behind schedule.

Boeing orchestrated many Lean tactics, like the institution of feeder lines and a commitment to just-in-time inventory, in order to make the moving line a realistic possibility. The fruit of all of these activities has been significantly improved performance as recognized in several key metrics at the 737 Renton facility:

Benefits achieved in final assembly (1999 to 2004)

Factory cycle time reduction	46%
Inventory reduction	
Stores inventory	59%
Work-in-process inventory	55%
Footprint reduction	21%

Benefits achieved in final assembly and suppliers (1999 to 2004)

Cost of quality reduction	61%

These are impressive numbers that most likely will continuously improve because the environment created with the moving line forces that to happen.

A host of other strategic initiatives exist within the Boeing Production System that foster ongoing continuous improvement. I will spotlight a handful of them to give you the essence of the supportive elements of the Boeing Production System.

One is the nine Lean tactics to improve operational efficiency. Bob Stanger, director of manufacturing and operations for the 717, explained that the nine tactics are the template for all of Boeing's activities. These Lean tactics were developed and adopted corporate-wide at Boeing in 2000. They represent an approach to increasing efficiency and the ability to manage flow in a manufacturing environment. These tactics are a culmination of years of lessons learned, and they create a discipline of thought and action that provides a common approach for improvement at the Boeing Company.

Another improvement approach that is part of the Boeing Production System is the *moonshine shops*. There are a number of these groups throughout the company that work full-time on coming up with creative outside-the-box solutions for improving manufacturing processes. They are chartered with the freedom to be different and unconventional in their approach to problem solving. There are no limitations on what they will tackle, and to date they have been involved in a wide variety of activities. Whenever they take on a problem, they are encouraged to use whatever resources are available to them. One example is the use of a garage door opener as an elevator to lift mechanics tools to point of use. Another is the use of a 1920s vintage air compressor motor with an old hay loader, to lift seats up from the floor to the airplane entryway. Mike Herscher indicated that the moonshine efforts have resulted in dramatic cycle time reductions for the manufacture of some of the tooling. Something that once took 18 months to manufacture now takes four to five weeks after being moonshined. The moonshiner in the hills competed for bragging rights as to who had the best moonshine. A similar competition exists at Boeing with its moonshine teams. There is an annual war between moonshine groups over bragging rights for the best moonshined activity. Senior management participates in this annual event by acting as judges in the selection of the best moonshine project.

Senior management is integrally involved with all aspects of continuous improvement at Boeing. There is a firm belief at Boeing that improvement begins at the top and is cascaded throughout the organization. We talked about a number of examples of senior management being directly involved with the business of improvement. One such example began in 1995 and continues today. Boeing has sent 1500 executives to Japan to study at Toyota with the Shingijutsu consultants. The Shingijutsu consultants are retired Toyota executives who consult on the principles of Lean manufacturing. Since the initial trips to Japan, Boeing has utilized the Shingijutsu consultants for 1600 weeks worth of consulting time. This has included both trips to Japan and on-site consulting in the United States. The high point of consulting activity was in 1998, when Shingijutsu was used for 350 consulting weeks. Today, the Shingijutsu consultants are called upon for approximately 120 consulting weeks per year. This intensive amount of training over the years has enabled Boeing to build up a strong internal resource of highly trained Lean consultants. Approximately 200 full-time Boeing employees are Lean experts, and 300 additional employees are well trained and operating in various areas of the organization. These Lean experts are called upon for a significant amount of the Lean direction. These days, Shingijutsu is utilized only for very complex issues.

The training with Shingijutsu surely was an influential factor in shaping the senior management level of involvement in the business of improvement at Boeing. Another example of such involvement is an internal Lean conference that is held twice per year, at which senior management usually gives either the keynote or one of the presentations. This is an enterprise-wide event, not limited to just commercial airplanes, and it is open to customers and suppliers. The first one was held in 2000 and about 120 people attended; about 500 people attended the most recent one. With representation from Lean leaders throughout the company and across the entire value stream sharing their lessons learned, valuable time and effort are saved not reinventing the wheel. These best practices are in turn taken from the conference and put into practice much sooner than would otherwise be possible. It provides a forum for the continued pursuit of excellence across the entire value stream using the common framework of Lean.

Another such forum that occurs almost every Friday at Boeing is an improvement team "report out." A "report out" is an encapsulation of a team's improvement activities, including the actions taken and the benefits derived. A vice president and/or general manager is present as an active listener to the team's report. This active involvement of senior management is driven from the top. Alan Mulally, president and CEO, Commercial Airplanes, starts each meeting of his direct reports with a review of improvement performance charts, and his direct reports follow suit. Dr. Deming and Dr. Juran would be proud to see such an active commitment from senior management to continuously improve.

An actively involved senior management can have a tremendous impact on the empowerment of the workforce. Providing the workforce with the skills needed to make improvement happen is paramount at Boeing. In the early 1990s, world-class competitiveness and 5S training was given by executive management to *every* employee in Boeing Commercial Airplanes. This 40-hour training program was a significant commitment.

Continuous training, senior management involvement, and continuous improvement team activities are all elements that support a continuous improvement culture. Boeing is constantly looking for ways to strengthen this improvement culture. Some are more innocuous than others, but nonetheless effective. The 717 Program co-located the back-office support personnel (engineering, supply chain, quality) in close proximity to the part of the aircraft they supported on a daily basis. In addition, the liaison personnel were all co-located on the shop floor next to the aircraft build position they supported. By doing so, they were able to align the goals and objectives, improve communication between the shop and office personnel, and improve problem resolution time frames. At Renton, the Lean initiatives put in place resulted in freeing up a fair amount of floor space that was previously filled with inventory. The plan was to utilize this space for offices of all support personnel that had anything to do with the airplane. This included manufacturing engineers, quality engineers, and even the vice president. The footprint required for the moving assembly line fit right into this plan. This close proximity to the assembly line promotes efficient communication and reinforces a focus of the plant's main purpose — assembling airplanes.

All of these cultural activities are focused on the common goal of improvement through the Boeing Production System, which is like an umbrella that oversees all aspects of improvement in a holistic fashion.

The discussion so far has focused primarily on the Lean activities at Boeing, but there is also a fair amount of Six Sigma activity. This activity is not so much factory floor oriented, but rather is research- or data-driven activity that drives improvement. The Renton facility alone has 50 Six Sigma black belts and 300 green belts.

How does Boeing plan to maintain this holistic management system and improvement culture in the years to come? Steve Westby indicated that it will not be difficult to convince the workforce of the importance of continuing to improve due to the competitive nature of the market. The commercial airline industry was one of the hardest hit industries after 9/11. In 1999, Boeing delivered 620 planes and in 2003 delivered 285 planes. To have endured such an impact on its industry is a testimony to the effectiveness of the Boeing Production System and the Lean manufacturing principles currently employed. Mr. Westby's message is that it is not going to get any easier, and hence the motivation to continuously improve is built into the business. Another supportive way of keeping the improvement train rolling along is to share success stories across the company. When you can understand why these Lean principles are being preached, it is easier to jump on the bandwagon.

Mr. Westby also acknowledges that the future of improvement at Boeing will include an increased amount of Lean office activity. In particular, engineering will work to improve the manufacturability of the product. Boeing has already made some inroads with Lean office applications, but much low-hanging fruit is still available. Look to see Boeing make a concerted effort in the future in both the office and the factory to become as Lean as possible.

It is this commitment to the future, a stellar improvement history, and the exciting activities of today that illustrate why Boeing is revolutionizing commercial airplane manufacturing.

Lockheed Martin

Creating a Culture of Improvement

Lockheed Martin is the world's largest defense contractor and largest manufacturer of military aircraft. It is also a leader in the design, research and development, systems integration, production, and support of advanced military aircraft and related technologies. Its customers include the military services of the United States and allied countries throughout the world. Products include the F-16, F/A-22, F-35 JSF, F-117, C-5, C-130, C-130J, P-3, S-3, and U-2. The company produces major components for the F-2 fighter and is a co-developer of the C-27J tactical transport and T-50 advanced jet trainer. Headquartered in Bethesda, Maryland, Lockheed Martin employs about 130,000 people world-wide and is principally engaged in the research, design, development, manu-facture, and integration of advanced technology systems, products, and services. The corporation reported 2004 sales of $35.5 billion.

As one of the leaders in the aerospace industry, Lockheed Martin is at the front of the pack when it comes to the establishment of an improvement culture. The effort that goes into the creation and the continual nurturing of an improve-ment culture is multifaceted and never-ending. As a leading-edge company, Lockheed Martin would be the first to acknowledge that it has not reached a level of comfort in its pursuit of perfection, but rather aggressively continues to pursue it.

Larry Pike, vice-president, deputy for production operations at Lockheed Martin Aeronautics, has been in the middle of the evolution of this improvement culture during his 32-year tenure. I spoke with him at length regarding the current state of improvement at Lockheed and where he sees it going in the future.

One of the many facets of creating an improvement culture is continuous learning. Learning is accomplished in a variety of ways, some of which include by the example of others, through educational training, and by observation of best practices. Learning by example is so powerful that it can transform the way we look at reality and be an impetus for positive behavior change — especially when the person setting the example is the CEO of the company. That is what happened at Lockheed in 2000 when then CEO Vance Coffman participated in a week-long training session on Lean and Six Sigma. All senior management participated in that same week-long class as well. It is difficult to say that you are too busy to learn about Lean for a week when the CEO is sitting next to you.

The leadership example set by senior management in regard to elevating a level of importance to Lean and continuous improvement has been integral to the workforce energy that drives the improvement engine at Lockheed. Larry Pike noted that if you have a committed workforce and you have established a culture that empowers people, then training this workforce on the "how-tos" of improvement will be easier.

Each employee becomes proficient in the "how-tos" by acquiring knowledge of the improvement tools and the analytical skills required for their value-added application. At Lockheed, this is done through ongoing continuous improvement tools training. The continuous improvement toolbox at Lockheed Martin combines Lean and Six Sigma as a program and draws upon Theory of Constraints when applicable. The use of these tools is integrated into the culture, which serves the corporate philosophy regarding the necessity to march to perfection in quality, then march to perfection in cost, and eventually march to perfection in schedule.

The best-in-class companies in all industries are driven by a similar pursuit of perfection and can be a valuable resource for learning as well. Lockheed Martin has learned best practices from the Toyotas of the world by going to their facilities and observing how they run their businesses. Sometimes this is the most effective approach for learning because you can see the theory or idea being applied. The art of learning to "see" Lean opportunities that exist is a necessity for ongoing improvement in a company with a mature improvement program. The more mature a company is in Lean, the harder it is to "see" new opportunities. Hence the need for continuous learning.

All of the continuous improvement learning at Lockheed Martin and the application of what is learned are governed through the corporation's oversight management system, known as LM-21. It is a holistic management system that integrates all of the elements relating to improvement, including the Lean, Six Sigma, and Theory of Constraints improvement initiatives. The guiding metrics for LM-21 are quality, cost, schedule, and people. The management-level activities that take place within LM-21 are oriented in a similar manner to those of the management review team responsibilities of AS9100. Lockheed Martin has 60 facilities worldwide, and each facility has a direct interface to senior management that is directly accountable for continuous improvement performance. This direct interface is also responsible for the deployment and oversight of Lean experts throughout the company as needed. This type of structure ensures that senior management is continuously involved with the business of improvement.

At the center of this business of improvement is quality performance. Quality is obviously paramount at Lockheed Martin because if its product does not perform as expected, the result could be catastrophic. The quality focus at Lockheed Martin is customer driven for obvious reasons. Lockheed Martin designs the quality into the product and processes utilizing Six Sigma initiatives that assure a high-quality product is delivered to the customer. The customer-focused quality does not end when the product leaves the shipping dock or is flown away. To show that the company stands behind its product, a Lockheed Martin representative accompanies every aircraft that is delivered to the customer and is there to assure that the product performs as expected. If any problem is found, the Lockheed Martin representative sends within hours a narrative of the problem, along with any necessary supportive information, digital pictures, etc. back to the department where the problem originated. This works to assure that the customer gets the product expected and also helps to prevent recurrent problems of a similar nature. The emphasis placed on any issues identified once the product reaches the customer can be characterized as a customer-focused kaizen blitz that initiates a flurry of activity within a matter of hours.

This type of customer-focused reaction is only possible with an empowered workforce that is in tune with the rhythm of the company. The empowerment of the workforce is a corporate objective, and the actions required to achieve it are part of the company's strategic plan. This is accomplished through training, coaching, and providing the employees with an opportunity to use their brains. One aspect of the workforce that helps with the objective of empowerment is the long tenure of the employees. One employee at the Fort Worth facility recently retired after 55 years of service, and there are many others with 20 or 30 years of service. Larry Pike believes that these long-term employees are proud to work for Lockheed Martin Aeronautics because it makes a product that is important to protecting the United States and 23 other countries. Making an impact on the world is good motivation for coming to work each day.

It is the company's products that eventually make the impact on the world by enabling the armed services that use them to protect and defend. The company manufactures a variety of products, but the shining star these days is the F-35, otherwise known as the Joint Strike Fighter. The F-35 is a stealthy, supersonic multirole fighter designed to replace a wide range of aging fighter and strike aircraft. Three variants derived from a common design will ensure that the F-35 meets the performance needs of the U.S. Air Force, Marine Corps, Navy, and allied defense forces worldwide, while staying within strict affordability targets. The three variants of the aircraft are a conventional takeoff and landing, a short takeoff/vertical landing, and a carrier variant.

Lockheed Martin is developing the F-35 in conjunction with its principal industrial partners, Northrup Grumman and BAE Systems. Companies worldwide are participating in the F-35's development. The aircraft that the F-35 will replace are the AV-8B Harrier, A-10, F-16, F/A-18, and the U.K.'s Harrier GR.7 and Sea Harrier.

Prior to the production of the F-35, Lockheed engaged in a number of upfront kaizen events in order to optimize the design in terms of manufacturability. These kaizens will prove to be time well spent once full production is up and running. Two of the reasons for this are parts commonality and the resulting lack of specialized tooling. Through the kaizens, the improvement teams were able to design the components for the F-35 such that 85% of all of the aircraft's components are common to the three aircraft used for the Air Force, Marine

Corps, and Navy. In addition to commonality of parts, these kaizens were able to design these common parts with mating fixtures that permitted them to be assembled without special tools. The actual benefit of these kaizens will be in the millions of dollars once the F-35 is in full production.

Another Lean manufacturing method that is being evaluated with the F-35 is the continuous moving assembly line instead of the traditional batch-and-queue approach to manufacturing military aircraft. If utilized, it will be the first-ever continuous moving assembly line for a combat fighter jet. Adopting such an approach could increase production efficiency, reduce floor space, and avoid an estimated $300 million in expenses over the life of the program. In late January 2004, members of the F-35 production team from Lockheed Martin, Northrup Grumman, and BAE Systems gathered on the Lockheed Martin factory floor in Fort Worth to begin laying out a preliminary plan for a continuous moving line. Using a full-scale F-35 model, the team simulated processes for installing aircraft systems as the jet crept along an imaginary track. Proponents of the continuous moving lines say they not only improve efficiency, but also force assembly problems to the surface, where they can be identified quickly and fixed permanently. This greater efficiency plays into the F-35's planned high rate of production — up to one aircraft per day and at least 2593 planes for the U.S. and U.K. military services.

One thing that a continuous moving line will force is the standardization of work. Larry Pike indicated that standardizing activity in relation to takt time is the number one challenge for Lockheed Martin right now. It is looking at standardizing the activity at the beginning of the Joint Strike Fighter program in order improve the efficiency of manufacturing and enable utilization of a moving assembly line if deemed appropriate.

The assembly will be performed at the Lockheed Martin Fort Worth facility, but the three F-35 partner companies are building major F-35 subassemblies, comprised of parts and systems from around the world. Northrup Grumman is producing the center fuselage at its Palmdale, California facility; assembly of the forward fuselage and wings is being done at the Lockheed Martin Fort Worth, Texas facility; and the aft fuselage and tails are being produced at BAE Systems in Samlesbury, England.

The first phase of the wing assembly at Lockheed Martin, Fort Worth began in late August 2004 with the skeleton. The completed skeleton will have the upper and lower carbon-fiber composite skins attached. It will then be mated to the other F-35 subassemblies beginning in the spring of 2005. Figure 1-3 shows the completed skeleton wing assembly, along with the proud wing assembly team members.

It is evident that the F-35 and all of the products being provided by the Lockheed Martin company are extremely sophisticated and therefore require

Figure 1-3. F-35 completed skeleton wing assembly and wing assembly team members. (Reprinted with permission from Lockheed Martin.)

optimum-performing manufacturing processes and systems. Innovation in manufacturing is a necessity in this type of business, and Lockheed Martin has its share of it.

One innovation is the sophisticated machinery it developed in concert with its machine manufacturers in order to achieve the required stealth features for the aircraft. New milling machines are accurate to within 50 microns — about one-third the width of a human hair. This machine will ensure that the F-35's outer shape is exact and meets its low-observability (stealth) requirements.

Another product Lockheed Martin developed was so successful that the company intends to market it. It is a patent-pending ultrasonic laser that enables the ultrasound testing for voids to be performed on an aircraft component without having to follow the contour of the part. As a result, an aircraft mechanic can check the aircraft components without having to remove them from the aircraft. This will be a huge time saver and provide as good or better quality performance.

Innovation and improvement initiatives are natural by-products of a culture of improvement. Lockheed's commitment to an improvement culture is bearing fruit in its manufacturing processes and systems, but what effect has it had in the office environment?

Lockheed Martin is committed to the Lean principles in the office environment as well. In particular, it has applied its 6S program (5S plus safety) throughout the office and has had some kaizen improvement activity in the office environment. The challenges of applying the Lean principles to the office are cultural and visual. Visual refers to having the ability to "see" opportunities for Lean. Nobody knows a process better than those actually doing it, so the company took an innovative approach to assist its employees in acquiring the ability to "see" Lean opportunities.

Through a survey of office workers, it was discovered that the majority had a strong interest in Indy and NASCAR racing, so arrangements were made for an Indy car team to visit Lockheed Martin. On the day of the visit, all of the office workers were asked to go down to one end of the factory floor. The Indy team started at the other end of the plant and drove down the center of it to the area where the employees were waiting. Once there, the team demonstrated a typical pit stop. The demonstration emphasized the Lean tool kit utilized for the pit. Standard work is a big factor in any pit stop that has a 10- to 15-second takt time, no setup, and no room for errors. Seeing the Lean tools from the perspective of the Indy team pit stop helped the employees with their ability to "see" Lean opportunities in their environment. As an offshoot of this effort, a handful of Lockheed Martin employees were given the privilege of spending some time at the track with the Indy team in an actual pit stop. These new eyes observing the process were able to identify opportunities for the Indy team that eventually resulted in reducing a few seconds off their time.

Lockheed has and continues to create a culture that fosters continuous improvement throughout the enterprise. Those in the armed services using Lockheed's equipment and those in the private sector being protected by it owe a debt of gratitude to this corporation's commitment to the pursuit of perfection.

Both Boeing and Lockheed Martin, two leaders in aerospace, have demonstrated their level of commitment to continuous improvement, and it is quite impressive. The future looks bright for aerospace, as the industry as a whole is committed to enterprise-wide transformation.

COMPUTERS/ELECTRONICS

One industry that is no stranger to positive reports about continuous improvement initiatives is the computer/electronics industry. It is one of the fastest paced industries in terms of introducing new products to market. That new computer you bought a mere six months ago now seems antiquated compared to the latest and greatest equipment available. It is mind-boggling how quickly the technology changes.

It's no wonder that the leaders in this industry are also leaders in transformation. Motorola was the company that introduced Six Sigma to the world, and it has since spread like wildfire. Let's take a look at a sampling of companies from this industry to examine their improvement initiatives.

Motorola

When most people think about Six Sigma, they naturally think of Motorola. Others, however, associate GE with Six Sigma. That is because GE, like so many other companies, has championed Six Sigma as a powerful tool for instilling excellence in a business. However, it all started at Motorola. It has been 20 years since Six Sigma was first used at Motorola, and the company is most certainly not reminiscing about the glory days when Six Sigma burst onto the scene. Motorola is practicing what it preaches and continuously improving upon one of the most powerful improvement tools of the 20th century.

I had the opportunity to pose some questions pertaining to the state of continuous improvement at Motorola to Tom McCarty, director of customer and supplier Six Sigma services:

> *Question:* As the creators of Six Sigma, I'm sure you have a robust Six Sigma program. Are you using any of the other tools, like Lean and Theory of Constraints?

> *McCarty:* Six Sigma is our "umbrella" for business improvement. That umbrella incorporates many of the methodologies often used independently, such as Lean, kaizen, Theory of Constraints, etc.

> *Question:* Oftentimes, I see reports of companies saving millions of dollars through the application of improvement tools. Has Motorola had any recent significant improvement gains?

> *McCarty:* We have documented and reported to financial analysts more than $1.2 billion in hard savings for the period of January 2003 through September 2004.

> *Question:* Would you describe the way you manage improvement as a holistic management system?

> *McCarty:* Yes. We apply Six Sigma as an overall management system and a structured approach for executing breakthrough business improvement driven from the office of the CEO.

> *Question:* What key metrics drive your improvement efforts?

> *McCarty:* We talk about key metrics as our "Big Ys," or the results that really matter. Currently, our three key Big Ys are:

- Engineering leverage
- Cost of poor quality
- Procurement effectiveness

Question: As a company with a mature continuous improvement program, what would you say are the three primary reasons you are able to continuously improve, given that the low-hanging fruit is gone?

McCarty: We still have strong leaders who sponsor and drive a "top-down" approach to business improvement, we conduct ongo-

---

Six Sigma Learning Topic: An Introduction to the New Six Sigma

Motorola University developed the New Six Sigma because we had to. We could see our Motorola businesses as well as our customers and suppliers struggling with the same critical issues. We knew that the classic Six Sigma methodology — focus on defects and variability reduction — had served our business managers quite effectively during much of the 1990s, and we had helped our customers and suppliers apply Six Sigma to dramatically improve their business processes.

But we could also see that Six Sigma was losing its relevance to many of our business leaders. They perceived the methodology as too complex, effective only in manufacturing and engineering environments, and too slow in yielding results. We could also see, however, that many of our leaders had taken the important elements of Six Sigma — like understanding customer requirements, continuously driving process improvement, and using statistical analysis to drive fact-based decision making — and moved them into a broader, integrated approach that flawlessly executed their full business strategies.

The New Six Sigma builds on the power of the Six Sigma methodology we pioneered in the 1980s and introduced to many businesses in the 1990s, yet it benefits from the lessons we learned as we helped our customers and suppliers implement the methodology.

The New Six Sigma solves the paradox that leaders find themselves in today of attempting to simultaneously achieve short-term financial gains through fast business improvement projects while building future capability in both key talent and critical processes.

The following four key leadership principles, discerned through studying organizations that successfully implemented Six Sigma, anchor the New Six Sigma.

Figure 1-4. New Six Sigma at Motorola. (From Barney, Matt and McCarty, Tom, *New Six Sigma: The Leader's Guide to Achieving Rapid Business Improvement and Sustainable Results,* 1st edition, ©2003, pp. 11–13. Adapted by permission of Pearson Education, Inc., Upper Saddle River, NJ.)

ing, rigorous reviews of improvement projects, and we have consistent application of the Six Sigma methodology.

Question: What are the ways you accomplish this?

McCarty: By always focusing on desired business results, the corporation's performance, and performance at the individual level.

Figure 1-4 discusses what Motorola is doing to take the company into the future. At Motorola, it is referred to as the *New Six Sigma.*

Align
- Using the performance excellence business model (based on the Malcolm Baldrige criteria), link customer requirements to business strategy and core business processes.
- Create strategy execution targets, stretch goals, and appropriate measures. The goal is to provide sustainable, measurable bottom-line results that drive business goal achievement.

Mobilize
- Empower teams to drive improvements using projects selected by executives, project management methodology, and Six Sigma methods.
- Organize team efforts with clear charters, success criteria, and rigorous reviews.
- Provide teams with just-in-time training and empower them to act.

Accelerate
- Employ an action learning methodology by combining structured education with real-time project work and coaching to quickly bridge the gap from learning to doing. The motivation to act is perishable yet essential for driving projects to timely results.

Govern
- Drive the execution of strategy by managing scorecard metrics. Structured review processes involve reviewing dashboards of results as well as drilling into process and project details where needed. Barriers lift when leaders share best practices.
- Create strategy execution targets, stretch goals, and appropriate measures. The goal is to provide sustainable, measurable bottom-line results that drive business goal achievement.

Hewlett-Packard

I had the opportunity to pose some questions to Jeffrey Ball, Master Black Belt, Corporate TCE & Quality at Hewlett-Packard, pertaining to the state of continuous improvement at HP:

> *Question:* Can you tell me which of three predominant continuous improvement tools — Lean, Six Sigma, and Theory of Constraints — HP uses?
>
> *Ball:* Of the three (which is a limited list), our program probably best matches Six Sigma, although it is important to understand that our methodology goes beyond the typical Six Sigma model.
>
> *Question:* Can you summarize what the benefits have been from your continuous improvement program?
>
> *Ball:* Right now, the annual impact has quite a bit of variance based on the projects that get selected for improvement. Some management teams prefer to focus on customer or employee improvement as opposed to making improvements in cost savings or revenue generation. We have had individual projects have as much as $120 million impact for the company. We also require our black belts to go through a formal financial review process so that any financial benefits can be mapped to a particular business group.
>
> *Question:* Where do you see HP going in the future with improvement initiatives?
>
> *Ball:* Right now, HP is continuing its development of tactical projects but placing a higher emphasis on leadership teams, starting from the definition of a purpose statement to match the needs of the customer, to viewing the organization as a system, to defining strategic objectives, and ending with constant monitoring of commissioned projects. Furthermore, HP has designed and/or adopted a host of methods that focus on inventing or improving the customer experience. While our approach to quality is based on the concepts of continuous improvement, our emphasis on the total customer experience balances the need for efficiency with the desire to provide the world's best customer experiences.
>
> *Question:* Do you see any benefit of incorporating a holistic management system that manages all three tools?
>
> *Ball:* As briefly noted in the first question, this is not a comprehensive list of methods. HP has based its improvement model on Deming's System of Profound Knowledge. It is key that we balance the theory of knowledge, systems thinking, psychology, and understanding variation.

Dell

Dell is one of the fastest growing manufacturers of computers, and much of its success is attributed to the management approach of Michael Dell and the company's overall commitment to continuous improvement. Figure 1-5 provides some insight into the management philosophies behind this success.[4]

When Dell CEO Michael S. Dell and President Kevin B. Rollins met privately in the fall of 2001, they felt confident that the company was recovering from the global crash in PC sales. Their own personal performance, however, was another matter. Internal interviews revealed that subordinates thought Dell, 38, was impersonal and emotionally detached, while Rollins, 50, was seen as autocratic and antagonistic. Few felt strong loyalty to the company's leaders. Worse, the discontent was spreading: A survey taken over the summer, following the company's first-ever mass layoffs, found that half of Dell, Inc.'s employees would leave if they got the chance.

What happened next says much about why Dell is the best-managed company in technology. At other industry giants, the CEO and his chief sidekick might have shrugged off the criticism or let the issue slide. Not at Dell. Fearing an exodus of talent, the two execs focused on the gripes. Within a week, Dell faced his top 20 managers and offered a frank self-critique, acknowledging that he is hugely shy and that it sometimes made him seem aloof and unapproachable. He vowed to forge tighter bonds with his team. Some in the room were shocked. They knew personality tests given to key execs had repeatedly shown Dell to be an "off-the-charts introvert," and such an admission from him had to have been painful. "It was powerful stuff," says Brian Wood, the head of public-sector sales for the Americas. "You could tell it wasn't easy for him."

Michael Dell didn't stop there. Days later, they began showing a videotape of his talk to every manager in the company — several thousand people. Then Dell and Rollins adopted desktop props to help them do what didn't come naturally. A plastic bulldozer cautioned Dell not to ram through ideas without including others, and a Curious George doll encouraged Rollins to listen to his team before making up his mind.

Walking Databases
To some, the way Michael Dell handled sagging morale might seem like another tale of feel-good management. But to those inside the company, it epitomizes how this Round Rock (Tex.) computer maker has transformed itself from a no-name PC player into a powerhouse brand. Sure, Dell is the master at selling direct, bypassing middlemen to deliver PCs cheaper than any of its rivals. And few would quarrel

---

Figure 1-5. Management philosophy at Dell. (Reprinted from November 3, 2003 issue of *Business Week* by special permission, ©2003 by The McGraw-Hill Companies, Inc.)

that it's the model of efficiency, with a far-flung supply chain knitted together so tightly that it's like one electrical wire, humming 24/7. Yet all this has been true for more than a decade. And although the entire computer industry has tried to replicate Dell's tactics, none can hold a candle to the company's results. Today, Dell's stock is valued at a price-earnings multiple of 40, loftier than IBM, Microsoft, Wal-Mart Stores, or General Electric.

As it turns out, it's how Michael Dell manages the company that has elevated it far above its sell-direct business model. What's Dell's secret? At its heart is his belief that the status quo is never good enough, even if it means painful changes for the man with his name on the door. When success is achieved, it's greeted with five seconds of praise followed by five hours of postmortem on what could have been done better. Says Michael Dell: "Celebrate for a nanosecond. Then move on." After the outfit opened its first Asian factory, in Malaysia, the CEO sent the manager heading the job one of his old running shoes to congratulate him. The message: This is only the first step in a marathon.

Just as crucial is Michael Dell's belief that once a problem is uncovered, it should be dealt with quickly and directly, without excuses. "There's no 'The dog ate my homework' here," says Dell. No, indeed. After Randall D. Groves, then head of the server business, delivered 16% higher sales last year, he was demoted. Never mind that none of its rivals came close to that. It could have been better, say two former Dell executives. Groves referred calls to a Dell spokesman, who says Groves's job change was part of a broader reorganization.

Above all, Michael Dell expects everyone to watch each dime — and turn it into at least a quarter. Unlike most tech bosses, Dell believes every product should be profitable from Day One. To ensure that, he expects his managers to be walking databases, able to cough up information on everything from top-line growth to the average number of times a part has to be replaced in the first 30 days after a computer is sold.

But there's one number he cares about most: operating margin. To Dell, it's not enough to rack up profits or grow fast. Execs must do both to maximize long-term profitability. That means products need to be priced low enough to induce shoppers to buy, but not so low that they cut unnecessarily into profits. When Dell's top managers in Europe lost out on profits in 1999 because they hadn't cut costs far enough, they were replaced. "There are some organizations where people think they're a hero if they invent a new thing," says Rollins. "Being a hero at Dell means saving money."

It's this combination — reaching for the heights of perfection while burrowing down into every last data point — that no rival has been able to imitate. "It's like watching Michael Jordan stuff the basketball," says Merrill Lynch & Co. technology strategist Steven Milunovich. "I see it. I understand it. But I can't do it."

How did this Mike come by his management philosophy? It started 19 years ago, when he was ditching classes to sell homemade PCs out of his University

Figure 1-5 (continued).

of Texas dorm room. Dell was the scrappy underdog, fighting for his company's life against the likes of IBM and Compaq Computer Corp. with a direct-sales model that people thought was plain nuts. Now, Michael Dell is worth $17 billion, while his 40,000-employee company is about to top $40 billion in sales. Yet he continues to manage Dell with the urgency and determination of a college kid with his back to the wall. "I still think of us as a challenger," he says. "I still think of us attacking."

It's not that Michael Dell leads by force of personality. He's blessed with neither the tough-guy charisma of Jack Welch nor the folksy charm of the late Sam Walton. Once, after hearing about the exploits of flamboyant Oracle Corp. CEO Lawrence J. Ellison, he held up a piece of paper and deadpanned to an aide: "See this? It's vanilla and square, and so am I." This egoless demeanor permeates the company. Everyone is expected to sacrifice their own interests for the good of the business, and no one gets to be a star. If Michael Dell is willing to modify the personality traits he was born with, other top execs are expected to be just as self-sacrificing. Frequently, Dell pairs execs to run an important business, an approach called "two-in-a-box." That way, they work together, checking each other's weaknesses and sharing the blame when something goes wrong. One such executive calls Dell's senior leadership "the no-name management team."

All this has kept Dell on track as rivals have gone off the rails. Since 2000, the company has been adding market share at a faster pace than at any time in its history — nearly three percentage points in 2002. A renewed effort to control costs sliced overhead expenses to just 9.6% of revenue in the most recent quarter and boosted productivity to nearly $1 million in revenue per employee. That's three times the revenue per employee at IBM and almost twice Hewlett-Packard Co.'s rate.

He (Michael Dell) maintains pinpoint control over the company's vast operations by constantly monitoring sales information, production data, and his competitors' activities. He keeps a BlackBerry strapped to his hip at all times. In the office, he reserves an hour in the morning and one each afternoon to do nothing but read and respond to e-mail, according to one former executive. "Michael can be a visionary, and he can tell you how many units were shipped from Singapore yesterday," says General Electric Co. CEO Jeffrey R. Immelt, a top Dell customer.

Rollins has the same attention to detail as Michael Dell. He is overseeing a Six Sigma transformation of everything from manufacturing to marketing that is expected to help cut expenses $1.5 billion this year. The emphasis is on small surgical strikes on defects and waste, not massive restructurings. Consider a Six Sigma meeting one balmy July afternoon. Rollins listened to John Holland, a technician in Dell's server factory, describe how his team replaced the colored paper it used to print out parts lists with plain white paper, saving $23,000. "Where else do you get a supervisor making $40,000 a year presenting to the president of a $40 billion company?" says Americas Operations Vice-President Dick Hunter, Holland's boss.

SUMMARY

Clearly, these companies are making significant strides to continuously transform their organizations. In an age in which our lives are becoming more and more dependent on electronic devices of one sort or another, it is comforting to know the commitment these companies have to achieving excellence.

We have looked at a variety of industries and gotten a perspective on how each of them approaches continuous improvement. All of them are admirable for a variety of reasons. When I was receiving this information from all of these great companies, I could not help but wonder what critical self-analysis each would do. What would each say about what it thought would be beneficial for it to do in the future? I interviewed a sampling of representatives from these companies and got responses that had a consistent theme around a couple of issues:

1. Expand the use of the continuous improvement tools across the enterprise.
2. Continue to foster an improvement culture through a holistic management system.

These issues are obviously noble activities to pursue in any organization. Let's consider the second item briefly at this point because it speaks to the focus of this book.

When speaking to representatives from these companies, it became clear that a majority of them believed that a holistic continuous improvement management system is beneficial in helping to sustain improvement. A lot of these companies have been doing this improvement business for quite some time, and the longer you do it, the harder it gets. Once the trees begin to be stripped of all that low-hanging fruit, it becomes harder to harvest additional fruit using the same tools.

Suppose you own an apple orchard. The rage of the apple orchard business is a new tool for picking apples, the ROBO picker. It is an automated tool that can pick twice as many apples as a person and does it in half the time. The manufacturer of the ROBO picker has offered to give you a prototype at no charge with the hope of getting future orders, and you decide to start using the ROBO picker at your orchard. It is everything that it was cracked up to be, and your savings in the first three months of using it are phenomenal. The only problem is that it cannot pick fruit any higher than five feet off the ground. Anyone who is familiar with apple trees knows that some of the best fruit can be found on the higher branches.

After three months, half of the orchard is picked clean five feet and below, but the apples higher up are still available for picking. The question is how to go about harvesting the apples that are higher up. Would you modify the ROBO to reach higher, utilize some pickers as you did in the past to harvest the higher apples with ladders, or try something totally different to get a jump on the competition?

You might decide to hire pickers as you have done in the past to reach the higher fruit with ladders. If you go down this path, then chances are you will not realize any additional gains beyond the combination of the ROBO and the pickers. The end result will be an initial big savings from the ROBO that levels off once the low-hanging fruit is gone.

You could decide to modify the ROBO to reach the higher fruit instead of hiring pickers, in which case you may be able to achieve additional benefits beyond using the pickers for the higher fruit.

On the other hand, you may decide to try something totally different than the ROBO and the pickers in order to achieve further optimization and financial gain.

The point is that once the low-hanging fruit is gone, the gains will not come as easily and the direction the organization should take to assure ongoing improvement becomes more challenging. If your goal is to rid your orchard of low-hanging fruit, then by all means get your ROBO and go at it. But if you have been using the ROBO for a while, you might want to consider a holistic management system to help you figure out how to optimize the utilization of the ROBO or any other tool available to you.

2

YOUR INDUSTRY STANDARD: A FRAMEWORK FOR LOOK FORWARD® IMPROVEMENT

Is your quality system "standard" driving your business to improve? Those in the automotive and aerospace industries have been conditioned over the years by the various mandated requirements flowed down through quality system standards, such as MIL-Q-9858, ISO 9001, QS-9000, TS-16949, AS9100, etc. The intent of any quality standard is to offer a prescription to follow in order to assure a desired level of enterprise-wide quality. Whether or not the standards of old or even the current ones accomplish this is up for debate. Clearly, true enterprise-wide quality is not some acknowledged summit reached by the successful indoctrination of various prescribed procedures. Rather, it is a culture that exists in which continual improvement is ingrained into the very nature of day-to-day business activities. Improvement is not an event or a project; it is a way of life.

I do not know whether or not all of the standards that exist today support the creation of and sustaining this type of culture. However, what I do know is that AS9100, which is the prevalent guiding standard for aerospace companies, does indeed create a strong foundation for building a culture of continual improvement.

If you are reading this book, you most likely are already familiar with ISO 9001:2000. AS9100 is ISO 9001:2000 and then some. It was initially published for aerospace companies in 1999 by the Society of Automotive Engineers and then further developed by the International Organization for Standardization (ISO), the Aerospace Technical Committee 20, and the American Aerospace Quality Group in the United States and the European Association of Aerospace Industries in Europe and other countries, including China, Japan, Mexico, and Brazil.

The additional requirements of AS9100 above and beyond those in ISO 9001:2000 are deemed necessary and critical for the aerospace industry. The following is a sampling of some of these aerospace-specific items:

- Additional requirements regarding company personnel, customer, and/or regulatory authority access to quality management system documentation
- Tighter controls on the association of standard requirements to documented procedures
- Some configuration management additional requirements
- An additional mandate upon management to *"ensure the organizational freedom to resolve matters pertaining to quality"*
- Some additional work environment comments
- Numerous product realization additions impacting design and development planning, inputs and outputs, review, verification, validation and changes, purchasing, production and service, identification and traceability, customer property, preservation of product, and control of monitoring and measuring devices
- A significant number of additions to the measurement, analysis, and improvement section as well, in particular pertaining to statistical techniques, internal audits, monitoring and measurement of processes, monitoring and measurement of product, inspection documentation, first article inspection, control of nonconforming product, and corrective action[7]

These extra requirements obviously contribute to establishing the character of any aerospace business and in an extraneous way, if embraced, contribute to fostering a climate of excellence.

The one additional requirement over ISO 9001:2000, which is italicized in the list above, is the one-liner in the management responsibility section which states that management must "ensure the organization freedom to resolve matters pertaining to quality."[7] If truly realized, this simple yet powerful statement results in an empowered workforce that is free to foster continual improvement. In terms of continual improvement, the standard states that it is to be achieved "through the use of the quality policy, quality objectives, audit results, analysis of data, corrective and preventative actions and *management review*."[7] The key is how this "management review" function is exercised within a company in order to foster continual improvement. How the Look Forward® method works to achieve this will be discussed later in this book.

The authors of this standard had the unique opportunity to shape and mold the nature of quality management systems across an industry for years to come. This is heady stuff and quite a responsibility. The impact these standards have had on changing the way companies do business likely exceeded the dreams of a Deming, Shewhart, or Juran, although when one reads these standards it is hard not to see the foundational teachings of the quality masters of ages past.

A prevailing theme of the teachings of all these quality giants has been the need for upper management's active involvement in the quality improvement process. Recall Deming's 14 obligations of top management:[2]

1. Create constancy of purpose for improvement of products and service.
2. Adopt a new philosophy; we are in a new economic age.
3. Cease dependence upon inspection as a way to achieve quality.
4. End the practice of awarding business based on price tag.
5. Constantly improve the process of planning, production, and service. This system includes people.
6. Institute training on the job.
7. Institute improved supervision (leadership).
8. Drive out fear.
9. Break down barriers between departments.
10. Eliminate slogans/targets asking for increased productivity without providing methods.
11. Eliminate numerical quotas.
12. Remove barriers that stand between workers and their pride of workmanship; the same for all salaried people.
13. Institute programs for education and retraining.
14. Put all emphasis in the company to work to accomplish the transformation.

Then there are Juran's success factors that senior management embraced in order to be effective leaders:[4]

1. The chief executives personally became the leaders of the quality revolution.
2. They trained the entire managerial hierarchy in how to manage for quality.
3. They opened up the annual business plan to include strategic goals for quality improvement.

4. They undertook quality improvement at a revolutionary rate, year after year.
5. They enlarged the executive report package to include reports on performance relative to the quality goals.
6. They provided opportunities for the workforce to participate in the quality revolution.
7. They revised the systems of recognition and reward to give greater weight to achievements in quality.

A consistent theme of both Deming and Juran is management involvement.

Clearly, management involvement resonates with the authors of the AS9100 standard and, for that matter, the ISO 9001:2000 standard. The authors challenge management to be actively involved in the continual improvement of the business through the propagation of eight management principles. These management principles are reflective of the teachings of Deming and Juran and are the solid foundation upon which a world-class quality management system can be built. The quality giants knew it, and the AS9100 authors have exercised their unique responsibility in order to effect change. The eight management principles, which are the focus of the standard, are as follows:[7]

1. Customer focus
2. Leadership
3. Involvement of people
4. Process approach
5. Systems approach to management
6. Continual improvement
7. Factual approach to decision making
8. Mutually beneficial supplier relationships

These eight principles could have been written by Deming or Juran themselves given the similar theme transmitted in their previously noted familiar points.

These principles are captured and eloquently formulated by the authors using an applied orientation in the eight elements that make up the standard. The last five of these elements are the heart and soul of the document from which all practical application of the requirements is initiated. The titles of the eight elements of the standard are:[7]

1. Scope
2. Normative Reference
3. Terms and Conditions
4. Quality Management System

5. Management Responsibility
6. Resource Management
7. Product Realization
8. Measurement, Analysis and Improvement

In this chapter, the focus is clearly on the "management responsibility" element and how the guidelines within the standard provide the building blocks for establishing a *world-class* quality management system.

The AS9100 authors waste no time in offering the reader these guidelines. To prove the point, one need only look at the standard's introduction. Although it is intended to provide a general overview of the standard's philosophy, it almost reads like a Lean or Six Sigma instructional document. The following is an excerpt from the Society of Automotive Engineers AS9100 standard:*

Process Approach:
This International Standard promotes the adoption of a process approach when developing, implementing and improving the effectiveness of a quality management system, to enhance customer satisfaction by meeting customer requirements.

For an organization to function effectively, it has to identify and manage numerous linked activities. An activity using resources, and managed in order to enable the transformation of inputs into outputs, can be considered as a process. Often the output from one process directly forms the input to the next.

The application of a system of processes within an organization, together with the identification and interactions of these processes, and their management, can be referred to as the "process approach."

An advantage of the process approach is the ongoing control that it provides over the linkage between the individual processes within the system of processes, as well as over their combination and interaction.

When used within a quality management system, such an approach emphasizes the importance of:

a. Understanding and meeting requirements
b. The need to consider processes in terms of added value
c. Obtaining results of process performance and effectiveness, and

---

* Reprinted with permission from SAE AS9100A. ©2001 SAE International.

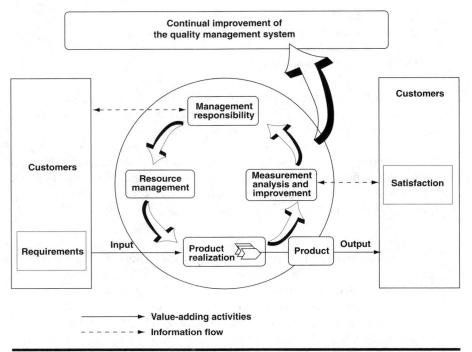

Figure 2-1. Model of a process-based quality management system. (Reprinted with permission from SAE AS9100A. ©2001 SAE International.)

    d. Continual improvement of processes based on objective
       measurement.

The model of a process-based quality management system shown
in Figure 2-1 illustrates the process linkages presented in clauses 4
to 8. This illustration shows that customers play a significant role
in defining requirements as inputs. Monitoring of customer satisfaction requires the evaluation of information relating to customer
perception as to whether the organization has met the customer
requirements. The model shown in Figure 2-1 covers all the requirements of this International Standard, but does not show processes at
a detailed level.

NOTE: In addition, the methodology known as "Plan-Do-Check-
Act" (PDCA) can be applied to all processes. PDCA can be briefly
described as follows:

Plan: Establish the objectives and processes necessary to deliver results in accordance with customer requirements and the organization's policies.

Do: Implement the processes.

Check: Monitor and measure processes and product against policies, objectives and requirements for the product and report the results.

Act: Take actions to continually improve process performance.

Dr. Shewhart and Dr. Deming would be proud to see PDCA incorporated in an aerospace quality system standard and prescribed as a normal course of doing business.

Prescribing the standard is just what the doctor ordered for an ailing company. The standard no longer is a counterintuitive force to the business, but rather provides guidelines that will help the business thrive. This thinking permeates the standard and provides the necessary tools for building a world-class quality system.

Building a world-class quality management system can be viewed as similar to building a house. When you think of what your dream house will look like, you think about its street appeal, floor layout, and amenities — in essence, the end product. However, the first step in making your dream home a reality is to build it on a solid foundation. The foundation is one of the most important aspects of a home, and its strength is critical for assuring that your dream home does not come crashing down. AS9100 is that foundation for a business upon which a world-class quality management system can be built.

So why isn't every company that is compliant to AS9100 world class? As with a house, the foundation alone is not sufficient. Your dream home is not four concrete walls in a hole somewhere. The foundation is the starting point from which to build. AS9100 is that starting point, which if embraced will support a transformation of your business such that the limitations on continual improvement are nonexistent.

The foundation, as critical as it is, in some ways is the easy part. The standard has well-thought-out prescriptions that give some guidelines for a path to success. But how do you go beyond the basics and make your company flourish? How do you erect the frame for your house, put up the drywall, and get it painted and polished so that it becomes that dream home?

To build your dream home, you need to contract with a builder, painter, electrician, plumber, and many other subcontractors. However, all of these activities need to be orchestrated properly so that they all complement each other. What you need is a general contractor to manage the various subcontractors available to you in order to optimize the building process.

Look Forward® sort of plays the role of a general contractor that can help you manage your business so as to optimize all of the business tools at your disposal. By the end of this book, you will see how a Look Forward®–managed business with a foundation of AS9100 or ISO 9001:2000 can be built upon, using the tools of Lean, Six Sigma, and Theory of Constraints, in order to achieve world-class levels of performance.

Someone who knows all about the role the standard plays in a company's continuous improvement program is John Sedlak, vice president and COO of Smithers Quality Assessments. Smithers is one of the leading registrars in relation to customer satisfaction (reference *Quality Digest* articles by Fredenberger et al.[3] and Carden et al.[1]). Over the years, Mr. Sedlak has seen the operations of many different companies, and from his viewpoint, the standard can be key to improvement if it is married to the overall philosophy of your company. Figures 2-2 and 2-3 provide a brief look at the impact the standard had on one of his clients, along with his views from a registrar's perspective.

As the global economy continues to emerge, the need for a firmly structured quality system cannot be underestimated. The implementation of ISO-based methodology has facilitated more thorough and effective planning and human resource development in all phases of our operation.

The teamwork approach has provided the basis for all disciplines within the group to become proactive members of process and system development.

The importance of training programs has become highlighted as critically important to the reduction of waste and improved operational efficiency.

Advance planning has promoted the launching of new jobs, on time and with a minimum of concerns.

We have found that implementing a system only to satisfy an auditor is not worth the time and effort and does little to improve a company. A truly effective system must become a way of doing business on an every day basis. When you get to the point that you are not scurrying around a week before an audit but are fully prepared every day is when you know you have an effective system that is fully integrated into your business.

Management commitment, organized planning, and human and material resource allocations are the keys to a successful QMS. It has provided for increased growth and profitability every year since our initial certification.

Don Tyler
Sr. Vice President
General Aluminum Mfg. Co.

Figure 2-2. The positive impact of a structured quality system. (Reprinted with permission.)

From the perspectives of a third-party registrar and its clients, the ISO 9001:2000 standard is the foundation upon which an organization can build and improve. Some organizations slow down when the basic system is in place, certified, and working effectively, viewing improvements as small, incremental steps. Others take a more aggressive approach, viewing certification as just the beginning. From this starting point, they aggressively pursue improvements in quality of product, design, delivery, and a host of other areas. These organizations utilize the appropriate improvement tools to achieve improvement, including Design of Experiments, Lean manufacturing, kaizen, Theory of Constraints, Six Sigma, five S, and so on. The key to their success is that their efforts are executed in a system that is grounded upon the requirements of ISO 9001:2000. Without this grounding, the results of improvement efforts are much like the tent pitched upon soft soil — improvements are only sporadic and at best are temporary.

In years past, there were many so-called improvement techniques introduced, such as quality circles, MBWA (manage by walking around), statistical process control, and zero defects, to name a few. While each of these had merit (and still do), they did not produce the expected results. Why? Because management saw each tool as an end-all or be-all. In fact, they were simply tools. When these valid tools were applied to a weak management system, there was little chance of success. However, since 1987, the ISO 9001 series of standards has provided organizations the means to create solid foundations upon which to build their improvement efforts. Now these tools have a much higher probability of success.

ISO 9001:2000 as a stand-alone system may not provide improvement, per se. However, an organization may realize some improvement via cultural changes. But certification to ISO 9001:2000 can provide the foundation upon which significant improvement efforts can be built. You can pitch a tent, you can build a castle, or you can build something in between. The choice is up to each organization. But if any organization believes that it can survive for any real length of time without practicing continual improvement, then it is suffering from a serious case of delusion. Why? Because in the meantime their competition is most likely passing them up.

Conclusion: How organizations run their business is up to them. There are as many approaches to organizational structure as there are fish in the sea. However, ISO 9001:2000 is a universally applicable framework that provides the foundation for success, short and long term. As such, organizations are encouraged to learn about it, implement it, get certified to it, and then utilize the tools of improvement on a continuing basis.

John R. Sedlak
Vice President, COO
Smithers Quality Assessments, Inc.

Figure 2-3. ISO 9001:2000 — the foundation for improvement. (Reprinted with permission.)

PART 2.
AN OVERVIEW
OF THE BIG THREE
CONTINUOUS
IMPROVEMENT TOOLS

SIX SIGMA

Over the last several years, Six Sigma has almost become a household word. It has been popularized by Jack Welch and others and was even used by the U.S. government to fight the war on terror. There are a plethora of resources that delve into what Six Sigma is in depth. This chapter will offer an overview of the methodology.

If you are not using these tools today, then this chapter will provide you with some insight into what they are and help you gain a clear understanding of their purpose. If you are currently using these tools, then this chapter will serve as a reminder of their effectiveness and, in conjunction with the remainder of the book, offer you an understanding of how they can be woven into the business fabric.

Let's start by looking at Figure 3-1. What comes to mind when you see this drawing? To put it another way: What is wrong with this picture? What is obvious? Clearly, using a single pulley and rope to lift a pallet of bricks is not the most effective method. How safe is it? Just look at those sandbags holding down the pulley post. It does not seem very safe. The obvious solution is that a hydraulic lift should be used to raise the bricks up to the working area. Right? Now, what is not so obvious? Step back and think about the whole process. It appears that the objective is to first transport the bricks from point A to point B. Is loading them in a wheelbarrow and rolling them along the best way to accomplish that objective? How could bricks be transported more efficiently? How do you suppose the competition is transporting bricks? If the competition is using a truck, will the company in Figure 3-1 be in the brick transportation business very long?

That is one of the aims of Six Sigma — to look beyond the obvious, identify the problem, and work toward achieving a solution. But that may not be what

Figure 3-1.   One brick at a time. (By Paul A. Piersa. Reprinted with permission.)

typically comes to mind when you think of Six Sigma. Where does the parts per million come into play, and where is all the statistical stuff? These surely are aspects of Six Sigma, but it is not limited to just that. In addition to crunching numbers, Six Sigma solves problems. The techniques and tools presented in this chapter are some of the ones in the Six Sigma toolbox from which the Six Sigma professional can draw.

Before getting into the tools, let's take a look at a definition of Six Sigma. According to Snee, "Six Sigma is a business improvement approach that seeks to find and eliminate causes of mistakes or defects in business processes by focusing on outputs that are of critical importance to customers."[16] Outputs that are of critical importance to customers are sometimes referred to as "critical to quality." Mikel Harry offers another definition of Six Sigma: "Six Sigma is a business process that allows companies to drastically improve their bottom line by designing and monitoring everyday business activities in ways that minimize waste and resources while increasing customer satisfaction."[7]

Mikel Harry was one of the chief architects of Six Sigma while working at Motorola in the 1980s. He is also the founder and chief executive officer of the Six Sigma Academy, Inc. and co-author of the book *Six Sigma: The Breakthrough Management Strategy Revolutionizing the World's Top Corporations.* His definition captures the essence of what Six Sigma is and what it is capable

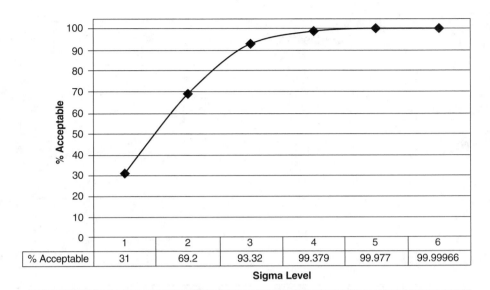

Figure 3-2. Sigma level versus percent acceptable. (Courtesy of Aircraft Braking Systems Corporation.)

of offering any organization that effectively implements it. At a minimum, it provides us with a conceptual understanding of Six Sigma. But from less of a conceptual point of view and more of a statistical standpoint, what does Six Sigma mean? Companies that are operating at Six Sigma are producing 3.4 defects per million opportunities, which results in 99.9997% acceptable output. Figure 3-2 illustrates the relationship between percent acceptable and the sigma level.

Most U.S. companies operate in the three- to four-sigma range. At first glance, three to four sigma doesn't seem all that bad, does it? Before answering that, let's look at how the sigma level equates to defects per million. Figure 3-3 illustrates the relationship between the sigma level and defects per million opportunities.

A transformation from a three- to four-sigma level to six sigma is somewhat of a quantum leap. Reaching six-sigma-level quality is no walk in the park and can only be achieved through a disciplined methodical approach to continuous improvement, which will be discussed in this chapter.

Given the difficulty of leaping to six-sigma-level quality, is three to four sigma good enough? In companies considering a six sigma approach, there is some debate as to the economic merit of making the leap. Of course, each

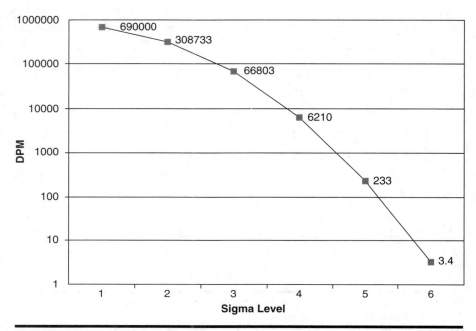

Figure 3-3. Sigma level versus defects per million opportunities. (Courtesy of Aircraft Braking Systems Corporation.)

instance is unique and must be evaluated as to the merit of six sigma. However, let's look at some statistics to consider when evaluating the pursuit of six sigma (99.9997% acceptance).

Can we live with 99.9% acceptance instead of 99.9997%? If we say yes, then we accept that we can live with the following outcomes each year:

1. 5400 arterial bypass failures
2. 31,536 commercial aircraft takeoffs aborted
3. 180 train wrecks a year
4. 50 visas issued to dangerous persons

Let's say we decide that 99.9% is just not going to cut it for the examples above and that we must have six-sigma-level quality. After implementing our Six Sigma quality efforts, the outcomes change to the following:

1. 18 arterial bypass failures
2. 107 commercial aircraft takeoffs aborted

3. Less than one train wreck a year
4. No visas issued to dangerous persons

What a difference a couple of sigma makes! This illustrates the impact Six Sigma can have on achieving the desired outcome. If you are on the customer end of one of the processes listed above, then your satisfaction level has just been bolstered significantly by your supplier's Six Sigma efforts. That is a major goal for any business — keep your customers happy and attract as many new customers as possible by exceeding their expectations.

Six Sigma projects should be customer focused. The key element of any customer-supplier relationship is a clear understanding of what the customer expectations are. Many a business has gone by the wayside clinging to the notion that because it is the authority, it can dictate to customers what they want. The message received from gaining a clear understanding of customer expectations is sometimes referred to as the *voice of the customer*. Rath & Strong suggest a process for collecting voice of the customer data:[14]

1. Identify customers and their needs.
2. Collect and analyze reactive and proactive data.
3. Convert collected data into customer needs.
4. Sort out the most important attributes that the customer wants.
5. Obtain specifications from the critical-to-quality characteristics.

How you decide to determine your customers' wants can be critical to your long-term survival. Whatever method you choose, let it be the focus of your continuous improvement efforts. We need to be customer-driven organizations in order to achieve world-class levels of quality. Our customers will make us better.

Since a successfully implemented Six Sigma program is focused on improvement projects that are relevant to the customer and positively impact the bottom line, where do we start with our efforts to implement Six Sigma successfully?

Every business system is made up of a series of business processes that have a variety of inputs and outputs. Some processes in your company churn along like a fine-tuned engine, never missing a beat, producing little to no scrap, and burdening the company with minimal operating costs. Others do not. That is where you want to focus — wherever the greatest economic and strategic benefit exists. No organization within your company should be exempt from Six Sigma improvement initiatives. Marketing, accounting, and R&D have just as many opportunities for improvement as the factory floor. The key is to identify the inputs and outputs to the processes involved and make them better.

However, before you run off and try to fix a process in marketing using Six Sigma, one critical factor has to exist — management support. For Six Sigma or, for that matter, any continuous improvement initiative to be successful, it is imperative that strong management support exists. The efforts expended must have buy-in from management because various resources will be utilized and personnel will be called upon throughout the project to invest time and energy. The commitment needs to be there or you are doomed to failure.

In addition to management support, the personnel involved in the project need to be adequately trained in the methodology of Six Sigma in order to properly apply the tools. The level of training is commensurate with the role an employee plays in the Six Sigma scheme of things. The typical roles that exist in the world of Six Sigma are black belts, master black belts, green belts, executive sponsors, champions, and process owners.

Once you have management support and the appropriate personnel have been trained, then the project teams are formed and the work of improvement begins. The project team members are typically made up of green belts, black belts, and people in the process who have received some related training. The remaining roles previously mentioned support the project team through mentoring, coaching, and sponsoring of the team's objective. A black belt differs from a green belt via an increased amount of training and knowledge in the tools and techniques of Six Sigma.

The objective or focus of the project team needs to be related to the organizational goals and result in a financial benefit to the company. In order to verify that the team's efforts have resulted in a financial benefit, it is imperative that effective metrics are evaluated. The act of measuring what you want to improve is obviously very important and not as trivial as it sounds. Harry and Schroederer introduced some Six Sigma metrics that are intended to accomplish the following:[7]

- Measure customer opinions (surveys, questionnaires, etc.)
- Determine customer critical-to-quality factors (critical-to-quality tree)
- Measure product outcomes (throughput yield, rolled throughput yield, normalized yield)
- Correlate process outcomes to critical-to-quality factors (measure processes with metrics that correlate to the company's fundamental economics)

These clearly desirable objectives for any company illustrate the importance of the metrics used.

The primary metric for driving any Six Sigma effort must have a dollar sign in front of it. If your effort does not save money, don't even bother with it.

Businesses are in business to make money. Any business improvement tool must improve the core purpose of the business's existence: to make money. All other nonmonetary metrics are secondary in nature, and their improvement should result in a corresponding financial benefit. If a metric does not, then do not use that metric, because it is not driving improvement in your business.

Once the project team wades through the maze of potential metrics and selects those most appropriate to the organizational goals, then the team is poised to initiate the project. A Six Sigma effort is a project that has a predetermined objective, a planned life cycle, and requires the allocation of resources for completion. Therefore, many of the basic tenets of "project management" apply to the execution of a Six Sigma project, and its successful execution and monitoring of status are accomplished in the same fashion as any other project, using Gantt charts, PERT charts, etc.

The execution of a Six Sigma project uses a structured method of approaching problem solving, normally described by the acronym DMAIC,[12] which stands for Define, Measure, Analyze, Improve, Control, or DMADV,[12] which stands for Define, Measure, Analyze, Design, Verify. DMAIC is the approach primarily used for improving existing processes, and DMADV is used for improving designs. Notice that the first three steps in each are the same.

A Six Sigma project typically will focus on a business system or process that may affect one or more functional areas. The key elements of any process, and the lifeblood to a Six Sigma project, are the inputs, outputs, and resulting feedback. These are all elements to consider within the Define phase of the project. That being the case, let's take a closer look at the Define phase to find out what it is all about.

DEFINE

In the Define phase of a project, a team is trying to get its arms around the extent of the effort required. The types of things that are determined in this phase include the scope of the project, the project charter, the metrics that will be used for the project, and most importantly, the problem statement.

The problem statement will address specifically what the team wants to improve. It provides a focus for the team's efforts and typically will include a representation of the current state, which clearly illustrates the need for the project and potential benefit. To use a travel analogy, it tells you what your city of origin is and gives you an idea of where you want to go. For example, if you are starting in New York and know you want to go to Los Angeles, New York is the equivalent of the current state of the process or system that you want to improve. Los Angeles is the amount of savings that you want to achieve as a result of performing the project. How you get from New York to Los Angeles is the variable that is determined by the team using the Six Sigma tools at its disposal. Getting to Los Angeles in this analogy is akin to the *goal statement* in the Six Sigma world. Both the problem statement and the goal statement are part of the overall *project charter,* which normally is one of the first deliverables of the project team.

Moen et al.[10] offer some recommendations for what should be included in the project charter:

- Business case (financial impact)
- Problem statement
- Project scope (boundaries)
- Goal statement
- Role of team members
- Milestones/deliverables (end products of the project)
- Resources required

The scope of the project is an attempt by the team to establish some boundaries of involvement to assist with maintaining the team's focus. It also serves the purpose of communicating clearly to those outside the team what the team's limitations are. Sometimes a project team can be viewed as a cure-all clearinghouse by those outside the team. The project charter helps to guard against that.

The next aspect of the Define phase we will discuss is the metrics that the team uses in order to illustrate the current state and also to validate the desired improvement. Typically, the metrics to be used are developed at this phase, but not completely finalized until the Measure phase. In determining the metrics to use, you would typically look for potential metrics from your suppliers, internal processes, and your customers. Eckes states that the basic metrics a team will consider involve aspects of quality, cycle time, cost, value, and labor.[5] Some methods for identifying metrics that a team may consider are the Pareto diagram, SIPOC, rolled throughput yield, voice of the customer, affinity diagram, Kano model, and critical-to-quality tree.[20] Let's take a look at SIPOC at this point.

SIPOC stands for Suppliers, Inputs, Process, Outputs, and Customers. It is a type of process map that provides a bird's-eye view across the entire supply and demand chain. An example of a SIPOC is shown in Figure 3-4. This approach drives you to identify those characteristics that are key to the process and thereby identify the appropriate metrics to use to drive improvement. We will fine-tune those metrics in the Measure phase, which is the next sequential phase of a Six Sigma project.

Suppliers	Inputs	Process	Outputs	Customers
Raw Materials Suppliers	Design Requirements	See Below	Aircraft Wheel Assembly	Airlines
Finished Part Suppliers	Delivery Requirements		Aircraft Brake Assembly	OEMs
Special Process Suppliers	Quality System Requirements		Brake Control System	Distributors

Process

Supplier produces material	Supplier delivers material	Parts machined & assembled internally	Orders processed for material	Send material to customer

Figure 3-4. SIPOC example.

MEASURE

It is within the Measure phase that a project begins to take shape and much of the hands-on activity is performed. This is also where the process analysis is performed and the data to be analyzed are gathered. Some of the tools that are utilized during this phase are process flowcharts, fishbone diagrams, descriptive statistics, statistical analysis, scatter diagrams, stem and leaf plots, histograms, measurement system analysis, and process capability.

The goal of the Measure phase is to establish a clear understanding of the current state of the process you want to improve. Think of it as similar to getting a physical examination. You might have an EKG and some blood work done. In addition to these basic measures, there are many other tests at the doctor's disposal in order to determine your current state of health. So too for the Six Sigma practitioner. There are many tools in the Six Sigma toolbox, some of which were previously mentioned, to draw upon in order to establish the current state of the process to improve. It is within the Measure phase that the metrics, which will be used to illustrate the improvement, are finalized. Clearly, these metrics will establish a baseline of the current state.

Many statistical tools are available to the Six Sigma professional, including probability analysis, box plots, scatter diagrams, and trend analysis. All of these measures will provide some understanding of how the data are distributed, but to really get a grasp on what the data are doing, you can go deeper using the probability density function and the cumulative distribution function. These will enable you to make intelligent decisions about how your data are behaving. The distribution that is associated with your data speaks volumes. Is it a normal distribution? If not, what is it? Is it a Weibull, Poisson, hypergeometric, chi-square, or student's t distribution? Are the data continuous or discrete? All of these may be questions you need to answer during the Measure phase of your project.

Measurement Analysis

No matter what tools you utilize to measure your data, it is important that you do not overlook the need for measurement system analysis. What is measurement system analysis? Measurement system analysis is an evaluation of the amount of variability that is being introduced into your data values as a result of the measuring equipment you are using. Your data are only as good as the measuring devices you are using. Typically, most manufacturers have gage calibration systems in place to assure a certain level of accuracy and repeatability in measuring devices. For everyday use, a calibration interval is established to perform a periodic verification on the measuring device before it drifts enough to cause issues with product acceptance. Other manufacturers may perform gage repeatability and reproducibility studies on their measuring devices in order to establish a measure of variability for the gage when in use. Gage R&R studies give some insight into the effect of the operator, the application of the gage, and the accuracy of the gage itself — in essence the entire measurement "process." Obviously, it is desirable to keep the amount of gage variation to a minimum. A word of caution is in order, then, to assure that the measuring system you use does not contribute significantly to data variation.

Process Flowcharts

It would be remiss to discuss the Measurement phase without giving consideration to process flowcharts. Whether you call it a process flowchart, process mapping, or value stream mapping, it is a valuable tool to use. Flowing a process and depicting it graphically gives you a road map of potential opportunities to focus on. The process of creating a process flowchart forces you to investigate the specifics about each and every step of the process. This activity alone can be an educational experience. Everyone is so busy these days that we rarely have the luxury of stepping back and looking at an overview of a process. However, when we do, it can be very beneficial. Creating a process flowchart should be one of the initial activities the team completes. With a completed flowchart in hand, the team may decide to utilize some of the other previously mentioned tools to complete the Measure phase of the project.

ANALYZE

The Analyze phase of a project is where you do the number crunching and evaluation of the data you measured in the previous phase. There are numerous statistical tools to analyze data, a sampling of which will be addressed in this section. We will take an overview look at simple linear regression, correlation coefficient, and hypothesis testing.

Simple Linear Regression

The regression line can be used to make predictions of how the data are going to perform based on the established regression line. In addition, it provides some insight into how well the data fit the line, thus giving you some insight into the level of confidence in your prediction. The better the fit, the higher the confidence.

Correlation Coefficient

The correlation coefficient, r, is a measure of how well two sets of data are related to one another. It is helpful in determining whether one factor in a process has an impact on another or if they are totally unrelated. The value of r will range from -1 to $+1$. A negative value of r indicates a negative correlation, and a positive value of r indicates a positive correlation. The closer the value to $+1$ or -1, the stronger the correlation between the two factors.

Hypothesis Testing

Hypothesis testing is used to evaluate the relationship between a statistic generated from sample data with either some known value or another sample statistic. Oftentimes, hypothesis testing is used to compare two means to determine if they are equal or if one is greater than the other. However, its use is not limited to testing means. It can be used to test variances and proportions as well.

Typically when performing a hypothesis test, there is a null hypothesis (H_0) and an alternative hypothesis (H_a). In the case of a test to determine if the means of two populations are equal, the null hypothesis is a statement that the means are equal, statistically speaking, and the alternative hypothesis is a statement that they are not equal.

When performing a hypothesis test, there is the possibility of error. There are two types of error to consider. Type 1 error occurs when the null hypothesis is rejected when in fact it is true. Type 2 error occurs when the null hypothesis is not rejected when it actually should be.

Depending on what statistics you are testing, your decision as to whether or not the null hypothesis is rejected is determined by the calculation of a test statistic from the data that is compared to a tabular value.

There are many other analysis tools including, but not limited to, multi-vari analysis, coefficient of determination, goodness of fit test, analysis of variance, nonparametric tests, the Spearman rank correlation coefficient, Kruskal-Wallis one-way analysis of variance by ranks, Mann-Whitney U-test, Levene's test, Mood's median test, etc. The challenge is to use the most appropriate tool for the situation in order to make the best decisions.

IMPROVE

Now that we have measured our data and performed some analysis on the data to know where our process is, it is time to improve it. There are three primary methods that the Six Sigma professional may want to consider when beginning to attempt to improve a process: design of experiments, response surface methodology, and evolutionary operations. In this section, we will take an overview look at what design of experiments is all about.

Design of Experiments

Experimentation performed without utilizing design of experiments actually only looks at one factor at a time, and conclusions are drawn based on the results obtained. Unfortunately, there are problems with performing experiments in this fashion. One is that any interaction effect that may exist between factors goes unnoticed; another is that without comparing various levels of all factors simultaneously, you have no visibility as to what the optimal combination of factor levels is. That is where design of experiments comes in.

With design of experiments, you can look at multiple levels of multiple factors simultaneously and make decisions as to what levels of the factors will optimize your output. There are various types of experimental designs you can draw upon depending on what you are trying to evaluate. Types of designs include randomized and randomized block designs, full factorial designs, fractional factorial designs, mixture experiments, and Taguchi designs. All of these except Taguchi designs are traditional methods of performing design of experiments. Taguchi designs were popularized by Dr. Genichi Taguchi and are argued to be more robust in their approach to experimental design.

When you decide that an experimental design is an appropriate tool to use, you need to approach the design in a methodical manner. First, you should identify the desired output of the design and/or process being studied. Second, brainstorm with all parties involved with the process to determine what the input factors and output factors are. Once you have done that, you are at a point where you can pick the most appropriate design for your application. After selecting your design, then execute it as prescribed and record your results. You may want to replicate some of the runs in order to validate the results you obtained. After you have run all of your experiments, crunch your numbers and draw your conclusions from them. It sounds simple, and in some sense it is, although some data that must be collected may require an interruption in operations. At the very least, it is an investment of time for the individual performing the experiment and analyzing the data, but a worthwhile one.

CONTROL

Our process has been measured, our data analyzed, and our process improved. Now we want to be assured that the improvements we have made will be sustained. We need to build an appropriate level of control into the process to assure that it does not backslide into an undesirable state. Tools that we can use to gain this assurance are statistical process control and some of the Lean tools. Let's take a brief look at each of these.

Statistical Process Control

Statistical process control (SPC) has been around for a while, initially developed by Dr. Shewhart in the 1920s. The purpose of SPC is to provide the operator with real-time feedback as to whether or not a process is functioning in control. There are a host of different types of charts that can be utilized depending on the type of data collection desired. Variable charts include X-bar/R, X/MR, EWMA, etc., and attribute charts include c, p, u, np, etc.

Instead of utilizing traditional SPC charts, you may want to consider using "precontrol" on your process. Precontrol is an easy method to evaluate your process whereby the specification range is divided into three sections. The middle section accounts for 86% of the data and is referred to as the target area. The outer two sections each account for 7% of the data and are the areas that drive your decisions on the process.

The precontrol rules are as follows:

- Setup: If five pieces are made within the target — okay to run.
- Running: Sample two consecutive pieces.
    - If first piece is within target — run (do not measure second piece).
    - If first piece is not within target — measure second piece.

□   If second piece is within target — run.
□   If second piece is not in target — adjust process — go back to setup.
□   Any time a reading is out of specification — stop and adjust.

Lean Tools

Some of the Lean tools may help you to maintain the improvements you achieved. These tools include the 5Ss, the kaizen blitz, kanban, poka-yoke, total productive maintenance, and standard work. They will be discussed in more detail in the next chapter on Lean manufacturing.

The purpose of the Control phase of a Six Sigma project is to maintain the improvements achieved in the prior phase. Whatever method you choose to use, consider the costs associated with it and the applicability to your process.

CONCLUSION

Congratulations! You have just completed all of the DMAIC phases of a Six Sigma project. Even though we have only scratched the surface of all the tools available in the Six Sigma toolbox, it should be clear that Six Sigma is a powerful tool.

Just as SPC charts and a stem and leaf plot are tools for a Six Sigma project, so too is Six Sigma itself a tool for the continuous improvement management system for your company. It is one of the three primary improvement tools addressed in this book. The other two are Lean manufacturing and Theory of Constraints. In the next chapter, we will look into some of the Lean manufacturing concepts you may want to have in your toolbox.

WAV Web
         Added
         Value™

This book has free materials available for download from the
Web Added Value™ Resource Center at www.jrosspub.com.

LEAN MANUFACTURING

Six Sigma is a relative "new kid on the block" in comparison to Lean. Some argue that the origins of Lean date back to 1913 when continuous flow was practiced at the Ford Motor Company's Highland Park facility. Henry Ford wrote the book *Today and Tomorrow*[4] in 1926; in it he addresses many topics we now refer to as Lean manufacturing. We will go into this further a little later. Although most would agree that the popularizing of Lean manufacturing can be attributed to the efforts of the Toyota Motor Company, Toyota's embodiment of Lean principles is known as the Toyota Production System.

Lean is a collection of practices that the Toyota Motor Company uses in its everyday operations. An essential by-product of being able to run your manufacturing processes in a Lean fashion is a reliance on a high level of quality performance from your internal processes and your supply chain.

Lean thinking has made the Toyota Motor Company the force it is today in the automobile industry. It has been able to continuously nibble away at market share that was once securely in the grasp of the "Big 3," although, as we saw in Chapter 1, the "Big 3" have adopted aggressive Lean and Six Sigma internal strategies of their own. As a result, the consumer wins by having more choices of higher quality automobiles that are backed by customer-friendly aftermarket service.

Jim Womack, Dan Jones, and Dan Roos popularized Lean manufacturing when they wrote the book entitled *The Machine That Changed the World*[18] in 1990. The title of the book was somewhat prophetic, if you consider how indeed the world has changed since its release. The unprecedented transformation of the automobile industry that has taken place has also begun in nearly every other major industry. We saw how Lean is improving the aerospace business and computers/electronics. Nowadays, if your company has not started its Lean journey, then you are being left behind. The world indeed has changed, thanks to the Toyota Production System.

What really is Lean manufacturing? Surely, as already stated, it is the Toyota Production System. But beyond that, what is meant by Lean manufacturing? How do we define it? It basically is the concept of doing more and more with less and less, by eliminating waste and improving quality. This is a broad definition that is somewhat simplistic, yet it speaks to the very essence of Lean.

The Toyota Production System is a way of life at Toyota. It is the model that others emulate in their attempt to incorporate Lean thinking into their companies. Typically, this involves the utilization of various tools that are associated with Lean. However, the Toyota Production System is much more than the execution of some improvement tools. It is a philosophy or culture that helps sustain any improvements that might be achieved from the utilization of the tools. Jeffrey Liker[9] provides unprecedented insight into the Toyota Production System in his excellent book entitled *The Toyota Way,* in which he outlines 14 principles that are at the heart of the Toyota Production System:

1. Base your management decisions on a long-term philosophy, even at the expense of short-term financial goals.
2. Create continuous process flow to bring problems to the surface.
3. Use "pull" systems to avoid overproduction.
4. Level out the workload.
5. Build a culture of stopping to fix problems, to get quality right the first time.
6. Standardized tasks are the foundation for continuous improvement and employee empowerment.
7. Use visual control so no problems are hidden.
8. Use only reliable, thoroughly tested technology that serves your people and processes.
9. Grow leaders who thoroughly understand the work, live the philosophy, and teach it to others.
10. Develop exceptional people and teams who follow your company's philosophy.
11. Respect your extended network of partners and suppliers by challenging them and helping them to improve.
12. Go and see for yourself to thoroughly understand the situation.
13. Make decisions slowly by consensus, thoroughly considering all options; implement decisions rapidly.

14. Become a learning organization through relentless reflection and continuous improvement.

These 14 principles portray a much broader aspect to Lean manufacturing than the standard tool set often associated with Lean. It is obvious from these principles that the Toyota Production System is much more than the utilization of some Lean improvement tools. I mean in no way to minimize the tools with this statement, but rather to acknowledge that the essence of the Toyota Production System goes much deeper than the tools themselves. Refer to *The Toyota Way*[9] to gain further understanding of these 14 principles.

The Lean tools that have been given to the world through their incorporation into the Toyota Production System are the mechanisms by which the Toyota philosophy is brought to life. These tools are techniques that will enable you to eliminate waste, improve quality, and do more with less — to become Lean! Therefore, let's take an overview look at some of the tools in the Lean toolbox.

KAIZEN

Kaizen is a Japanese term that basically means changing for the good. Kai means "change," and zen means "good."[6] It is probably one the most frequently used terms in the Lean world because it is at the very heart of what Lean is all about — continuous, incremental improvement in processes, which is effected by all parties associated with the processes. Kaizen never ends. It is fueled by the ideas and the creativity of workers and managers. Therefore, a natural prerequisite of it is an engaged workforce that has mutual respect for each other and a common focus. If this is not an aspect of your culture, then the success of kaizen will be a greater challenge. You will have to strengthen your foundational communication channels first in order to facilitate the execution of kaizen.

Many companies practice kaizen in a much more dynamic fashion than I have described. This practice is commonly referred to as a kaizen event. Typically, a kaizen event consists of a focused approach on a particular process or problem over a short period of time. There is no hard and fast rule on the length of time, but generally a kaizen event lasts five days. Resources from all areas that affect the particular process being focused on are brought together in a concerted effort to achieve improvement. Typically, because such events occur in such a short period of time, the improvement is measured in the elimination of waste. Long, in-depth evaluations that might be characteristic of a Six Sigma project are not the focus of a kaizen event.

A kaizen event can serve to energize those who are involved by achieving measured success and improvement in such a short period of time, thus empowering them with the confidence that will prove to be valuable as they participate in future kaizen activities. Not only does a kaizen event energize the workforce, but it also results in real, measurable improvement that reduces waste and helps the bottom line. Isn't that what this improvement stuff is all about?

The heart and soul of kaizen is the PDCA cycle. Let's take a closer look at what it is.

PDCA

The American statistician and thinker Dr. W. Edwards Deming was welcomed in the Japan of the 1950s when it was trying to rebuild its manufacturing base. Dr. Deming and his ideas were not treated with a similar level of enthusiasm at the time in the United States. His gospel was viewed as nice but not necessary to most U.S. manufacturers, because the postwar economy was booming. On the other hand, industry in Japan was all ears, and Dr. Deming was a willing teacher.

One of the approaches to continuous improvement that Dr. Deming introduced was the PDCA cycle,[2] which stands for Plan, Do, Check, Act. It is an approach that can be used to attack an underperforming manufacturing process or new product development. It is a closed-loop cycle which, if followed religiously, will ensure that the desired "plan" is achieved or will make it apparent that an alternative course of action should be considered. What occurs at each step in the cycle is self-explanatory. Fostering the discipline to follow through with each step such that it is ingrained into the culture is the greatest challenge. PDCA is predominantly what is used for kaizen, and it is the very essence of the Toyota Production System.

VALUE STREAM MAP

The value stream map is one of the most effective and powerful tools within the Lean toolbox. If you decide you want to take a vacation that requires you to drive into an area you are not familiar with, you most likely would not set out on your journey without first acquiring a map. Sure, you would probably be able to get by without a map, maybe by asking some questions if you get lost, but the probability of the objective of your trip being met is greatly enhanced if you have a map that shows you where to go.

The same is true for an improvement journey you embark on with the objective of improving a process within your company. Where do you start, and what is up ahead? Are there any intersections you need to be concerned about? What is the quickest way to get there? There is no way to know without a map. The beauty of the value stream map is that it not only provides you with a clear indication of the current state of a process, but it also enables you to identify activities within the process that are not adding any value to the overall objective. Hence the name value stream map. Once the value stream map for the current state has been created, then the focus of your improvement efforts has been identified. The map will illustrate those activities that add value to the process and those that do not or simply are not desired by the customer.

An example of something not desired by the customer can be illustrated with an ordinary spoon. A spoon has certain functional requirements: the size and shape need to be within specified dimensions, the material needs to be per the required properties, and the finish needs to be acceptable for aesthetic purposes. Suppose as a spoon manufacturer you decide to go all out on this last requirement, aesthetics. Not only are you going to make your spoons pleasing to the eye, but you are going to gold plate them so that they are the nicest spoons your customers have ever seen. Clearly, gold plating the spoons will add cost to the process, but the general public, which makes up the majority of customers for spoons, has no desire to have their spoons gold plated. The gold plating in this case does indeed add value to the spoon, but the customer does not desire it. How many gold-plating-type activities do you have in your enterprise? Does your customer want them?

The value stream map helps to sort out what to keep and what to eliminate. Figures 4-1 and 4-2 are examples of a value stream map for the current and future state of a quoting process.[3]

5S

The 5S tool is a Lean tool that is not necessarily one of the primary Lean tools but rather more of a supportive one that nonetheless plays a key role in establishing the continuous improvement culture. When utilized, this tool will ensure that the working environment is clean and clear of any encumbrances that would negatively affect continuous improvement. At one time or another, we all have heard the saying "a place for everything and everything in its place." This is the battle cry of the 5S tool.

Let's take a look at each element of the 5S:[1]

1. Sort
2. Straighten
3. Shine

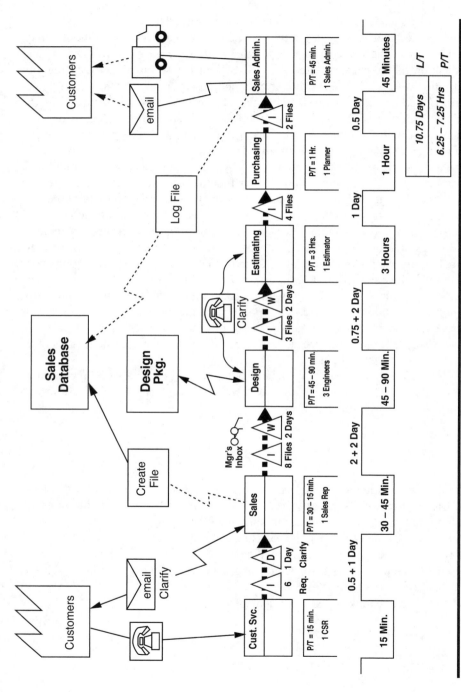

Figure 4-1. Current state map for product quoting process. (Courtesy of Duggan & Associates, Inc. Reprinted with permission.)

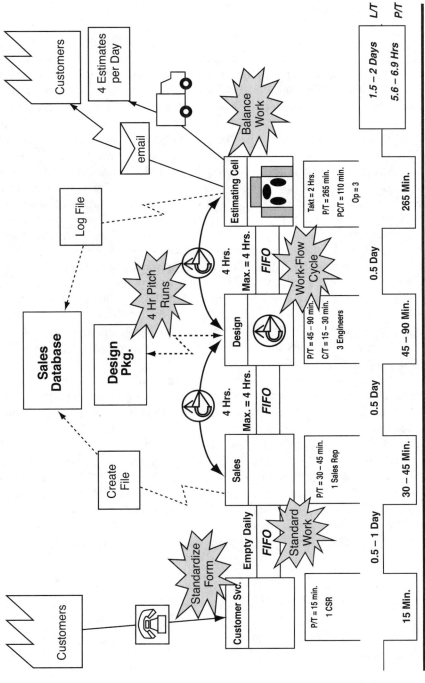

Figure 4-2. Future state map for product quoting process. (Courtesy of Duggan & Associates, Inc. Reprinted with permission.)

4. Standardize
5. Sustain

The intent of "sort" is to eliminate unnecessary items in the work area by removing them and keeping only those that are necessary to perform the task at hand. Once we have identified what items in the work area are truly necessary, we need to consider where they should be located. That is where "straighten" comes in.

Straighten means evaluating what the optimal location of these items should be and placing them accordingly. For example, a tool that is frequently used to make adjustments to a machine should be located in close proximity to the machine, thus preventing any unnecessary movements that would be a waste of time. This plays to the very heart of Lean — the elimination of waste.

In addition to keeping only necessary items in the work area and placing them in an appropriate location, it is important to keep the working environment as clean as possible, which is the third "S": "shine." Chips and dirt in a machine center can be contributing factors to machining nonconformances, which require rework, another form of waste. If a work environment is clean and neat, then people will feel good about working in it. Nobody wants to work in filth. The level of cleanliness also sends a message to outside observers visiting your facility. I have gone into numerous facilities over the years, and the first impression of a clean facility helps to validate other company characteristics revealed after a deeper look.

The next "S" is "standardize." This means that once you come up with an approach that works for your company for sort, straighten, and shine, you should standardize that approach throughout the facility. This keeps everyone on the same page and also will work to promote a self-policing mentality among the workforce. Everyone knows what the expectations are.

Finally, the fifth "S" is "sustain." With sort, straighten, shine, and standardize, you have created a program that will facilitate a clean and efficient working environment, which will enhance continuous improvement and waste reduction. But you cannot just step back and let this program run on autopilot. It needs to be sustained. How you choose to sustain your program will be unique to your facility, but typically will involve some management oversight and recognized accountability.

5-WHYS

Why is the 5-whys included in the Lean toolbox? Why is it effective in identifying core issues? Why? Why? Why? Why? Why? It is a simple and direct way to get to the underlying root causes of a problem. Asking why several times does not permit the luxury of stopping at a superficial solution to a problem. For example, the cause of a nonconformance could be an error by the operator. But is that the "root cause"? *Why* did the operator make the error? Was it because the operator did not have adequate training for the function being performed? Perhaps so. If that is the case, is that the "root cause"? *Why* didn't the operator have adequate training? Was it because the internal policies did not require the operator to receive the training before being assigned to this job function? Then *why* didn't the internal policies require that adequate training be given prior to assigning this operator to the job function? You get the picture.

A popular commercial that aired a couple of years ago touted the company's prowess at innovation and creativity. The theme of the commercial was that innovation was attainable because the company's personnel had an unceasing motivation to constantly ask *why*. The commercial ended with a voice repeatedly asking why, why, why, why, why. It is a simple approach but effective.

KANBAN

More often than not, when you go to the grocery store, there is always an adequate supply of the items you need on the shelves. That is because grocery stores use a kanban system to control their inventory. When Taiichi Ohno visited the United States in the 1950s with the objective of learning the good and bad about how business was run, he was intrigued by the American grocery store, in particular how stores controlled their inventory and also how the demand for goods was established. Grocery stores are a classic "pull" system, where the customer's selection of items off the shelves identifies a need for restocking. This need is determined by some predetermined restocking level.

The grocery store approach was brought back to Japan and incorporated into the production system of the Toyota Motor Company. Today, it is known as the kanban approach. Kanban is the Japanese term for "tag" or "ticket."[12]

The term "tag" or "ticket" is appropriate because the method incorporates the use of physical signs or cards in order to identify the need for replenishment from upstream processes. Buffer inventory is maintained between operations at a minimum level, but enough to prevent flow interruptions. When a customer "pulls" from the existing inventory, then a replenishment order is issued upstream, similar to a grocery store. When you pull a box of cereal off the shelf and pay for it, a replenishment order is issued to restock the shelf.

This replenishment order is communicated to upstream operations through the use of cards. When downstream operation B removes a widget from the buffer inventory to process a customer order, a kanban card is issued to upstream operation A to replenish the buffer inventory with a widget. The kanban card issued for the replenishment travels along with the processed widget so that it is clear what demand is being satisfied with this particular widget.

In this day and age of enterprise resource planning systems and high-tech electronic solutions, this may sound a bit antiquated at first glance. However, it is effective in controlling inventory and allowing a process to be driven by the "pull" of the customer as opposed to the "push" of a schedule.

Clearly, in order for this approach to be most effective, the processes in your operation should be producing a high level of quality product so as to prevent interruptions in flow due to nonconforming material.

PULL

The difference between a "push" and a "pull" manufacturing system is the philosophy that drives the scheduling of operations. In the non-Lean "push" approach, a company forecasts the expected demand, manufactures the product and thereby creates inventory, and then "pushes" the inventory to customers through its sales force.

In the Lean "pull" approach, the execution of manufacturing operations is set in motion as a result of customer demand. The final manufacturing process then "pulls" the upstream processes to create replenishments as the demand comes in from the customer. The operations are "pulled" by the customer demand.

STANDARD WORK

Consider the following: A manufacturing facility runs a three-shift operation that makes a machined component for a first-tier aerospace supplier. The component is fairly complicated in that it requires a number of tight tolerance dimensions and fine finishes. The company is trying to progress along its Lean journey and as a result has developed a continuous flow process for this component. A series of operations are executed on this component, and an operator is required to support the functioning of each workstation.

Suppose there are three workstations. Work has progressed smoothly at stations 1 and 3, but recently some problems have become apparent at station 2. Looking into the cause of the problems, it was found that a new operator was recently hired at station 2 for the second-shift operation. This operator had experience making a similar part at another company and had some specific ideas about how it should be done. The problem was that his approach was totally different than that of the first-shift operator, and the result was that parts were being produced with product discrepancies and interrupted flow.

This is a simplistic example of not using standardized work. Standardized work is a tool that will help to assure a consistent outcome from processes day in and day out. It also establishes a foundation that can be built upon with continuous improvement efforts. When an optimal approach has been established for performing a process, then this valuable information should be made available to all parties involved in the process. It should be standardized.

This standardization is not limited to factory-floor-level activities. It applies to any process in an enterprise. Those in highly regulated industries like aerospace have probably been standardizing their enterprise processes for quite some time now. The procedures for manufacturing and nonmanufacturing operations are typically addressed in a procedures manual that receives a regular periodic cross-functional review for continuous improvement.

The benefit of standardization is the establishment of some degree of order within a process. When the work is performed in an orderly fashion to begin with, successful execution is more likely, and future improvement opportunities will become more evident.

ONE-PIECE FLOW

One-piece flow is one of the hallmarks of Lean and when feasible is one of the most effective tools for achieving high-quality, fast delivery to the customer. Ideally in a one-piece flow operation, the sequential operations are organized in close proximity with one another so as to minimize the need for transportation. Waste. Because the operators have a lot size of one, they pay special attention to each and every piece they produce.

One-piece continuous flow utilized in conjunction with a kanban customer pull system is the optimum. Obviously, in order for this to be effective, quality has to be built into the process such that it is producing a consistently high level of quality product.

Figures 4-3 and 4-4 illustrate some of the benefits of one-piece flow. In this simplistic example, the benefits of one-piece flow are clearly evident. The time required to process the same amount of parts over the same work centers drops from 20 hours with the batch flow approach to 6.5 hours with the one-piece flow approach. That is a tremendous gain in throughput. As mentioned before, the nature of this approach tends to assure a high level of quality output due to the special attention given to the lot size of one.

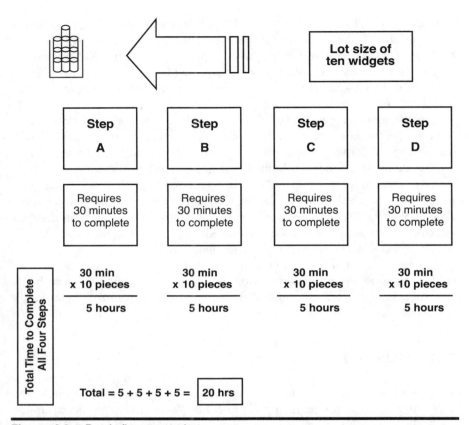

Figure 4-3. Batch flow example.

POKA-YOKE

Can you think of a device you encounter on a daily basis that has the express purpose of preventing you from making a mistake? Surely there are many of them, but we typically go through life taking them for granted. That means they are accomplishing their intended objective.

One that comes to mind is the 3.5-inch diskette used in a computer. Have you ever tried putting it in the slot in your computer upside down? Apparently some people have, because the diskette manufacturers have incorporated a poka-yoke or error-proofing device in diskettes. As a result, if you try to put a diskette in upside down, it will only go in about half way and stop. It does not allow you to make that error. Wouldn't it be nice to have error-proofing

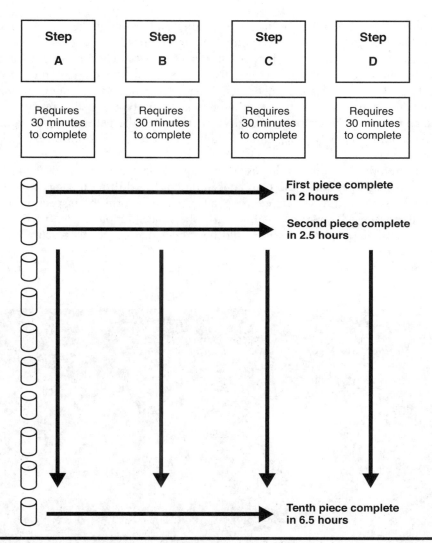

Figure 4-4. One-piece flow example.

devices for everything so that we could go through life error free? It sure would. Then don't you think it would be just as wonderful to incorporate error-proofing devices in every conceivable situation in your company so that all of your processes are executed error free? Most certainly.

Sometimes it may not be feasible to build in an error-proofing device that will prevent you from making an error. In these cases, the next best thing is to incorporate an inspection function at a strategic location in the process to let you know if you are on the verge of making an error.

An example of this is a periodic in-process check of fluid concentrations performed in surface treatment tanks that are used to coat parts with protective coating. Perhaps it has been determined that excessive particle counts of contaminants in surface treatment solutions can impact the quality of coating, thereby making the coating ineffective at providing the necessary protection. This could be a costly proposition if allowed to occur, as a result of extensive rework expenses.

Therefore, a periodic in-process inspection of the concentration of the tanks will alert the operator if the tank concentrations are drifting too far from the desired levels. In this example, an operator could perform the inspection or a monitoring device could be used to verify the concentration levels. If a device is used, an alarm of some kind could be triggered when levels reach a point of concern.

Some examples of error-proofing devices are provided in Figures 4-5 to 4-7.

Figure 4-5. In-cycle probes verify that the wheel is mounted correctly. (Courtesy of Aircraft Braking Systems Corporation.)

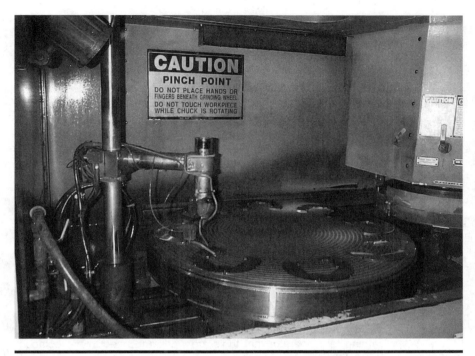

Figure 4-6. Thickness gage stops machining at a precise preset thickness. (Courtesy of Aircraft Braking Systems Corporation.)

TOTAL PRODUCTIVE MAINTENANCE

Total productive maintenance is an approach to maintenance that uses many of the Lean tools previously mentioned. It takes an aggressive approach to machine maintenance and, using the PDCA cycle, works to determine what the predictive maintenance is for machines and eventually how to design machines to reduce or eliminate the need for maintenance.

If you are trying to incorporate a Lean operation, the performance of your machines becomes more critical than ever. Any excessive downtime could bring a process to a screeching halt. The total productive maintenance approach to machine maintenance will assure that this does not happen.

VISUAL FACTORY

Stop and think for a moment about all of the visual signs you are exposed to each day with the purpose of either providing you with needed information or

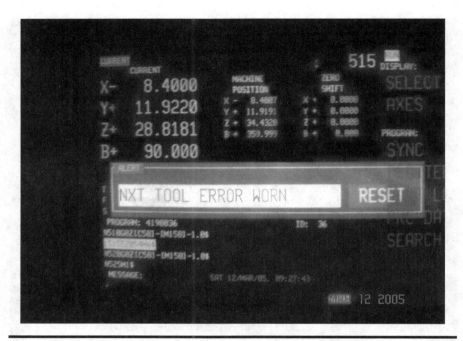

Figure 4-7. Warning tells operator that tools are worn and need to be replaced. (Courtesy of Aircraft Braking Systems Corporation.)

directing you to behave in some fashion. A song popular with the counterculture movement of the 1970s says it best:

> Sign, sign, everywhere a sign
> Blocking out the scenery, breaking my mind
> Do this, don't do that — can't you read the sign?
>> The Five Man Electrical Band[14]

When you think about it, signs are everywhere, telling us what to do and what not to do: Keep off the grass. No parking. Left lane ends, merge right. No trespassing. Open. Closed. We are influenced by visual stimuli such as signs and typically will modify our behavior accordingly when confronted with them.

Why not bring what works to inform us and direct us in our everyday life into the workplace to accomplish the same objectives. Communication and a common understanding of the appropriate direction to take are imperative for keeping a sense of order and velocity. Imagine driving down the road without any signs directing you where to go. You would go much slower and struggle to find your way.

Use visual signs as much as possible in your operation to provide direction when necessary, along with information. These signs could be as simple as graphical displays of how to install a particular part. Sometimes a picture is worth a thousand words. Another example is a board that includes a variety of information pertaining to a particular process or commodity, such as production schedule, quality performance, capacity, etc.

Signs are intended to be working tools that affect behavior. A board with production schedule information could serve as the focal point for daily meetings with all pertinent personnel to review the current status. However you choose to use them, make them work for you to make you better.

POLICY DEPLOYMENT

Lean tools can have an impact on any aspect of your organization. The temptation for the newly indoctrinated is to rush out and start using them everywhere. Any improvement approach that you undertake should be in concert with the overall policies of the company. Therefore, in order to bear the most fruit from the improvement efforts expended, a strategic plan should be deployed that aligns the improvement efforts with the corporate policies.

This deployment is referred to as policy deployment in Lean terminology, although it goes well beyond simply the communication of corporate policies. The Lean philosophy remains prevalent in policy deployment, ensuring that the improvement activities meet the established objectives. Monitoring of effectiveness is accomplished through periodic reviews and ongoing communication.

The general flow of the policy deployment process is illustrated in Figure 4-8.[8] This monitoring is captured using an elaborate documentation structure that provides a concise picture of the improvement initiatives, all on an 8.5-by-11-inch sheet of paper. Figure 4-9 provides an example of a blank template used for documentation.[8] The individual sections within the template are self-explanatory. The approach is simple but effective.

As you can see, policy deployment functions as an oversight methodology to assure that the improvement efforts under way using various other Lean tools are on track and on target.

Obviously, these are not all of the Lean tools that are available, but rather a sampling of some of the frequently used ones. There is one more Lean concept to touch on before the close of this chapter: value stream management and the role of value stream managers.

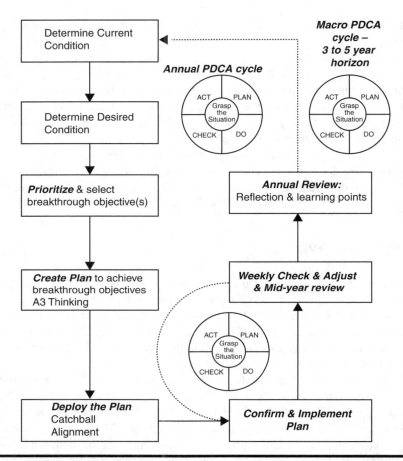

Figure 4-8.   Policy deployment process. (Courtesy of Lean Productivity Systems. Reprinted with permission.)

VALUE STREAM MANAGEMENT

James Womack addresses the need for a manager who has responsibility for overseeing the entire value stream across departments.[15] He argues that this role should be structured organizationally within a company's hierarchical structure. The objective is to establish an individual who is accountable for the success of the value stream and not burdened by the functional responsibilities of a particular functional area.

There is much value that is readily apparent in establishing a value stream manager position, including accountability, focus, and a single-mindedness that

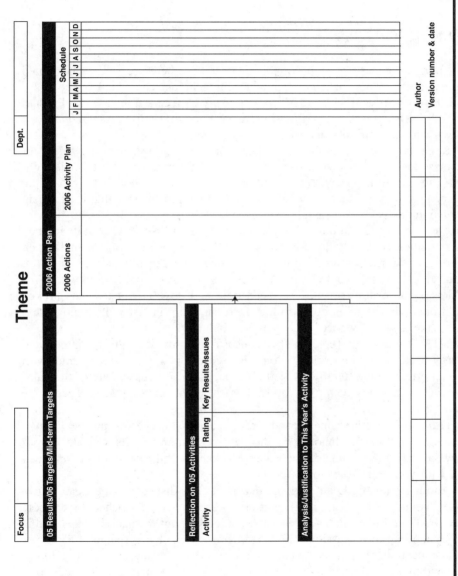

Figure 4-9. Policy deployment template. (Courtesy of Lean Productivity Systems. Reprinted with permission.)

will surely reap long-term benefits. The approach is similar to the Look Forward® management approach, which will be addressed in Chapter 7, although some slight nuances exist.

LEAN RESOURCES

I mentioned at the beginning of this chapter that there are some who would argue that the origins of Lean manufacturing techniques date back to the 1920s with Henry Ford and the Ford Motor Company. A recent rerelease (by Productivity Press) of the book written by Henry Ford in 1926 entitled *Today and Tomorrow*[4] has stirred some of this debate.

Regardless of where the Lean ideas originated, the important thing for business leaders to realize is that they can make a company better. It is wonderful to see so many companies embracing the Lean methods with a passion. Henry Ford and Eiji Toyoda would be pleased with the energy that is prevalent in their industry as well as almost any other industry.

The spread of Lean throughout all industries is still somewhat in its infancy but nonetheless already quite impressive. The aerospace industry is making an aggressive effort to incorporate Lean techniques in order to transform the entire industry. At the forefront of this effort is the Lean Aerospace Initiative (LAI). LAI is a consortium of industry, academia, and government that has broken traditional barriers in an effort to transform an entire industry. Its membership looks like a who's who of the aerospace industry.

MIT is a driving force in this consortium, providing the resources and energy to keep the train rolling along. It even offers a doctorate program with a Lean orientation at the Sloan Kettering School of Business. One of the valuable gems that has come out of LAI is the book entitled *Lean Enterprise Value*.[11]

LAI serves as a breeding ground for ideas and approaches for practical implementation of Lean techniques in the aerospace industry. Its website (http://www.lai.org) offers a number of valuable resources and tool kits that can assist you with your transformation efforts.

Another valuable Lean resource that is at your disposal is the Lean Enterprise Institute (LEI). LEI is a nonprofit organization established to promote Lean thinking in any industry. It was founded by Jim Womack in 1997 and is run by a group of professionals with impressive Lean backgrounds. LEI serves as an educational outlet for Lean techniques and acts as a global Lean community within which Lean experiences are shared among members. The best part of joining the community is that it is free. A number of valuable resources are available in the forums and libraries on the LEI website (http://www.lean.org)

that can help guide you along your Lean journey. Those at the beginning of their Lean journey can learn from the experiences of others who have already been down the road. In addition to the resources available on the website, LEI has an excellent staff of trainers who provide regularly scheduled courses on Lean methodology. You can't go wrong with LEI if you are looking for a Lean training resource.

One other Lean resource that perhaps is not as recognizable as LAI or LEI is the National Institute of Standards (NIST), Manufacturing Excellence Partnership (MEP). It offers a resource for providing 360vu accredited Lean training, which is a standardized approach to Lean training for small and medium-size industry and is overseen by NIST MEP. As industry in the United States heads in the direction of becoming more Lean, the MEP 360vu training centers located throughout the country will be a good resource to draw upon. The resource section at the back of this book provides further information.

THEORY OF CONSTRAINTS

When you look at all the information that comes across your desk about continuous improvement awareness, you could easily be persuaded that Lean and Six Sigma are the only effective improvement tools at your disposal. The widespread adoption and popularity of these tools are unprecedented, and the impact they are having will change the future of all sectors of the societal infrastructure that hop on the bandwagon. The groundswell has been so great for both methods that large segments of industries have become rabid proponents of them — so much so that the obvious strengths of Lean and Six Sigma have been combined and packaged as Lean Six Sigma in order to give you the best of both worlds.

Companies that have adopted Lean Six Sigma are striving to produce a near-perfect product with a process that has a minimal amount of waste. What company wouldn't want that as its credo? Indeed, these are lofty goals, and without question, Lean and Six Sigma are some of the most effective tools available to help your company achieve them.

However, these tools do not comprise the limit of your continuous improvement arsenal. A continuous improvement method that is equally powerful, if not more so, but perhaps somewhat less popularized is known as the *Theory of Constraints*. It is an improvement approach that focuses on alleviating the constraining elements of an operation in order to allow a business to perform at its optimal level. Every business, process, or activity of any kind has constraining elements that prohibit it from performing at a higher level.

Consider a five-person relay team that participates in a long-distance race throughout a city. Let's say that each of the team members covers the same distance along the course, and team members are selected at random. If the objective of the team is to finish the race as quickly as possible, then you might say that the slowest member of the team is the constraining factor in achieving the desired objective. If the slowest person improves his or her time, then what was constraining the team's performance has been improved upon or elevated, thus improving the team's ability to achieve its objective — a faster time.

However, as soon as the constraint is lifted (i.e., by the team member improving his or her speed), a new one emerges. In our example, the team member whose speed improved is no longer the slowest, and a new team member is now identified as the slowest or the constraint. The focus is now on that team member to improve his or her time in order to lift the constraint of the team's slower speed and help the team achieve its objective.

Note that the constraints are identified as impediments to achieving an objective. In the relay team example, the objective of the team was to complete the race as quickly as possible. What if the objective was not to complete the race as quickly as possible but rather to cover the distance at a casual pace and enjoy the camaraderie of fellow runners?

Let's look at this same team again. Perhaps four of the five runners are average recreational runners, and the fifth person on the team is a world-class runner. He or she is passionate about speed and wants the other runners on the team to share this passion. This runner may try to get the other four members to change their recreational approach to running and improve their speed.

That's all well and good in and of itself, but how does it impact the team's stated objective? Recall that the objective of this team was to cover the distance at a casual pace and enjoy the camaraderie of fellow runners. Clearly, the approach of the world-class runner would be an impediment to the objective of the team. In essence, the world-class runner would be the constraint of the team.

The constraint is not always clear-cut. If the world-class runner was on the team in the first example, then that team member would most certainly not be a constraint to the team. However, in the second example, that team member is clearly the constraint.

Your constraint is determined by your objective. What is the objective of your company? To build widgets? Perhaps. To provide a service? Maybe. To offer opportunities for employment? Most likely. But are any of these the primary purpose of your business? Of course not. The primary purpose of your business is to make money. If you are successful in making money with your business, then these secondary objectives will be achieved naturally.

This point was so eloquently made in the multimillion-selling blockbuster book entitled *The Goal*,[3] the book that introduced Theory of Constraints to the world. It was a first-of-its-kind business novel, written by Eliyahu M. Goldratt, who is widely recognized as the father of the Theory of Constraints.

Dr. Goldratt has no qualms about breaking the mold and pursuing the nontraditional path. He has been described by *Fortune* as a "guru to industry" and by *Business Week* as a "genius" (see the review on the cover of *The Goal*).[3]

Goldratt, a physicist by education, obtained his bachelor of science degree from Tel Aviv University and his master of science and doctorate of philosophy from Bar-Ilan University. In addition to his pioneering work in business management, he holds patents in a number of areas ranging from medical devices to drip irrigation to temperature sensors.[5]

If you are reading this book, chances are pretty good that you already are aware of Eli Goldratt and the impact he has had on achieving business excellence. So why do you suppose Theory of Constraints is not as well known as Lean or Six Sigma? Or perhaps it is.

Let's start by taking a look at what Theory of Constraints actually is. I touched briefly on a description of what it is in the relay team example. It is a methodology or business philosophy that focuses on identifying the constraints that impact a business. Once identified, the theory purports that the organization's efforts should be expended on elevating or overcoming the constraint in order to alleviate whatever impediment it facilitated. This analysis and execution are not intended to be a finite iteration of activities that continue until all opportunities of constraint removal have been exhausted, but rather it is a continuous cyclical approach used to uncover new opportunities to improve a business by alleviating the most prevalent constraint keeping a business from achieving its goal — making money.

Theory of Constraints requires an intimate association with the business processes being improved and, contrastingly, a concurrent understanding of the global elements that contribute to the desired outcome. It forces you to think and to look at your business in ways you never may have done before. It fosters revolutionary change that transforms a company by providing a methodology for enabling its employees to focus their efforts on a common goal.

Theory of Constraints is not as black and white as some of the other methods may be and by its very nature is somewhat elusive in being tagged with a clear-cut characterization. The following is an additional description of Theory of Constraints from the Goldratt Marketing Group website (http://toc-goldratt.com/index.php?cont=13):[5]

> TOC is a multifaceted management philosophy...a systematic reexamination of some of the most fundamental beliefs in today's man-

agement, culminating in a new approach to address problems facing us today.

Theory of Constraints "is more than a set of tools or techniques, though it certainly contains these. It is more fundamentally a paradigm shift which demands that we think about our problems and solutions, our goals and objectives, policies, procedures and measures, in a different way."[7]

Constraint(s) Management, Synchronous Flow Manufacturing (SFM), Synchronous Production (SP), and OPT are other terms sometimes used synonymously with Theory of Constraints, but are more correctly used to describe the earlier components of Theory of Constraints rather than the more recent parts, such as the Thinking Processes.[7]

Hopefully, my attempt to describe Theory of Constraints along with this additional reference provides you with a rough understanding of it, although, to me, Theory of Constraints is like a living and breathing approach to improvement that has some core values that are used as the springboard for action. The rest is up to you.

You may be wondering about the history of Theory of Constraints. What circumstances preceded the introduction of this approach? Where did it come from, and when did it happen?

As previously mentioned, Eli Goldratt was a trained physicist. However, in characteristic fashion, he did what one would least expect from a physicist. He developed and implemented early in his career a production scheduling system that had amazing results.[6]

Goldratt obviously realized that this effective scheduling system could benefit many other companies. Thus it was introduced to U.S. industry as a production planning program known as OPT (Optimized Production Technology). Goldratt's planning program was successful because of the logic he built into it. It was apparent to Goldratt that his analytic approach could have a much broader impact on business than improved planning and scheduling. To communicate his philosophies so as to have the most widespread impact, he chose to write a book that encapsulated his theories. However, what he wrote was not a technical book that documented his formula for success, as one might expect from a Ph.D. in physics. Rather, it was a novel entitled *The Goal,* which told a story of the everyday operations of a business faced with real challenges. That is not so unusual today, some 20 years after its release, but back then it was unheard of. That is typical Goldratt though — doing the unorthodox but achieving phenomenal results. The book has sold well over three million copies and is still popular. *The Goal* was the real launching pad of the mass appeal for Theory of Constraints. Theory of Constraints has been embraced by many companies striving to achieve excellence, and it thrives today as one of the leading improvement methodologies of our day.

That provides a little background on the history of Theory of Constraints, but what is at the heart of it? What are the tools within the tool, and how do you measure effectiveness?

THEORY OF CONSTRAINTS TOOLS

The theory behind the philosophy of Theory of Constraints is understandable, but getting from theory to application is not necessarily intuitively obvious. Some of the Theory of Constraints tools that will be discussed in this chapter are helpful in enabling the practitioner to put Theory of Constraints into practice. The five tools that will be addressed are as follows:[2]

1. Current reality tree
2. Conflict resolution diagram
3. Future reality tree
4. Prerequisite tree
5. Transition tree

Sometimes it is difficult to tell the forest from the trees, but I shall do my best. Let's start by looking at the first tree.

Current Reality Tree

The current reality tree is a type of flowchart that depicts the cause-and-effect relationships that exist for the object of interest. The tree is normally built using a storyboard-type approach, starting with a listing of the effects to be remedied. The contributing factors that perpetuate these effects are associated with them and listed accordingly. This type of analysis is performed again on the perpetuating factors and is continued until what in essence would be the root cause of the problem can be identified. This simplistic explanation can become quite convoluted in practice when the situation under study has multiple effects to remedy and many associated contributing factors. It is normally through brainstorming activity involving all parties associated with the situation of interest that a beneficial list of factors can be developed. For a more detailed explanation of how to construct a current reality tree, refer to a fine text written by William H. Dettmer entitled *Goldratt's Theory of Constraints: A Systems Approach to Continuous Improvement.*[2]

One of the expected outputs of creating a current reality tree is to identify the root causes that are perpetuating the effects to be remedied. Once these causes are identified, then they provide a focus for subsequent efforts. Speaking of which, let's take a look at our next tool: the conflict resolution diagram.

Conflict Resolution Diagram

Inevitably, when you begin to take a look at an undesirable condition of any kind, you will unearth some issues that need to be addressed in order to alleviate the condition. More often than not, these issues will have competing interests within the organization that inherently conflict with one another. Otherwise, the undesirable condition would not exist in the first place.

The conflict resolution diagram picks up where the current reality tree left off. The output of the current reality tree was the identification of root causes that contributed to some undesirable condition. For example, the root cause of accidents on a street corner is that people cannot see the stop sign that is covered over by branches of a tree. This particular tree has become overgrown because there is infighting between the city streets department and the parks and recreation department. Each claims that the other has responsibility for maintenance of the tree, and neither has actually done anything. Thus the undesirable condition of a tree blocking the visibility of motorists driving down the street is what needs to be addressed. That being said, the desired outcome of any subsequent activity would be a clearly visible stop sign. This is an example of what is referred to as the *objective* for a conflict resolution diagram.

The goal of utilizing the conflict resolution diagram is to be able to arrive at a win-win solution. A win-lose result and a compromise are possible solutions, but not the preferred result. The conflict resolution diagram utilizes an analytical approach to try to get the parties in conflict to arrive at a mutual consensus. In the tree example, let's say that in order for either the streets department or the parks and recreation department to issue a work order to trim the tree, a maintenance order must be approved by the city council. This activity would be referred to as a *requirement.* To achieve the desired objective, typically one or more necessary requirements must be satisfied. In the tree example, nothing will be done without a written maintenance order, approved by the city council. The written maintenance order is a necessary "requirement.

One of the keys of the conflict resolution diagram is to try to identify all of the pertinent requirements that impact the desired objective. The requirements give us insight into the path that leads to the source of the conflict. Continuing down this path a little further, we will want to determine what needs to take place before a requirement can be accomplished. This activity is referred to as a *prerequisite.* Again using the tree example, in order for the city council to approve and issue a maintenance order to trim the tree, the request must be submitted to the council with justification. Any maintenance order must be approved by a two-thirds majority vote of all council members. This is the prerequisite.

The stalemate over trimming the tree has occurred because half of the people on the council in this small town are also employees of the streets department and half are employees of the parks and recreation department. The streets department employees have a bone to pick with the parks and recreation department employees. The latter comprise a council subcommittee that has the responsibility for approval of all capital equipment expenditures, like tree-trimming equipment for example. It has been 20 years since this subcommittee has approved any new tree-trimming equipment, so whoever has to trim the trees will be required to use equipment that is somewhat antiquated.

This irks the streets department employees on the city council, because it is obvious to them that either one or the other of the following is taking place. One thought is that the parks and recreation department employees simply do not have a clue about what it really takes to trim a tree and do not want to spend money on the needed tree-trimming equipment because they want the money used for something else or not at all. It is an election year, and a lot of them are campaigning on the issue of keeping the city expenditures down to keep the tax base low.

The other thought is that the parks and recreation department employees know exactly what it takes to trim a tree but are on a power trip. Perhaps they get some sadistic pleasure out of making the tree-trimming activity as difficult as possible for the streets department. These statements are what is referred to as an *assumption* in the conflict resolution diagram analysis.

The world clearly is not black and white, and when we apply analytical reasoning to activities involving the human dimension, we need to take that into consideration. When we establish the requirements that are needed to achieve the desired objective and what prerequisites are necessary to accomplish the requirements, we are inherently making some assumptions about all of these. It is important that the underlying assumptions that drive the establishment of requirements and prerequisites are documented and included in the analysis. It is these very assumptions that could be the impetus for change.

In the tree example, the two assumptions of the streets department employees regarding their perception of the parks and recreation department employees may be the farthest thing from reality, but they are held deeply as being true, so much so that the streets department council members are willing to stick their heels in the ground and not support a vote to trim the tree, when in fact it has actually become a safety issue in the community. However, if these assumptions are brought out in the open, they could be overcome and no longer be an impediment.

We often hear employees say they know what management "really" wants in certain situations when perhaps they do not. Personal biases can be the source of these hidden assumptions. The same holds true for management's perception of employees. Those in management may think they "really" know what the employees are up to or thinking, when it is the farthest thing from reality. No one group has a monopoly on the quirks of human behavior. Uncovering any assumptions that may exist will help resolve any conflicts more expeditiously.

Once uncovered, then something has to be done about them. Perhaps it is crystal clear what to do and a designated action can be identified. In the tree example, the assumptions dealt with the streets department employees' perception of the parks and recreation department employees. It turns out that once these assumptions were surfaced and discussed, it was clear that they were far from the truth. The reality was that the revenue flow into the city coffers had consistently been on a downward trend over the last several years due to businesses and young people leaving the small community. Money was tight. In fact, it just was not there to spend on anything, including tree-trimming equipment.

Once the streets department council members came to accept this as the true reality and abandoned their previous assumptions, they became more willing to work together to come up with a solution. After all, a stop sign was covered up and people were getting hurt on a frequent basis. The situation could not be allowed to continue until the tax base took a turn in a positive direction. That could be years away. Something had to be done immediately!

To make matters worse, this was no ordinary tree. It was a rather large one with convoluted twisting branches that made it almost impossible to trim with 20-year-old equipment. The city council had a challenge on its hands, but at least both sides were now working together toward the common goal of trimming the tree, and all previous underlying assumptions were abandoned. The council members had absolutely no clue as to how they were ever going to get it done, but they had a common focus.

The first thing they did was establish a community action task force and petition all the members of the community for assistance in solving this pressing problem. That proved to be a saving grace because, unbeknownst to the council, one of the newer residents in the community turned out to be the owner of a private tree-trimming company that had all of the latest equipment. As soon as the owner heard about the problem, he offered his services on a gratis basis. He had moved to this community from a big city because he loved how people in small communities got involved with one another to solve shared problems. He was thrilled to help.

In this example, the establishment of the community task force by the city council would be referred to as an *injection* in the conflict resolution diagram.

Injections are conditions or actions that occur in the future and are geared toward overcoming any underlying assumptions that prevent the achievement of the objective.

This gives you a little flavor of the conflict resolution diagram. It is intended to work off of the current reality tree by establishing an objective that would overcome the identified root cause and then determining how the objective would be accomplished.

Now let's take a look at the next tool utilized after the completion of a successful conflict resolution diagram: the future reality tree.

Future Reality Tree

Using the current reality tree, we identified the existing conditions that needed to be changed and then we honed in on what the root causes were. Then, using the conflict resolution diagram, we identified an objective to counter the effect of the root causes and developed a plan of attack for achieving the objective. At the core of this plan of attack was the injection that, if followed, assured our path to success.

With the future reality tree, we begin at this point and develop a more detailed analysis that considers what may or may not happen at each step along the way toward the expected outcome. The work done with the current reality tree and conflict resolution diagram provides us with pieces of the puzzle within the future reality tree. The starting point with the future reality tree is the injection identified in the conflict resolution diagram.

The future reality tree helps fill in the blanks when going from point A to point B. The result can be a multitier tree that illustrates the effect of the proposed injection applied to the current reality. In an ideal world, if the stated injection is applied to the current reality, then the expected outcome is immediately achieved. In the real world, however, the result may likely be somewhere in between but closer to the desired objective.

This iterative process is continued until all scenarios are considered between the initial injection and the final expected outcome. In other words, in the new world that shows some improvement, a new injection would be applied that would be geared toward directing this new reality closer to the final desired objective. Clearly, the imposition of any injection upon the current reality will not always result in a positive nudge closer to the final expected outcome. A proposed injection potentially could have a negative outcome. That needs to be taken into consideration and any negative outcome scenarios incorporated into the tree. The iteration process is the same as previously described; however, a negative result could require more decision or injection points than might otherwise occur without it.

When creating your tree, be realistic. Do not be afraid to include those negative outcomes if they are true possibilities. It is better to try to brainstorm solutions to them in this planning stage than in the heat of battle, so expose them and go after solutions to them.

This gives you a little insight into the future reality tree. It is a detailed planning tool that helps to simulate what might happen in practice when certain actions are initiated toward achieving a desired outcome.

Now let's move on to the next tool, the prerequisite tree.

Prerequisite Tree

The prerequisite tree is a tool that can be used independent of the other Theory of Constraints tools or in concert with them. Its purpose is to help identify obstacles that exist between the current state and the desired objective. Once identified, it offers a means for determining an approach for overcoming the obstacles. It is certainly possible that a prerequisite tree may not be necessary for a simple objective that previously has been addressed with a current reality tree, conflict resolution diagram, and future reality tree. However, if a high level of complexity is associated with the problem under analysis, then the prerequisite tree may be in order.

The focus is on overcoming obstacles that prevent you from achieving the ultimate desired objective. If you were to list all the obstacles that lie in your path at first glance, you may begin to think of ways to overcome each of them independently. For instance, consider the following example.

Every year, thousands of enthusiastic participants dive into the Pacific Ocean in Hawaii at the beginning of the Iron Man competition. The event consists of swimming 1.2 miles, jumping out of the water and bicycling 100 miles, and hopping off the bike and running 26.2 miles. The ultimate objective of most participants is completing the event, but for the elite participants the objective is winning it. In either case, there are clear obstacles that must be overcome all along the way. The obvious ones are just finishing each leg of the event. The not so obvious ones are hidden within each event. In the swimming event, the participants need to try to keep the salt water out of their eyes and avoid the sharks, for starters. Once on their bikes, they need to assure that their bikes perform as expected mechanically throughout and need to know what to do if they get a flat tire. Going into the marathon run, the athletes need to dress appropriately so they do not overheat and assure that they take in an adequate amount of liquids so they do not become dehydrated.

There are many, many obstacles that need to be overcome in order for you to successfully achieve your ultimate objective. To overcome these obstacles, you establish intermediate objectives that are focused on the specific obstacles.

The prerequisite tree is a compilation of these intermediate objectives and their associated obstacles. Obviously, it can be a good planning tool for considering your options when faced with all the intermediate stumbling blocks thrown at you.

Now let's take a look at the last of the five Theory of Constraints tools in this section, the transition tree.

Transition Tree

The transition tree is similar to the future reality tree with the exception of a couple of key points. The transition tree is intended to be used for a final implementation plan, whereas the future reality tree is used as a planning tool to help simulate what might happen in practice when certain actions are initiated toward achieving a desired outcome. The transition tree is used when you have completed your simulation activity and are ready to go forward with a plan. It is basically another project management planning tool. Consequently, as you might expect, the transition tree contains a greater amount of detail than is typically found in the future reality tree. With the transition tree, you go beyond the postulating and into the strategic planning.

Summary

That was a quick look at some of the Theory of Constraints tools that relate to the thinking process associated with the Theory of Constraints. For an in-depth analysis of these tools, refer to the Goldratt Marketing Group (http://toc-goldratt.com) and/or the excellent text entitled *Goldratt's Theory of Constraints*[2] by William H. Dettmer.

Now that we have examined some of application tools associated with Theory of Constraints, let's explore what measurements Eli Goldratt promotes for determining whether or not these expended efforts are effective.

MEASUREMENTS

There are three primary measurements that Dr. Goldratt promotes as being at the core of any business. If you are performing well at these measurements, then it is safe to say that your business is performing well. The measurements are as follows:[4]

1. Throughput
2. Inventory
3. Operating expense

Let's take a look at Goldratt's definition of these three metrics:

- **Throughput** — The rate at which the system generates money through sales
- **Inventory** — All the money the system invests in purchasing things the system intends to sell
- **Operating expense** — All the money the system spends in turning inventory into throughput

Clearly, we can see from these definitions that two of them directly influence the traditional big three global company measures: net profit, return on investment, and cash flow. These two are throughput and operating expense.

Let's look at throughput first. If you are generating money at a higher rate through sales, then the amount of profit or return you will realize will also be higher. All things being equal, if there is an increase in annual sales, then your profits, return on investment, and cash flow will increase.

Next is operating expense. If the money spent to turn inventory into throughput goes down, then the profit margin, return on investment, and cash flow obviously go up.

What about inventory? Does it have an impact on the big three global measures? Of course it does, although the extent of the impact is not always as blatantly clear as it is with throughput and operating expense. Followers of the Toyota Production System or Lean manufacturing are zealots for the abolishment of inventory. It is waste, and its elimination is facilitated by the just-in-time approach to doing business. Most companies are modeling some form of just-in-time these days. If not, then they are probably storing up some inventory to handle expediting, poor quality, and process problems. Goldratt speaks at length to the issue of inventory in the book entitled *The Race*[4] and also in *The Goal*.[3]

You can use whatever metrics you want to track your improvement efforts, but Goldratt argues that if they do not have an impact on throughput, operating expense, and inventory, then perhaps your improvement efforts are in vain or at least are not having an improvement effect on the overall health of the company. These three simple and straightforward metrics indeed will drive overall improvement of your company.

FIVE-STEP PROCESS OF ONGOING IMPROVEMENT

We have looked at the tools that are used in the Theory of Constraints thinking process and how we measure the effectiveness of our efforts. Now it is time to take a look at the Theory of Constraints process of ongoing improvement.

Anyone who has read the book *The Goal* is familiar with this process. Again, it is simple and straightforward, but powerful nonetheless. The five steps[3] of ongoing improvement are:

1. Identify the constraint
2. Exploit the constraint
3. Subordinate everything else to the constraint
4. Elevate the constraint
5. Go back to step 1 and identify the constraint

Let's take a brief look at each of these steps.

Identify the Constraint

A constraint is anything in an organization with a demand that exceeds its capacity. Obvious examples are machines on the factory floor that are in high demand due to their capabilities, but are unable to produce to the desired demand because of capacity limitations. Constraints are not limited to the factory floor, however.

Consider an engineering change approval process that requires sequential approval of a change by designated functional representatives. Perhaps the quality representative on the approval routing is buried with many other additional responsibilities in addition to change approval. As a result, his or her cycle time for review of change and approval documentation is much longer than someone from another functional area who may have very little else to do. The demand placed upon the quality representative for the approval routing exceeds his or her capacity. The quality representative in this example is a constraint.

There can be multiple constraints in a business that impact the ability to improve its performance. On the factory floor, look for the area that has the most work in process. Chances are, you will find a constraint that is causing it. In the office, look for the desk with the largest stack of papers that require action of some kind (i.e., review, approval, etc.). Again, chances are, that individual or position is a constraint in a process. For companies that operate in a paperless environment, look at the electronic in boxes.

The first step in the Theory of Constraints approach is to identify the constraint. Once the constraint has been found, the next step is to exploit it.

Exploit the Constraint

The phrase "exploiting the constraint" sounds like it has a negative connotation. However, that is not the case at all. When you exploit the constraint, you are working to get everything possible out of it. In the case of a machine, you are looking for ways to increase its capacity. Perhaps that means coming up with creative ways to reduce the amount of built-in idle time (shift change, lunch, etc.) and thereby increase the amount of productive time. Perhaps that means adding an in-process inspection point to assure that the constraint is fed only good parts to process, thereby eliminating any time lost due to nonconforming material.

Whatever you choose to do to exploit the constraint, the objective is to max it out as much as possible. Sometimes this can be accomplished just by making it known to all parties involved that the process is a constraint or bottleneck. When everyone knows that a particular operation impacts the overall performance of the facility, people pay special attention to it.

This also pertains to any white-collar activity that is identified as a constraint. The key is to try to optimize the performance of the bottleneck as much as possible. Once the bottleneck is performing at peak levels, the next step is to begin to take a look at all of the other nonconstraint processes.

Subordinate Everything Else to the Constraint

We have identified our constraint and exploited it to the point where it is now running on all cylinders. But what about all the other processes? Recall that these can produce at a higher rate than the bottleneck, and left unchecked, that is exactly what they will do. The obvious result of that would be the creation of excess work-in-process inventory. Therefore, it is necessary to subordinate everything else to the pace of the constraint, even if that means allowing a machine to sit idle. Everything needs to march to the drumbeat of the constraint.

This establishes a steady synchronized product flow that has had outside interruptions minimized. It also creates a baseline for future continuous process improvement efforts. How do you make this steady flow faster? You have to get a process in control before you can begin improving its capability.

The next step in improving performance is to elevate the constraint.

Elevate the Constraint

An overall process is improved by elevating the constraint. Elevating means doing whatever it takes to increase throughput through the bottleneck. An example would be to redirect some of the load on the constraint to another capable resource so as to increase capacity. Another example would be to transfer some duties to another capable person with excess capacity.

Once you are successful in elevating the constraint, then in essence it is no longer a constraint to the process. This is at the crux of the continuous improvement aspect of the Theory of Constraints, because it does not stop at alleviating one constraint. In a perfect world, there would be no constraints to achieving the ultimate goal of a business — to make money. With no constraints, a business can make an infinite amount of money. How many businesses do you know of that are pulling in infinite amounts of money?

There will always be constraints that can be overcome. This thought brings us to the last step in the Theory of Constraints process.

Go Back to Step 1 and Identify the Constraint

The fifth and final step creates the endless do-loop in this analytical process. It fosters the notion that there is no pinnacle to reach with your improvement efforts. You do not eliminate a constraint or two, declare that the company is pretty darn good, and then not do anything further. Of course, any efforts expended should not cost more than the benefit gained. You cannot lose sight of the goal of a business, which is to make money.

It is fair to say that the more improvements you make, the harder it will be to make further strides. But difficult is not the same as impossible. In the Theory of Constraints world, as long as there is any constraint that works against the company making more money, then there is still opportunity for improvement.

After reviewing the Theory of Constraints, it is apparent that it is a thought-provoking method of continuous improvement that can help you achieve world-class performance. Some 20 years after it was first widely introduced in the book *The Goal,* it is more popular than ever. This speaks to its staying power and its effectiveness in achieving real results.

For further information on how you can learn more about the Theory of Constraints, visit the following websites: http://www.toc-goldratt.com, http://www.rogo.com, and http://www.tocinternational.com.

PART 3.
LOOK FORWARD®:
BEYOND THE CONTINUOUS
IMPROVEMENT TOOLS

6

THE CHALLENGE OF MAINTAINING CONTINUOUS IMPROVEMENT

We all have heard stories of the millions, even billions of dollars saved by companies that have successfully implemented Lean, Six Sigma, or Theory of Constraints continual improvement tools. The numbers are staggering and speak loudly to the impact the tools can have on a company and also to the state companies were in prior to transformation. Just think of it — the bottom lines of our companies were being hit with billions of dollars of waste before transformation. How in the world did we even survive? It makes you wonder. Without transformation, many of us certainly would not be around today.

The only problem with transformation is that the more you do it, the harder it becomes to sustain. The low-hanging fruit gets picked quickly, and before long, the tree starts to look pretty barren. As change agents, we want to harvest a plentiful amount of savings each and every season. Is there a point where there are no longer any more benefits to obtain? That point would be perfection, and I'll go out on a limb and say that no company has yet achieved perfection. There is always room for improvement.

That reminds me of a story. A man is standing against a wall of a room facing the opposite wall. The objective is for him to begin walking and reach the opposite wall. There is only one rule that guides him as he attempts to walk across the room. He must repeatedly walk half the distance to the wall and then stop. How long will it take for him to reach the opposite wall? Clearly, he never will because the distance can always be reduced by half. That is a good analogy for the pursuit of perfection. It can be a goal and you can keep moving toward it, but it is never totally obtainable, because when the waste is completely squeezed out of your current processes, then you can think of smarter, faster, and more efficient approaches.

As with any effort expended in a business, the justification for performing it is based on the return it offers. When the big initial returns become yesterday's news, there is always the option of doing nothing more. Maybe that is the right thing to do for some processes. Maybe not. Certainly, that is not the appropriate course of action across the board for any company.

Consider the following company motto:

> At Company XYZ, we have improved our processes as much as we can such that the widgets we make are pretty darn good. We are comfortable with the level of quality and service we provide and do not anticipate expending any effort to make any further improvements.

Obviously, no company would ever publicly have such a motto, but some may privately say something similar. This improvement stuff is hard. Human nature tends to direct us to the path of least resistance, which is not naturally the most difficult approach. The decision to go further in improvement pulls at your very being, because if you have been at it a while, have already made significant accomplishments, you can rationalize resting on your laurels a bit. It is somewhat like the New York Yankees. In Major League Baseball, there are 30 teams in the American and National leagues. If you are a baseball fan, you know that year after year the Yankees will be contenders for the world championship. Does that mind-set exist because of past success? Partly, but what about the Angels or the Marlins? Sure, they will probably have a good team and a chance at the playoffs, but world champions? I am from the Cleveland area, and the Indians haven't won a championship in 50 years. The team has made significant improvements over the past decade and has come close to winning a championship, but has not won.

Even before the season starts, the perception exists that the Yankees have the greatest likelihood of being the world champions, because they are constantly and continuously improving their ball club so as to stack the deck in their favor. There is no resting on one's laurels in the Yankee front office. Of course, the Yankees have the revenue that affords them the opportunity to acquire the highest paid players, but that's an argument for another day. The point is the mind-set of continuous improvement. The Yankees organization has won more

World Series championships than any other team in baseball, and the way they aggressively work to create a winning team makes you think they are scratching to win their first.

Don't we all want to be the Yankees of our respective industries? There is no reason why you cannot be. Never be satisfied with past success, and continuously try to stack the deck in your favor to achieve success. So far in this book, we have looked at some of the elements that will help you stack the deck in your favor, namely the continuous improvement tools. The continuous improvement tools are like the high-paid players on the Yankees. They are the best business tools that are available to you. We will learn more about Look Forward® in the chapters to come, which is analogous to the Yankee management organization. It is the holistic management structure needed to optimize the performance of your company and assure ongoing continuous improvement.

There can be a point in your improvement journey where "innovation" is necessary in order to make the next leap. Maybe you have squeezed all the waste that you possibly can out of a process and have it performing at its highest possible capability. What's next? Maybe it is a breakthrough innovative way of accomplishing the objective of the current process. Maybe it is a new innovative product to replace a current one.

Imagine a management improvement team discussion at a typical horse-and-buggy manufacturer of years gone by. Some of the topics of discussion could have been about how to make the buggy wheels roll smoother, how to make the ride more comfortable, or even how to get the horses to go faster. Of course, the discussion would be geared toward trying to give the company an edge over other horse-and-buggy competitors. Unfortunately, someone came along with the bright idea of transporting people using the innovative machine called the automobile, which obviously was the beginning of the end for the horse-and-buggy business. It is important to bring everything to the table when you are evaluating improving your company, including the possibility of an innovative breakthrough.

The continuous improvement tools themselves (Lean, Six Sigma, and Theory of Constraints) are innovative business improvement tool breakthroughs. We looked at these tools in earlier chapters, and each has its unique aspects that make it a powerful weapon in your arsenal. The passion that these tools elicit among some of their true believers is equally impressive. When this passion for a particular tool becomes pervasive among the leadership of a company, then the company adopts an identity that intertwines itself with the tool. You might hear someone refer to his or her company as a Lean company, a Six Sigma company, or a Theory of Constraints company. Typically, when a company adopts the identity of a tool, it is because people have been sold on its philosophy and believe that it will assure continuous improvement. One of the unfortunate offshoots of such a path is that the tools not adopted are ignored. For example, those in a Lean company may not pay much attention to Six Sigma or Theory of Constraints, although that does not happen as much anymore as perhaps it did 10 or 15 years ago. In fact, many companies have adopted a Lean Six Sigma identity in their improvement efforts in an attempt to have the best of both worlds. Why not? They are both very powerful tools that have their unique benefits. Why ignore one over the other?

In our baseball analogy, we would not identify a team based on one player, regardless of how much he contributes to improvement. The Yankees are not a Derek Jeter organization (although some Derek Jeter fans may argue this point). The Yankees are an organization that has equipped itself with the best tools available, including the Derek Jeter tool, the Mario Rivera tool, the Joe Torre tool, etc. Each one of these tools or individuals has truly demonstrated

---

This achievement report describes, in the Shingo Prize format, changes made and resulting achievements at Delphi Packard Electric's Ohio molding operations since 1997.

Injection molding of plastic parts has always been a cost-competitive business for Delphi Packard. Because almost all customers were internal, Packard's wiring assembly plants acted as quality filters for nonconforming plastic parts. Therefore, the focus on plastic historically has been one of cost, while quality and responsiveness received substantially less focus. In addition, Delphi Packard's business had primarily been selling wiring assemblies. The component operations, including plastic molding, played a supporting role.

In the 1990s, sales of components to outside customers grew substantially. Product design and performance, price, and cost levels facilitated this continuing growth. Product quality was an issue with several customers. At the same time, Packard's wiring assembly plants began to put substantial pressure on component plants to improve quality rapidly. Customer expectations had simply outrun our ability to improve quality levels within our plastic molding operations.

During the Business Review process in 1997, Ken Ellsworth, then plant manager of Plant 3, and his staff analyzed the state of the molding business in all respects, including customer expectations, cost, safety, delivery, responsiveness, and competitiveness. The only conclusion they could reach was that quality and responsiveness must improve drastically. The team faced a "fix the business or lose the business" decision.

Ken and his team formulated a concept and plan to replace the obsolete molding operation with one that is truly world class. Because of their experience, a brainstorming session quickly identified a long list of necessary improvements.

Figure 6-1. Summary of achievements at Delphi Packard Electric's Cortland Molding Operation, Plant 45. (Courtesy of Delphi Packard Electric. Reprinted with permission.)

that he will facilitate improvement on his own. Some of the other teams in Major League Baseball might say that if they had the Joe Torre tool or the Mario Rivera tool, they could be champions also.

Is that all it takes to be successful at maintaining ongoing continuous improvement — having the right tool in place in your organization? Some would argue yes, and indeed there are some convincing examples that strongly support their claim. Figure 6-1 highlights a success story at the Delphi Packard Plant in Cortland, Ohio. The company's efforts were so successful that it earned the honor and recognition of receiving the Shingo Prize. Delphi is no stranger to winning the Shingo Prize; it has won seven of them at its Packard facility. You can find out more about all of the good things that are happening at Delphi by visiting http://www.delphi.com. This is an excellent example of how the application of Lean methodology can help achieve phenomenal results.

Quality opportunities were primarily equipment capability, tooling, system, environment, and infrastructure related; cost opportunities included machine uptime, material handling, and labor savings; responsiveness could improve with quicker changeovers, improved cycling capability, and improved operational availability; safety improvement potential existed in ergonomics, equipment layout, and material handling. A cross-functional group was formed to identify anything that might prevent us from being at an ideal state and to lay a plan to correct everything identified.

Numerous options were analyzed; the spectrum went from a renovation of the existing facility, to upgrading other existing facilities, to constructing a "greenfield" facility. This analysis was very extensive and took many months. In the end, the best option, renovating the existing 22-year-old Cortland plant, was chosen. Detailed planning for that facility began while a formal Appropriation Request was developed to pay for the project.

In July of 1999, renovation of the facility began, with production beginning on March 28, 2000. Cortland was scheduled to take 100 machines worth of business from Plant 3 and to insource 32 machines from outside suppliers. This work would be done on 120 machines due to improvements in efficiency, utilization, and uptime. As the business that existed in Plant 3 began to move to Cortland, machines in Plant 3 were shut down.

The Cortland plant is currently taking the remaining tooling from Plant 3 and outside suppliers. The following list is an attempt to identify accomplishments associated with the team that has managed this business for the past five years:

- Using the Business Review process as it was truly intended to be used, to listen to the customer and take a serious, honest look at the operation.

- Taking advantage of the expertise of a truly cross-functional team in identifying what the operation should look and operate like if we were to truly exceed our customers' expectations both now and in the long term.
- Setting very high goals and expectations for the operation and the employees. Many goals were extremely difficult to attain, such as zero blocked cavities and zero returned rejected parts per million (RRPPM), as discussed in the body of the report.
- Assembling a team of motivated individuals, all working as a team to both start up the Cortland plant and then continuously improve it.
- Selecting the optimal mix of automated and manual systems to minimize total cost.
- Taking risks with technology and systems, such as live labeling at the press, to attain goals such as zero misidentified containers.
- Working with our supplier of raw material to minimize the cost of raw material handling and storage.
- Innovations such as the returnable raw material bin, low volume material vessel, automatic regrind blending, and single container flow.
- Continuous improvement activities such as improved material drying, improved layout, ergonomic workstation designs, outstanding housekeeping, and reduced inventory levels.
- Improving changeover time from 2 hours and 18 minutes to 37 minutes.
- Establishing a facility with world-class housekeeping, so that existing and potential customers say "Wow!" when they visit.
- Having all equipment and systems in the facility on preventive maintenance programs.
- Applying error-proofing techniques extensively throughout the operation to eliminate the most common sources of quality problems.
- Extensive use of visual control.
- Implementing a comprehensive information technology system to allow the plant to operate with substantially fewer personnel than previously.
- Applying Six Sigma techniques to improve process performance.
- Performing at 0 RRPPM to all outside customers since start-up.
- Performing at 12 RRPPM to all customers since start-up, in a business that has historically run between 800 and 1000 RRPPM.
- Having zero mis-IDs since start-up.
- Reducing scrap by 68%.
- Improving first-time quality by 62%.

Figure 6-1 (continued).

However, the question is not whether the tools or any combination of them will enable a company to achieve significant improvements over the long haul. The question is whether or not all of the tools at your disposal can be utilized in harmony in a fashion that fosters a holistic management culture that lives and

- Reducing unit cost by 2.5%, with a projection of 10% total by year's end.
- Achieving outstanding schedule utilization performance of 95%.
- Insourcing work above and beyond the planning level, saving the division over $15 million annually.
- Executing zero blocked cavities since start of production, increasing output by 6% and drastically improving quality performance.
- Being awarded the 2000 Global Excellence Award, Delphi Packard's most prestigious internal award.
- Being nominated by Microsoft for the *Computerworld* Honors 21st Century Award.
- Performing well enough that Delphi has chosen to build a greenfield operation nearby to take the remaining work from Plant 3 — groundbreaking is September 2001.
- Having the courage to do what is right for the business by focusing on total cost, even though at times it conflicted with an organizational desire to suboptimize one or more metrics.
- Establishing an attitude and culture of always striving to be the best. The team in the Cortland facility has improvement plans right now to make the operation even better than it is. Continuous improvement is a way of life with the Cortland team.

In summary, we feel that the improvement in the molding business in the Ohio operations has been nothing less than outstanding. While the performance has and continues to improve drastically in the areas of safety, quality, delivery, and cost, we recognize that no matter how much improvement we make, there is always more room to improve.

The greatest achievement for the group is in attitude. The molding team has exhibited extraordinary diligence and persistence in dealing with a very challenging, complicated, and difficult operation. Every challenge is met with constructive attitudes, and problems are addressed as opportunities.

No operation, including the Cortland operation, is perfect. Visitors will undoubtedly find areas that can improve and systems that may not fit with their own personal philosophies about manufacturing systems. But very few operations have the collective attitude that this facility's team does in constructive discussion, debate, and openness to change. We feel that these people, with this attitude, are what makes that plant great and will keep it world class long term.

breathes improvement. If the answer is yes, then the next obvious question is whether it would be worthwhile to pursue.

The answer to that question seems to depend on whether each of the individual tools is perceived as having merit. Clearly, there are plenty of people who are true believers in all three of the methods. It is just as clear that each of the methods has its own unique benefits that it brings to the table, so why not use all of them if it will make your business better?

One reason why not would be the orchestration that would be required in order to assure that all three methods were being implemented properly. Another would be that the lack of focus on a particular method could lead to confusion from one method to another and bog down the whole process. We will take a look at these reasons and some others as well a little later in an attempt to evaluate if they are legitimate concerns. But before we do, let's take a look at some of the more general factors that affect sustaining a continuous improvement program.

THE DRYING UP OF THE LOW-HANGING FRUIT

This first and foremost is probably the biggest stumbling block to sustaining an effective continuous improvement program. This is when it becomes really tough to make any significant improvements. Up to that point, it is easier to get the troops to jump on the bandwagon. People get excited about being acknowledged for contributing to a project that saved the company thousands or even millions of dollars. It is hard to find someone who doesn't want to be a part of that. It is an ego boost and viewed as a good move politically.

The term low-hanging fruit implies that a minimal amount of effort is required. All you have to do is walk by and scoop it up. In reality, that may not necessarily be the case. Just because it is low-hanging fruit does not mean that you will not have to work for it. But if you use a fair amount of due diligence in the application of the continuous improvement tools, chances are you will harvest some of that low-hanging fruit.

The tools will serve you well even after the low-hanging fruit is gone, although making further inroads will put the old gray matter to the test. You will have to think outside the box, above and below it, and all around it in order to develop a new way of looking at a long-standing problem. Recall the horse-and-buggy example. Maybe a breakthrough innovation will be required. Whether product or process related, one thing you can be sure about is that it will not be easy. Sprinkle in a little good old-fashioned ingenuity along with the powerful continuous improvement tools and you will come up with the right recipe.

The problem that the members of your improvement teams will have to deal with when they reach this point is frustration. At least you hope that is the problem they will have. At this point, they have gone year after year chalking up success after success, and now they have gotten bogged down. They should still have expectations for successful results, and not obtaining them would be the source of frustration. This frustration, if left unchecked, can kill any positive momentum an improvement team has in its favor.

That is why some additional coaching of the improvement teams may be necessary when they reach this point. At a minimum, management needs to help them work through their frustration in order to free up their thought processes for developing solutions. They need to have just the right amount of rope at this point — enough that the creative juices are spurred on, but not so much that complacency over past success creeps in. Perhaps the scope of the improvement objective may need to be broadened in order to effect change. Maybe cross-team brainstorming may be required if the issues have grown beyond the teams' initial scope.

Whatever the issue, it most likely will require some management coaching, mentoring, or whatever you want to call it. Once the logjam is broken, the natural abilities of the improvement team will kick into gear.

THE CORPORATE PERSONALITY

What is the corporate personality? In the next chapter, personality characteristic traits will be discussed in relation to team members, but that is not what corporate personality refers to. What is the personality of your company? Did that question conjure up some notions when you read it? I bet it did. Why wouldn't a company have a personality? It is made up of numerous individuals, all of whom have distinct personalities. It is a living and breathing entity.

The personality of a company will have an impact on maintaining the positive momentum of its continuous improvement program. In the next chapter, we will talk about the four primary personality characteristic traits that are prevalent in people:[5]

1. Take charge
2. Care taking
3. Detail orientated
4. Fun loving

These same characteristics apply to the personality of a company. Not that long ago, one of the objectives of a company was to be somewhat of a caretaker to its employees. Human resources designed program after program to help employees in one fashion or another — the corporate gym, cafeteria, resort, etc. — anything to assure some level of comfort and to communicate that the company truly cared. The personality of such a company would clearly be caretaker. Do any of those companies still exist today? I am sure some do, and if they have the finances to justify it, more power to them. But does that type of approach foster ingenuity, elimination of waste, and a passion for continuous improvement? Maybe, but I'm not so sure. I tend to think that it would support a sense of entitlement, somewhat of a corporate welfare type of mentality. This is counterproductive to instilling a passion for improvement. Obviously, some perks are a good thing for employees, and a company should take every opportunity to reward them. Employees are a company's most valuable asset. The problem arises when the perks are handed out to an excess. At that point, they become counterproductive to all aspects of a business, including the continuous improvement program.

Paralysis by analysis occurs when people become so caught up in the details of something that they are overwhelmed to the point of paralysis. That brings us to the detail-orientated personality of a company. It is most prevalent in highly technical companies in which the analysis of details is the essence of what they are. Such companies cannot ignore the details and typically are in the types of industries that should not ignore the details, like aerospace, medical equipment, pharmaceuticals, etc. However, there are many other industries that do not have to function at the same level of detail. The key from a management perspective, regardless of the industry, is to be sensitive to when detail analysis is or is not required. If it is not, then the improvement teams should not be impeded by a mentality of overanalysis. This can be counterproductive to moving forward with improvement efforts.

As a leader of your company, you are a take-charge kind of person. You make things happen and you get things done. If the company on the whole has this type of mind-set, then that normally plays well for your continuous improvement program. The team members on your improvement teams need to be able to feel like they can make decisions and move things forward. When this behavior is modeled to them, they tend to adopt it. It is a kind of behavior that builds upon itself as well. It is contagious. When it is fostered and supported, before you know it, you have a bunch of leaders making decisions about all kinds of things.

With all of the decisions that have to be made and all of the daily stresses of the job, is it possible to still have fun at work. Some leaders firmly believe that work is supposed to be fun, and that attitude most likely is an offshoot of their fun-loving personality type. When the corporate personality is fun loving, then everyone feels like they have the freedom to have fun at work — to laugh, joke around, and enjoy the camaraderie of peers while still accomplishing the required tasks of the business. This type of corporate personality can work both ways in regard to a company's continuous improvement program. The fun-loving freedom can foster creative ideas that may turn out to be breakthroughs that result in innovative changes. However, if taken to excess, work can turn into a big party. If this is the personality of your company, then you will have to walk the management tightrope to assure that things don't get out of hand. However you decide to do that, make sure that you have fun doing it!

THE CORPORATE CULTURE

We have talked about how a company can have a personality of its own; now let's take a look at the culture of a company. How does that differ from the personality of a company? It differs in the same way that the culture of any group of individuals differs from their personalities. The United States is the great melting pot, and Americans come from different cultures. You can trace your ancestral family tree to discover the culture from which your family line originated. Americans come from eastern European, western European, Asian, Mexican, and African cultures, to name a few. If you do not want to go back that far, just look at the culture of the world we live in today: suburbia, inner city, rural, etc. All of these environments have a unique culture associated with them. A company is no different. The personalities that the people within the culture exhibit are unique to them and do not define the culture.

To help illustrate what corporate culture means, let's consider a few examples of the different types of corporate cultures.

The Functionally Oriented Culture

The functionally oriented culture is more of the traditional model for the corporate environment. The engineering department does its thing, the accounting department does its thing, as does purchasing, etc. Activity takes place mostly in silos, with a lot of territorial underpinnings flowing through all the interactions between functional areas. This is without a doubt the most counterproductive culture in terms of the ongoing maintenance of a continuous improvement program. This probably is not a news flash to anyone, but the funny thing is that even though most people know this, it still is a prevalent corporate culture. That just illustrates how hard it is to change human dynamics in the corporate setting.

But it can be done, even without changing the organizational structure from a functional standpoint. The key is not who people report to along the corporate food chain, but rather how they execute their assigned duties. If they are executing their duties as if there were no functional boundaries or silos, then what difference does it make who they report to? They can still report to their respective functional management, yet operate as if they are structured by process, organizationally. How can this be done? In the next chapter, we will see how this is done using the Look Forward® management approach, although as long as an organization is structured functionally, it is important to be attentive to breaking down any silo walls. This is not a one-shot deal either; it is ongoing and continuous. Human nature is funny. When people have been functioning for years in a certain way, if the opportunity exists for them to revert to old behaviors, they may have a tendency to backslide. That is why you need to encourage the positive cross-functional interaction and continue to break down those silo barriers.

The Benevolent Dictatorship Culture

Sometimes when a company is struggling or finds itself in circumstances that are less than favorable, the leadership is called upon to exert an appropriate amount of influence in order to right the ship. I refer to this as the benevolent dictatorship culture. Typically, this results in the company turning the corner and getting back on the right track, but not without a cost. The cost is the empowerment of the employees. The benevolent dictator is viewed as the company messiah and the source of anything that will have a significant impact on improvement. Within a company that has this culture, there can be the "grand pooh-bah" benevolent dictator, who has many subjects who also are benevolent dictators to a lesser degree.

The general idea is that the grand and glorious ideas flow downward for the troops to implement. This environment is counterproductive to sustaining ongoing long-term continuous improvement. The real breakthroughs that are needed to sustain improvement after the low-hanging fruit is gone will come from those most familiar with the processes, not the benevolent dictator. If this is the culture of your company, you need to begin a transfer of power to make improvements to those who can sustain them.

The "It's as Good as It Gets" Culture

How good is good enough? In Chapter 3 on Six Sigma, we looked at some statistics for various industries. How many train wrecks are acceptable? How many improperly issued visas? Clearly, how good a company needs to be from a basic product safety or functional standpoint should be apparent. Where it starts to get a little gray is when you go beyond that point. Obviously, cost will be a driver. If it costs more to implement an improvement than you gain from it, then the business decision should be not to do it, as long as all factors enter into this costing evaluation, especially the voice of the customer.

At this level, however, things are not always black and white, and the subjectivity of customer perception enters into the picture. In addition, some of the future gains from an expense could be speculative. Take, for example, training in the continuous improvement tools. There clearly is an expense incurred in committing to train employees and/or the supply base. What assurances of a return are there? Some will argue that there definitely will be a return, and the skeptics will take the doubting Thomas position and say there is no need for it. It's as good as it gets!

The key to overcoming this roadblock to continuous ongoing improvement is the metrics. You have to be able to show that your invested time and talent will have a direct impact on some metric that relates to the health of the business. If you cannot do that, then you are standing on shaky ground. Just having the metric is a good start, but it is no guarantee that performance will change in the appropriate direction. That is where the management review comes in, which will be discussed in the next chapter.

HERD MENTALITY

The last impediment to ongoing continuous improvement is herd mentality. It refers to large or small groups of people falling into the trap of thinking alike. Everyone just goes along with the program so as not to rock the boat. It is a sure recipe for keeping improvement initiatives stuck at status quo. There is never enough critical thinking or competing ideas to move things off of dead center.

How do you counteract the herd mentality? By finding ways to get the key players involved in the decision-making process, to express their unique opinions. Ideally, you want to bring this out within a group setting, so as to create a dynamic that fosters this behavior among the group members.

These are some of the general factors that can have a deleterious impact on sustaining ongoing continuous improvement. Obviously, there are many more that you will have to face at one time or another. The good news is that none of them can permanently stop your improvement effort. They most certainly can bring it to a crawl, but can be overcome if addressed head on.

MANAGING MULTIPLE TOOLS

Let's revisit the previously raised concerns for not using all three tools simultaneously. They were: (1) the orchestration required to assure that all three methods are implemented properly and (2) a lack of focus on one particular method can lead to confusion and bog down the process.

Continuing with the earlier baseball theme, consider that a lot of teams have not followed the Yankee model. Some baseball teams make the organizational decision to go after one particular type of tool to assure their successful performance. The Cleveland Indians and Atlanta Braves of the 1990s each chose a different tool to be identified with. For the Indians, it was hitting. They stacked the deck in their favor with power hitters. There was Albert Belle, Manny Ramirez, and Jim Thome. The Indians were recognized as a tremendous hitting team during the 1990s, one of the best ever.

The Braves, on the other hand, made the organizational decision to be strong in pitching. Their pitching staff included John Schmoltz and Greg Maddux. The Braves were recognized as a pitching team during the 1990s, one of the best ever.

Both teams had powerful tools. The Indians had such strong hitting that they would kill the ball every game. The Braves pitching staff was so intimidating that runs by opposing teams were few and far between. Both teams realized success from the tools they implemented in their organizations. An analogy would be to equate hitting to Six Sigma and pitching to Lean. Just as the Indians and Braves had success in the 1990s, so have many companies that have adopted either Six Sigma or Lean.

The success of the Indians and Braves during this time frame was such that they faced each other in the 1995 World Series. It was a classic matchup — great hitting against great pitching. The pundits argued back and forth about which team would win. Those enamored by hitting were confidant that the powerful bats of the Indians would overcome the Braves pitching. Those enamored by pitching knew that good pitching always beats good hitting. The bantering is reminiscent of the arguments heard from true believers of either Lean or Six Sigma; each side knows without a doubt that its favored approach is better than the other.

As it turned, out the Braves won that series in six games. Their tremendous pitching overpowered the strong bats of the Indians. There was talk that this was the beginning of a dynasty for the Braves, but things didn't quite turn out that way. The Braves haven't won a World Series since. Their focus and dedication to having the most powerful pitching staff of all time was not enough to sustain continued success.

As for the Indians, their powerful hitting was potent enough to take them to the World Series again in 1997. Unfortunately for Cleveland fans, the result was the same. The Indians lost the series, this time in seven games to the upstart Florida Marlins. The organization's focus and dedication to having the most powerful hitting lineup of all time brought some success for a period, but it never won a championship. Since the Indians never won the world championship, they obviously never sustained improvement as well. In fact, it has been over 50 years since the last Indians championship.

But what about the Yankees? Love them or hate them, you have to acknowledge their success — not just periodic success, but rather ongoing, continuous success. If we take a closer look at the approach the Yankees have chosen, we see that they have utilized the best tools that are at their disposal. These tools impact all facets of the organization, not just pitching or hitting. Certainly, the Yankees have had good pitching and good hitting over the years, but it seems that their teams are well balanced. It is not just the athletes in the organization that they optimize, but the coaching staff, farm system, etc. This organization pulls together the best tools available and manages them in concert in order to foster ongoing, continuous improvement.

If your company is strong in hitting, then do not ignore some of the free-agent pitchers that are available to you. Go out and get them to make your company better. Once you amass all of your tools, then decide as an organization what you will consider to be success. Do the Yankees think it was a successful year if they make the play-offs? No way. For the Yankees, anything less than winning the World Series is an unsuccessful year. In your business, determine what measures your success for the year and track it. Do not settle for making the play-offs. Go for the championship.

But how do you do all of this for the whole organization? How do you manage it such that the improvement effort is in concert with the activities of the business and drives it to continuously improve? It is no different than running the Yankees. You need an executive-level management body that oversees the improvement efforts and is actively involved. Other than George Steinbrenner and your hometown team's owner, how many owners of baseball teams can you name off the top of your head? Not too many, I'm sure. You need to execute leadership and have an understanding of where you want the team to go. Management needs to be actively involved on a continuous and ongoing basis.

This is very difficult to do. Even the Yankees do not win the world championship every year. Do not be discouraged if you have a bad year or two along the way. This is a marathon, not a sprint. You are in it for the long haul, so make your decisions to assure long-term ongoing continuous improvement.

Management's role in optimizing all of the best ballplayers (the continuous improvement tools) the world has to offer has never been needed more. Today's competitive world market demands higher quality products and services delivered quicker than ever. Companies can only do this by optimizing the assets they have, the greatest of which are their people.

Jim Womack is the founder and president of the Lean Enterprise Institute as well as co-author of *The Machine That Changed the World, Lean Thinking,* and a host of other books on Lean. As co-author of *The Machine That Changed the World,* he was instrumental in introducing the Toyota Production System, or Lean, to the world and is considered to be one of the foremost thinkers when it comes to Lean. In a presentation to the Association for Manufacturing Excellence in November 2000, he acknowledged the need for continuous improvement management that is ingrained into all aspects of the business in order to take Lean to the next level.[6] He also proposed that in order to make the "next Lean leap," we are going to have to start to look at managing the entire process and not just a particular improvement project. Rather than designating someone or some team as the focal point for overcoming a problem using one of the continuous improvement tools, he recommends designating someone as the value stream manager. Instead of managing a specific problem to correct, the value stream manager would manage the entire value stream for a particular part family. These value stream managers would be supported by cross-functional representation and work to eliminate waste and improve the flow of their assigned part family. The concept of value stream management is further addressed by Jim Womack and Dan Jones in the 2003 revised and updated version of *Lean Thinking.*[7]

What are some of the other voices out there saying about continuous improvement management? Pete Robustelli is Six Sigma Qualtec's executive vice-president and managing partner. He has over 20 years of experience working in the improvement arena in all facets of improvement both in the United States and internationally. In an article entitled "Beyond Six Sigma," published in the September 2003 issue of *Quality Digest* magazine,[4] he addresses the need for a holistic management system to be in place in order to sustain improvement, whether it involves using Six Sigma or any other tool. He calls upon the leaders of the company to take holistic strategic measures to achieve the company's overall mission. He goes on to say that:

> This means implementing a management system to plan and execute actions and designing that system to change with the changing times. If a major problem-solving tool is needed, perhaps Six Sigma should be implemented, but maybe not. It all depends on what's best for

the business, and what's best depends on its leaders and the system by which they live.

That brings us to the next chapter, which addresses the Look Forward® management approach to continuous improvement. Look Forward® establishes a culture that promotes ongoing improvement and requires active accountability from the management team and the cross-functional improvement teams for sustained success. Look Forward® offers you the opportunity to manage your business in a manner akin to the Yankees organization, such that year in and year out you can expect your company to be the world's best at what you do.

This book has free materials available for download from the Web Added Value™ Resource Center at www.jrosspub.com.

LOOK FORWARD®: THE ABSC WAY

On a hot afternoon during the summer of 1996, Senior Vice-President of Operations James "Tank" Williams initiated a meeting to discuss how Aircraft Braking Systems Corporation (ABSC) was going to break through the current continuous improvement logjam. ABSC had historically been a high-performing company and now found itself at the point where its rework- and scrap-related costs were not getting any lower. The company was flatlined at $2 million for two consecutive years. Granted, the cost of these "bad goods" in relation to sales was not all that bad in comparison to benchmarks for manufacturers in the industry. In fact, it was 0.8% in 1996. This was *world-class* performance according to the metrics published in the November 2001 issue of *Industry Week* magazine. Regardless of how ABSC compared to other benchmark statistics, it was extremely annoying to be flatlined on its bad goods metric. Besides, $2 million is $2 million, a significant amount of money in anybody's book. The $64 million question was how to take it to the next level and break through the $2 million barrier. The obvious answer available at the time was to establish a directive that mandated the adoption of one of the predominant continuous improvement methodologies: Lean, Six Sigma, or Theory of Constraints. To do so would have established ABSC's identity as a "Lean" company or a "Six Sigma" company, and the challenge from then on would have been to educate everyone in the company as to what their new identity was.

This would not have been a new path for ABSC to go down. It had already been through the quality circle era, world-class manufacturing, and total quality management. Each of these has merit and is all well and good on its own, but none took hold and became a part of the way of life at ABSC. With this background in mind, a clear hesitation existed to adopt another off-the-shelf continuous improvement methodology and try to fit ABSC into it. But what to do as an alternative?

The meeting was held in the office of Mark Graham, director of quality at ABSC. It required abandoning all previously conceived notions as to how to approach continuous improvement. Starting with a clean slate, what would be the best approach for ABSC? What would capitalize most on the strengths of the company and overcome any of the weaknesses? How could ABSC jump-start its most valuable asset — its people — to reach the next level of performance? The answer to all of these questions evolved into the Look Forward® management approach. Evolved is the appropriate word because it was not one of those ingenious ideas that popped into someone's brain and then shared in the meeting down to the most finite level of detail. Rather, the foundation of the Look Forward® approach was conceptualized and the organization given birth to by the end of the meeting. The vision was to develop a homegrown approach to continuous improvement that would empower the workforce and by its nature instill a high degree of ownership among those involved. The results today are phenomenal, but the path to the current state had its share of twists and turns that challenged the core purpose of the vision along the way. I will share with you some of the adventures we encountered along our journey to provide some insight into some of the continuous improvement opportunities you may face within your company. First, let's look at the background of ABSC and the state of the company leading up to this initiative.

ABSC has been in the aircraft wheel and brake business for over 75 years, getting its start in 1925 as Goodyear Aviation Products. It was the first major manufacturer of aircraft wheels and brakes and a pioneer in the industry from the very beginning. Some notable firsts for the company are:

1930s	First multiple-disk brakes
1940s	First automatic adjusters for single-disk brakes
1950s	First trimetallic brake and electronic antiskid system
1966	First carbon brake lab test
1970	First carbon brake production contract
1974	First brake-by-wire system
1983	First electric brake
1984	First FAA-certified composite main wheel
1985	First digital brake-by-wire system
1988	First nose/main gear carbon brake management system
1991	First taxi brake select system

1992	First phase change/carbon brake
1993	Deceleration feedback control
1994	High rejected takeoff coefficient long-life carbon
1997	Thermal management ceramic technology
1998	First high-energy-capacity carbon brake prototype
1999	First successful iteration of a brake control system into a third-party modular avionics unit system
2000	Development of NUCARB® carbon disks
2001	First electric brake system for space vehicle
2002	Debut of NUCARB® breakthrough carbon technology

Clearly, innovation was a way of life at ABSC and, as with most technology-oriented businesses, a necessity for survival. Seventy-five years of survival equates to being a leader in innovation. As a result, ABSC is the world leader in carbon brakes. It was the first aircraft wheel and brake manufacturer to use carbon brakes, which now are used on over 5000 aircraft. In addition, ABSC is the world leader in steel brake equipment, and its product is on more than 20,000 aircraft.

Much of ABSC's growth and development occurred as a division of the Goodyear Tire and Rubber Company. In 1974, Goodyear Aviation Products joined with the division of Goodyear known at the time as Goodyear Aerospace Corporation. The Goodyear Aerospace years were good ones, and the division was a valued asset of its parent company. However in 1987, Sir James Goldsmith attempted a corporate takeover of the Goodyear Tire and Rubber Company by purchasing a majority share of stock. In an attempt to fend off Sir James, Goodyear Tire and Rubber divested itself of some of its assets. The Goodyear Aerospace division was one of those assets. The company was purchased by Loral Corporation in 1987, which marked another turning point. The spirit of innovation that had been so prevalent at the company since its inception was now accelerated as never before.

Whoever coined the phrase "necessity is the mother of invention" was very astute, and in some sense, that is where the company was. It had just been through an unprecedented corporate raid of one the world's largest manufacturers and now found itself under new management looking to take it to new levels. The company was being called upon to reinvent itself.

At the time, the company was the world's leading provider of aircraft wheels and brakes, so you might wonder what the problem was. Why reinvent a company that is leading the world? The answer is obvious and speaks to the very soul of ABSC. If you want to continue to be the best in the world, you need to be constantly and exhaustively continuously improving. Yesterday's ideas and accomplishments are history. A world leader is constantly looking for the next edge and never settles into complacency.

It was with this mind-set in 1988 that ABSC embraced the initiative to orient the manufacturing facility with a cellular manufacturing concept. The objective of this effort was to cut out all of the nonvalue-added transportation and processing activity. The one activity of transforming the machining centers into cells was a boon to the company. This initiative drastically reduced cycle times, lead times, and operating costs. Figure 7-1 is a representation of how things were before consolidation with cellular manufacturing. It gives you an idea of how product moved between plants during its life cycle, logging miles upon miles of travel. These aircraft wheels and brakes were frequent flyers before they even made it out of the facility. Figure 7-2 illustrates how the product flow occurred after cellular manufacturing consolidation.

When ABSC went down the path of cellular manufacturing, it did not just identify machines to be consolidated and then cluster them into cells. This activity was optimized as much as possible. Martin Ferrell, vice-president of manufacturing, and Joe McCutcheon, plant manager, decided that they wanted to work with the machine manufacturers and develop machines that optimized performance at ABSC. Doing so required an exchange of ideas between ABSC and the machine manufacturers such that the unique needs of ABSC could be addressed. As a result, ABSC was instrumental in the development of machining centers, which were the first of their kind. These centers provided ABSC with a level of performance never before achieved.

Pushing the technology window with the machine tool manufacturers is another example of ABSC innovation and leadership. Leadership, innovation, and an exhaustive spirit for continual improvement are the key elements that comprise the core value of the company. This was clearly apparent to Bernard Swartz, who was CEO of Loral Corporation at the time. In 1989, the company was sold by Loral to become a privately owned entity. Now known as ABSC, it was privately owned by Bernard Swartz and Sheerson Lehman Hutton. With a strong management team in place during this transition, the company maintained the long-standing tradition of being a leader in the aircraft wheel and brake market. It was for this reason that the Aurora Capital Group was attracted to ABSC in late 2004.

The Aurora Capital Group is a Los Angeles–based investment firm formed in 1991 that acquires and builds companies in partnership with operating management. Aurora believes that the most important element in its investment process is to identify and align itself with outstanding and principled management teams. Aurora acquired ABSC in November 2004 for $1.06 billion.

Throughout all of these business-related transformations, the company has always had a solid quality management system that assured the manufacture of

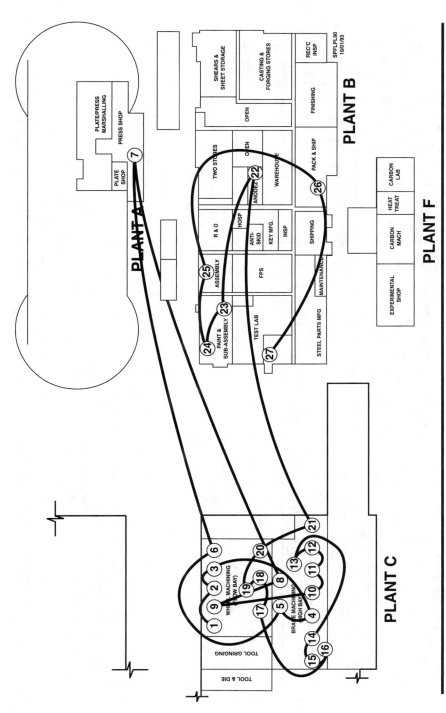

Figure 7-1. Product flow prior to cellular manufacturing consolidation. (Courtesy of Aircraft Braking Systems Corporation.)

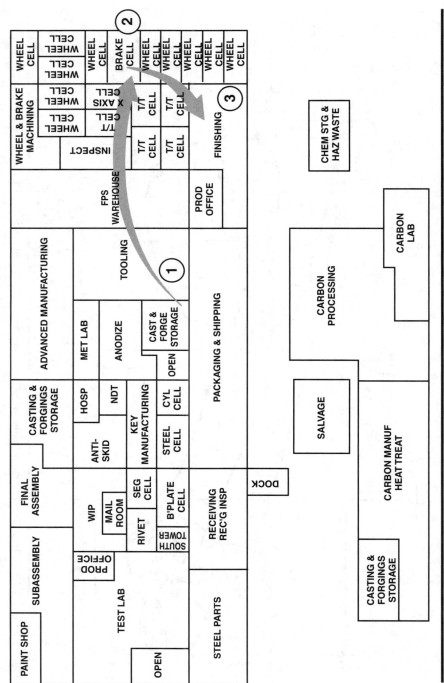

Figure 7-2. Product flow after cellular manufacturing consolidation. (Courtesy of Aircraft Braking Systems Corporation.)

a high-quality product and regulatory compliance. ABSC has been a leader in the world of quality management systems as well. The following summarizes some of the quality management system highlights over the years:

- In 1992, ABSC became the first aircraft wheel and brake manufacturer to be certified to ISO 9001.
- ABSC was one of the first companies to pilot the Federal Aviation Administration Aircraft Certification Systems Evaluation Program system audit.
- ABSC was the first company to be accepted by Douglas Aircraft Corporation's Total Quality Supplier Team.

These quality management system highlights reflect an organization that is striving to be at the forefront of implementing quality systems that foster continual quality improvement. However, even with this structure in place, ABSC's quality performance was flatlined in the 1995–1996 time frame.

Up to that point, ABSC had a traditional corrective/preventive action system in place that identified problems and assured the implementation of effective resolution. A corrective action chairman and a cross-functional team met periodically, evaluated the nonconformances the company was experiencing, assigned responsibility for resolution, and oversaw implementation of the appropriate root cause corrective or preventive action. Although this traditional system met all of the requirements of a corrective or preventive action system, it was not effective in taking the company to the next level.

In addition, during this time frame, production/manufacturing management would meet monthly with executive management to review their performance. The meeting typically consisted of the manufacturing manager going to great pains to make a presentation (dog-and-pony show) that would put him or her in the best light possible in order to avoid the wrath of the executive managers if performance was below expectations.

Quality management made a separate presentation on reject rates and bad goods cost. The motivation was similar to the manufacturing manager's. The quality assurance manager needed to show that he or she had met the management-imposed goal — or else! This type of approach promoted a silo mentality, polarized manufacturing and quality assurance, and did nothing to empower the workforce. That being the case, this approach managed to achieve continual improvement during the years when there was low-hanging fruit to grab. Figure 7-3 depicts this performance. Notice that in 1990, bad goods costs (costs associated with scrap rework and repair) were over $6 million. Bad goods costs as a percent of sales were 2.4%. By 1996, bad goods costs dropped to $2 million dollars, and bad goods costs as a percent of sales improved to 0.8%.

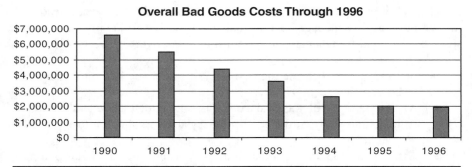

Figure 7-3. Bad goods performance chart. (Courtesy of Aircraft Braking Systems Corporation.)

ABSC had a long history of continual improvement, during which most of the low-hanging fruit was picked, leaving only those elusive opportunities that required a bigger ladder. The challenge was to determine what ladder to use to get at the fruit higher up in the tree. Should ABSC become a Six Sigma company or a Lean company? Should all of its efforts be focused on becoming a Theory of Constraints company?

The answer was none of the above. By that, I do not mean that we thought these methods were inadequate. On the contrary, at this time we already had pockets of applications of Lean and Six Sigma methodology. The question was whether or not to establish the corporate identity as a Lean or Six Sigma company. A toolbox analogy will help to illustrate the dilemma. Imagine that in your toolbox in your basement or garage, you have a screwdriver, a hammer, and a pair of pliers. As a homeowner, opportunities to fix things constantly arise. If you are a parent, then you are fortunate enough to have some helpers in the form of your children. You can pass your knowledge about how to fix things on to your children. These young minds are like sponges, seeking direction on the most appropriate way to fix a particular problem.

Suppose you have a certain affinity for the hammer in your toolbox. Perhaps it was handed down to you from your father, and it has some sentimental value. The pliers and screwdriver may have no such significance. Your feelings about your hammer are so strong that you decide to instruct your children to use the hammer to fix all of the problems that come up and to ignore the pliers and screwdriver. You proudly proclaim your household to be a "hammer household" that uses hammers to fix all problems and to make home improvements. Does that sound silly? Of course it does, although it is not too far off the mark from a decision to solely use a particular continual improvement tool. Taking the analogy further, suppose that your children have some degree of mechanical aptitude and through the transfer of your genetic strain have been endowed with a boatload of smarts — they are just oozing with potential and innate ability to figure out how to fix things. Instead of making all of the best tools known to man available to them and fostering their inherent strengths, you proudly proclaim that you fix things with a hammer in your house. Although there are a lot of things in a house that can be fixed with a hammer and done so in the most efficient manner, using a hammer to put screws in is not the most effective approach. The screwdriver is the better tool.

That is one of the reasons why ABSC did not want to pick a particular continual improvement tool and make the identity of the organization fit what characterized that particular tool. The second and most important reason for not selecting an off-the-shelf method was ownership. As previously mentioned, the company had already been through implementation of total quality management, quality circles, and world-class manufacturing, none of which seemed to stick. Although of these methods clearly have high ideals and are well-intended methodologies, they were viewed as flavors of the month, and when introduced to the workforce, they rolled off like eggs in a Teflon pan.

The key to empowering the workforce with an energy to sustain an ever-evolving continual improvement effort is *ownership*. The people who make things happen must feel like they have some influence on the direction of the company's improvement effort. This is risky business from a management perspective, because it requires a deliberate decision to intervene less, a must in order to create a culture that nurtures empowerment. Of course, there is a fine balance between the level of oversight and when to back off and let things happen. Where this balance point is becomes glaringly apparent as you progress down the path.

In the beginning, ABSC set out to empower the workforce by taking the following first step:

> *Eliminate the corrective action chairman position and the quality and manufacturing presentations to upper management*

This initial step was perceived by those involved as a liberating activity. We all have done things in our careers that seemed like we were doing them just because they had to be done, not because they added value. That is what the perception of these activities evolved into over the years, so eliminating them set a positive tone for what was to come.

The next step was to:

> *Create a cross-functional team for each major part commodity with members from manufacturing, quality assurance, and engineering*

When the teams were first started, the idea was to begin with the basics and build upon them. That is why the team members initially consisted of representatives from manufacturing, quality, and product design engineering. At the time, these functional areas obviously interacted with one another, but they were strongly silo oriented. Overcoming this approach to doing business and fostering a process-based work method was no easy task. I will speak to some aspects of that later in this chapter, but first let's look at what was done to monitor the teams' effectiveness.

With parts per million and bad goods cost as metrics, each team was to establish its improvement goals for each year.

■   Goals were not to be "dictated" by upper management.
■   *All* team members were to be held accountable for the metrics.
■   Teams were encouraged to "Look Forward®" to prevent rejections.

Again starting with the basics, *rejection rate* and *bad goods cost* were chosen as the two primary metrics for the teams. One of the big differences from the previous way of doing business was that the teams were challenged to establish their own goals, instead of management dictating an expected level of performance. Obviously, some rationale had to be included in the established goal. The results were surprising. The teams came up with projected goals that were more aggressive than those previously imposed on them by management. To help assure that these proposed goals had substance to them, each team member was held accountable for the team achieving its goals via his or her individual performance appraisal. This has served to be a good tool to instill functional organization accountability into the process-oriented activity of the teams. All team members, regardless of their functional affiliation, were encouraged to Look Forward® in order to evaluate future rejection opportunities and prevent them before they happen. Recall that with the traditional corrective/preventive action system, past problems were evaluated for root cause and appropriate corrective action implemented. Now we were going beyond that and making what's coming down the road the primary focus, with the past as a guide.

Lastly, these newly created teams were to be structurally responsible to a cross-functional executive management committee. The ABSC management review team (MRT) naturally filled this role. At first, teams were required at a minimum to submit annual goals during the first month of each year and to meet with the MRT once per year. This level of oversight was modified accordingly as required for any particular team. This whole process has evolved over the years and continues to do so. The makeup of the team members has expanded to include representation from industrial engineering, production planning, materials, plant maintenance, and other areas on an as-needed basis. In addition, the scope of the teams has evolved from meeting their parts per million and bad goods cost objectives to include establishing and meeting goals for lead time performance, owning supplier issues that affect the team's commodity type, and providing input into the engineering drawing standards for the particular commodity. The teams have basically taken responsibility for all aspects pertaining to their commodity type and own the issues from cradle to grave throughout the product's life. They basically run their own little commodity-type businesses within the overall business of ABSC. That's *ownership!*

The periodic meetings between the part family Look Forward® teams and the MRT have evolved to become more value added. They are less dog-and-pony show and more status/working meetings that set the tone for the coming months. The MRT itself is a cross-functional team made up of vice-president- and director-level personnel. The role of the MRT is one of the most challenging aspects of the Look Forward® management approach. It is the MRT that must establish the boundaries within which a continual improvement culture can grow. This is accomplished by coaching a common focus on value-added activity both within the MRT Look Forward® team meetings and throughout any given working day.

At ABSC, all links in the demand and supply chains are represented on the MRT. Therefore, there is a high level of continuity in the communication between executive management and the Look Forward® teams. This information transfer fluidity works to improve the velocity at which any desired activity can be effectively implemented. Communication is always a two-way street, and it is imperative that open and honest communication prevails. The teams use the MRT meeting as an avenue to let executive management know where they have been and where they are going.

In addition to a periodic meeting with the MRT, there is significant visibility regarding team performance to the established metrics. Each team's performance is published to all team members, all levels of management, and customer representatives in a monthly publication. The MRT has additional visibility to the activities of the teams through distribution of its meeting minutes. The meeting minutes typically include much *continual improvement* activity. Continual improvement is used here in the AS9100/ISO 9001 context. The bottom line is that the activity and focus of the team members are continually fostered and reinforced on a constant basis. Even though the individuals on the teams are organizationally structured in functional silos, they operate and are reinforced in a manner that is process driven. The culture has been modified to the extent that day-to-day activities are as seamless as possible in terms of functional boundaries. Each member brings his or her functional expertise into the mix, but all accept some accountability for overall performance, whether quality, delivery, design, etc. The manufacturing representative on the team is as passionate about the design features of the product as the product design engineer, and the product design engineer feels strongly about the manufacturability of the part. In essence, everyone begins singing out of the same hymnbook, and a common goal is ingrained.

When the Look Forward® teams were created, the structure of team meetings was set up so as to have some basic common elements that tend to help direct the overall focus of a team's efforts. Clearly, any team is unique, and the issues that arise will be quite diverse. The core of this approach, however, was to be rooted in a few basic concepts that have evolved over the years.

For now, let's take a look at the initial framework for a team's focus. One of the concepts to be established was an evaluation of problem issues that occurred in the past and impacted the product, process, or activity for which a team was accountable. On the product teams, this consisted of a review of the part family reject run for a designated time period (previous month, two months, six months, etc.). The review served several purposes. It provided all the team members with an overview of how well they performed and what specific issues affected their performance. In addition, this cross-functional evaluation of specific problems brought together the collective insight necessary to identify root cause issues and to effect change. This is one of the foundational steps upon which the rest of a team's efforts are built.

Another concept was for the teams to turn their gaze in the opposite direction and begin to Look Forward® to determine what in the future may impact their world and possibly provide opportunities for error. The teams would have to be able to identify on a continuous basis activities that would prevent future errors.

Once these activities to fend off future problems were identified, the next step was to implement them. It was a simple concept that was challenging to incorporate into the business culture. But we did it!

Now that we have looked into the origins of Look Forward® to some degree, let's talk about some of the current application tools that are inherent in the Look Forward® management approach. Look Forward® is a *FREE* and *EASY* approach that will cause your company to *ROAR* as never before and in the end create a perpetual state of *UTOPIA* for the workforce and management. This metaphor may sound like something out of the sixties or like an advertisement for Woodstock, but trust me, it is not. Let's take a look at the four primary methodologies of the Look Forward® method: *FREE, EASY, ROAR,* and *UTOPIA.*

FREE

Dr. Crosby told us that quality is free, and indeed it is, although that is not what free means in the Look Forward® context. FREE stands for:

Forecast
Review
Evaluate
Execute

This is at the heart of the day-to-day activity of the Look Forward® teams at ABSC. As mentioned previously, each Look Forward® team is accountable for all aspects of its particular commodity type from cradle to grave. Therefore, a team is basically running its own company within the company and needs to be concerned about all aspects of its commodity. One of the first and foremost concerns a team has is the forecasted demand from its customers. In some cases, the customer will be internal, and in others external. That is the starting point: What are the future customer needs? With this knowledge in hand, the team as a whole is now in tune to what is coming down the pike in the world of its commodity.

With this as its guiding light, the team then looks backward to determine what problems it may have previously encountered with any of the forecasted customer demands. This is the review step. It consists of an evaluation of reject history, manufacturing or tooling history, planning or industrial engineering issues, etc. Once a comprehensive review of any of the issues relating to demand has been completed, then the team moves into the evaluation stage.

In the evaluation stage, the past issues are evaluated and a determination is made as to whether a proper fix has been implemented to prevent future occurrences. In addition, a broader look is directed at the forecasted demand to determine if there are any potential new unforeseen problems that may arise from the perspective of the cross-functional team. This forward-thinking preventive-type approach goes a long way in optimizing the process and preventing issues before they happen. This is where the team will draw upon any one of the valuable continuous improvement tools — Lean, Six Sigma, Theory of Constraints, or any other problem-solving methodology.

Once the evaluation of fixes for past issues and possible fixes for any potential new issues is completed, then it is time to put these fixes in place. This is where the team moves into the execution phase of its activity. In the execution phase, the corrective and preventive activity is implemented in preparation for the subsequent stream of customer demand. Processing is changed, operations are removed or added, nonvalue-activity is eliminated, drawings are modified, and a host of other pertinent activities are done. When this up-front forward look is accomplished in a systematic fashion, the resulting benefit is a smooth-flowing process that is nearly defect free.

The *FREE* approach is also applied to a specific activity that the ABSC product-oriented Look Forward® teams get involved in. This activity is the review of drawings created for a team's part commodity before release. In addition, the team performs a periodic review of drawing standards that pertain to its part family. Recall that a team functions as if it were a company within the company; it has a variety of inputs and the completed part commodity as its primary output. One of the key inputs is the product design. In essence, the product design team is part of a Look Forward® team's supply chain. Obviously, it is critical to involve the supply chain as early as possible in subsequent processes that are impacted. The Look Forward® teams do this for their part design suppliers. Before a drawing is released, it has been concurrently evaluated by the appropriate Look Forward® team members, along with the respective product design personnel. If the part is purchased, then the appropriate representatives from the supplier are consulted to identify the issues that will impact manufacturability. The voice of the end customer is brought into the mix through the product support engineers. Therefore, the entire supply chain is represented. The end result is a product design released to manufacturing that has been thoroughly evaluated and created to optimize manufacturability and performance. The benefit of having the Look Forward® team drive this activity is that the team has a high level of ownership in the part commodity and is measured on the execution of transforming all inputs into the desired output. The team functions as its own company within the company. That is the essence of empowerment.

EASY

Now let's take a look at the next application tool, *EASY,* which stands for:

Encourage
Abandoning
Silos
Year-round

Encouraging the abandonment of silos year-round is an activity that resides in the management element of a company. At ABSC, it is accomplished through the MRT, which at ABSC consists of director- and vice-president-level personnel along with a few strategic middle managers. The MRT has oversight over the Look Forward® process, and one of its many responsibilities is to encourage the abandonment of the silo mentality. This is not done with the cross-functional team for a specific finite project, but rather is mandated as a way of doing business on a day-to-day basis. This may sound simple, but it is easier said than done. It requires leading by example and the establishment of a mutual trust that continuously needs to be reinforced. Sometimes this is accomplished in subtle unassuming ways and sometimes in direct overt encounters. The key is for the MRT members to be in lockstep and consistent with their message. This can be a threat to an executive manager's fiefdom, but it must be risen above. For a Look Forward® team to have the freedom to work on a day-to-day basis in areas that cross traditional functional boundaries requires the establishment of a corporate culture that not only nurtures such activity but applauds it.

Does that mean the organizational structure has to be revamped to be process oriented around part families in order for this dynamic to be prevalent? No. The functional areas within an organization definitely have their value, and we don't want to throw the baby out with the bathwater. Granted, there are impediments in a process-driven organization that is structured on a functional basis, but the focus should be on fixing those impediments and not on the abolishment of the functional environment.

If the MRT does nothing else and is successful in accomplishing the abandonment of the silo mentality on a day-to-day working basis, then it has earned its weight in gold. The acronym for this activity, EASY, is somewhat of an oxymoron. It is not easy and requires a commitment from top management to keep going forward and not look back. It may not be easy, but it is doable. Does anything truly beneficial come painlessly?

ROAR

Okay, so you acknowledge that it is hard work and think this stuff is all well and good, but how does a company go about making the transformation to this type of corporate culture? I will get into that a little later, but before I do, let's take a look at the next Look Forward® application tool, *ROAR,* which stands for:

Replicate
Other
Acceptable
Resolutions

With this tool, focus is shifted back to the Look Forward® team's activity. Recall that the primary objective of the FREE approach taken by the team was to implement a solution that would pave the way for future product coming down the pike, prevent the repetition of past defects, and head off the generation of any new or unforeseen defects. That's fine, but is that where the effort should stop? The answer is clearly no. Are there any similar parts within the part commodity family that could benefit from the evaluation performed during the FREE activity? Nine times out of ten, the answer to this question will be yes. And even if it is not, a conscious effort needs to be expended to rule out the possibility. Time is such a valuable commodity in the workplace these days, and whenever it can be optimized, you are farther ahead. If you have already invested the lion's share of the time necessary to evaluate and implement an effective resolution, then take the additional small portion of time required to determine if the fix is appropriate for other parts, even if there currently is not any customer demand for them. At some point, your customers will want them, and there is no better time than the present to make them better. Even though in the short run it is an expenditure of time, in the long run it is a generator of it. The time saved by not having to deal with future problems will far outweigh the time invested at this point in the game. Be smart. Replicate good solutions.

UTOPIA

That brings us to the last application tool. It is actually the pinnacle of all that is embodied in the Look Forward® management approach. It is where we all want to be — *UTOPIA,* which stands for:

Upward
Transfer
Of
Potentially
Ingenious
Activity

As an executive manager, what would you conceptualize as your ideal working business environment? Is it an empowered workforce? Most of us would agree with that, but what does an empowered workforce mean? One of *Webster's* definitions for empower is "to give official authority to: commission, authorize."[7] Although we may have a general idea of what it means and more often than not can recognize it when we see it, it remains a somewhat nebulous or subjective concept.

Let's begin by thinking of the concept on a micro level of a business organization: the basic employee-manager relationship. As an employee, my level of satisfaction and my sense that my efforts actually have some importance are directly proportional to my perception of the level of freedom I have in performing my required duties. The greater the freedom or responsibility, the greater the impression I have that I am making a difference. As a result, my motivation, enthusiasm, and passion for what I do progressively increase to my maximum potential. Empowerment! Granted, this freedom is bestowed upon those who have previously demonstrated a propensity to flourish in this environment. However, freedom is an attractive concept, and seeing others live it out serves as a motivator to change in order to become a participant.

Now, let's look at the employee-manager relationship from the manager perspective. As a manager, my ideal situation would be to have a workforce made up of people who are self-motivated, passionate about what they do, are continuously seeking to improve, and require minimal direction.

If as a manager my experience is quite the opposite such that my employees constantly need to be motivated, seem to exhibit no strong feelings about what they do, and do not naturally seek self-identified improvements, then I will feel drained, less satisfied, and unfulfilled in my position.

Clearly, the reality will fall somewhere in between these two extremes. My goal as a manager would be to get as close as possible to the ideal stated above. The closer I am to that goal, the more empowered I feel as a manager.

If the employees and managers within your company are feeling empowered, then you have the closest thing to *UTOPIA* that you will to find in any business. ABSC has had some success in empowering the workforce, and this success is reflected in how effective the Look Forward® teams have been.

The first year of operating with the Look Forward® teams as the continuous improvement engine for ABSC resulted in a 19% reduction in bad goods cost. This was just what the company was hoping for, and the success of this first year was an excellent motivator for future Look Forward® efforts. The results of these efforts are indexed with sales in Table 7-1.[6]

The bottom line was that back then ABSC wanted to bust through the $2 million bad goods logjam and set its sights on additional gains. That is exactly what has happened and continues to happen. ABSC got what it wanted: continuous improvement, bad goods dollars reduction, and an empowered workforce. How's that for the business equivalent to *UTOPIA*?

But there is still a long way to go. Although the bad goods cost improvements have been significant over the years, there still is room for more improve-

Table 7-1. Bad Goods as a Percent of Sales

1996 ABSC bad goods costs as a percent of sales	0.8%
2003 ABSC bad goods costs as a percent of sales	0.35%
World-class manufacturer median*	1.3%

* World-class metrics provided by the *Industry Week* magazine and Manufacturing and Management Performance Institutes 2003 Census of Manufacturers. Copyright The MPI Group, Inc. Reprinted with permission.

ment in additional bad goods cost reduction as well as other metrics. As the Look Forward® approach is expanded throughout the enterprise, ABSC is confident that it will be able to accomplish this.

This confidence comes from the improvement breeding ground that is fostered by the Look Forward® approach. In addition, it is supported by an underlying spirit of humility that does not permit being self-satisfied, but rather promotes continuously striving to be better. A dedication to the Look Forward® methodologies of *FREE, EASY, ROAR,* and *UTOPIA* along with the power of the three primary continuous improvement tools will assure that ABSC continues to get better.

These methods provide you with the directions, but you still have to drive the car to get where you are going. It all comes down to execution. Your workforce can be knowledgeable about all of the most powerful improvement tools in existence, but if people are unable to execute them, you have gained nothing.

One monitoring approach that has been found to be effective in assuring the execution of continuous improvement is the Boardwalk.

BOARDWALK

One of the key elements of Lean manufacturing and/or the Toyota Production System is visual control. It is a simple activity that, when religiously executed, serves to help sustain overall improvement activities. The *Boardwalk* at ABSC is the daily pilgrimage to the information board for a particular commodity. The information board is centrally located within the manufacturing area for a particular commodity. The board contains key information that provides a snapshot of the current activity of the work in process as well as any problems that need to be addressed. The daily discussions can be very brief or last for about 30 minutes, depending on the issues that need to be addressed.

The mix of the attendees that participate in the Boardwalk is comprised of representation from the MRT, typically at the vice-president or director level, along with all of the members of the cross-functional Look Forward® team. This dynamic daily interaction between executive management and members of the cross-functional team works to support the continuity of improvement activities. Normally, this meeting is more of a status meeting that enables everyone to be on the same page about key activities pertaining to the commodity. It is not a meeting where management directs the team members about what to do. It supports the ongoing continuous improvement culture. As a rule, the Boardwalk is not conducted for every commodity that is controlled by a Look Forward® team. It is only used where it strategically makes sense to do so. As with any other tool, it is only used when necessary.

TEAM DYNAMICS

The real key to this approach is not any particular tool or hard analytical methodology, but rather the people involved. The makeup of the people within your teams will impact the level of success you achieve. Clearly, personality strengths and weaknesses will affect the level of interaction that takes place. Whether someone sees the glass as half full or half empty can overshadow evaluation of a problem or the path chosen going forward. I once heard at a conference that you should not have any "CAVE" people (an acronym for Citizens Against Virtually Everything) as members of a continuous improvement team. Change agents have to be possibility thinkers, not people whose mantra is "It can't be done!"

Let's take a look at the people side of the equation in any continuous improvement program. There is no doubt that people are the most valuable asset in the success of any continuous improvement program. In fact, they are more critical to the success of the program than all the continuous improvement tools combined. Yet, people seem to receive the least amount of attention when discussing continuous improvement. Your people can be educated on all of the methodology of the continuous improvement tools, but if they are unable to successfully interact in a team environment, then your chances of success are compromised.

The reason why team interaction is so important is not because of some warm and fuzzy, let's hold hands and sing kum-ba-yah reason. Rather, it is because everyone brings to the table their unique and valuable knowledge and experience that helps put together the missing pieces of the puzzle, where the puzzle to solve is how we get better.

If we accept the premise that we must draw upon each other's strengths as a team in order make significant improvements, then it makes sense that we should figure out how to work well with each other in order to optimize the performance of the team activity. Consider any sports team and how important it is for the team members to have almost a sixth sense about each other. What are each team member's strengths and weaknesses? How does each team member communicate to the rest of the team what he or she is thinking? What does the particular behavior of each of the members mean? Should all team members have the same personality? The soft-skills side of things gets complicated, more so than the hard-skills side of things.

In addition to all the personality and behavior characteristics that affect team performance, the office politics factor must be included in the mix. With all these unique variables and potentially volatile aspects of the process, it is amazing that any team is able to get anything done.

One aspect of the soft-skills equation is how personality traits can affect team performance. There are four primary personality characteristic traits. They have been described in a variety of different ways by experts in the field, but the one I have found to be the most clear and concise comes from Gary Smalley, president of the Smalley Relationship Center.[5] He categorizes them as follows:

1. **Lions** — The leader, take-charge-type characteristics
2. **Golden retrievers** — The care-taking, nurturing-type characteristics
3. **Beavers** — The detailed-oriented-type characteristics
4. **Otters** — The fun-loving, happy-go-lucky-type characteristics

In an ideal world, we would all have an equal portion of all of these characteristics and be perfectly well rounded in how we relate to others. Since we do not live in an ideal world, the reality is that typically one or two of these traits will be predominant, accompanied by a smidgen of the others. Anyone who has kids can bear witness to this wonder of nature. A family of four can have a variety of animal characters living under the same roof. This fact tends to support the idea that we are born with a particular orientation that is a part of who we are, even as adults.

The good news is that we have it within our power to modify our behavior characteristics by gaining an understanding of what they are and how they manifest themselves in our relations with others. But why bother? Is there really anything to this psychobabble mumbo jumbo? Again, if you are a parent, you already know that an individual's personality comes with a unique type of wiring right from the get-go. If you are not a parent, then certainly you have interacted with enough people by now to realize that everyone is different.

If we accept that, then it is in everyone's best interest to gain a better understanding of what makes us tick. With that premise, let's take a look at how the various personality characteristics can influence team dynamics.

Lions

People who are predominantly lions tend to be leaders. They get things done and can make decisions. They have the ability to project a vision and garner the support of others to execute the vision. The problem with people who have too much of this characteristic is that they can come across as overbearing and demanding and can actually have the opposite effect on those around them. One way to describe it is having a Napoleon effect on one's co-workers. This may have worked back in 18th century France, but it doesn't go too far nowadays. If you have too much of this characteristic and your objective is not to be a detriment to the team you are involved with, then you can work at cranking it down a notch or two. On the other side of the spectrum, if you recognize that you can use a boost in the amount of lion you exhibit, you can consciously work at trying to be more decisive in your team environment.

Golden Retrievers

If the golden retriever characteristics are predominant in your personality, then you are naturally concerned about the feelings of others. As a result, you may exhibit care-taking-type behavior that may or may not be beneficial to the team. If someone on the team is struggling, then you would be the one trying to figure out how to help the person along. All of us at one time or another go through a slump. When we do, the support of our teammates helps us out of it. Just ask any Major League baseball player. However, when this characteristic is exhibited to an extreme, it turns into a negative for the team. When care taking turns into carrying the duties of someone else in addition to your own for an extended period of time, then it becomes a detriment to the team. If this is your predominant personality characteristic, you need to guard against practicing it to an excess. Keep it in check.

Typically, as a general rule, you can get an idea of what your weaknesses are by taking a look at your strengths. Your weaknesses may simply be your greatest strengths pushed to an extreme, like the lion who turns into Napoleon or the golden retriever who is doing all the work for the team. This is something to keep in mind when in a team meeting.

Beavers

Beavers are valuable assets to any organization. They are the people who see to it that things get done right. The battle cry of the beaver is "If you're going to do something, then do it right." Beavers typically need to have some sort of reliable reference to use as a guideline for establishing what the "right" way is. They are the people who actually read the instructions before putting something together.

Beavers need to be careful about permitting their desire to do something "right" to evolve into irritating perfectionism. Granted, some things are black and white and must be done in a particular manner. However, many things are not black and white and are open to interpretation. In these situations, beavers need to guard against their opinions becoming the absolute "right" approach. Nothing is more annoying to nonbeavers than to have a beaver invalidate their opinion on a subjective matter. When working in teams, all team members need to feel comfortable that their opinions are relevant. An overzealous beaver can stifle this dynamic.

Otters

Did you ever meet someone who seems to go through life with a twinkle in their eye, a smile on their face, and a fascination with people? These people are the otters. They love life and consider everything to be an adventure. They treat you as if you are their best friend the first time you meet them. They are the idea people who love to offer their ideas up to a captive audience. When business leaders spread the message that work can be fun, the otters are right there saying they knew that all along. Not only is work fun, but everything is fun to the otter. The mind-set of otters is future based, always anticipating the next new and interesting activity they will be involved in.

Otters are optimistic about almost everything. The risk for otters is that this fun-loving mind-set is taken so far that any consequences associated with their actions are considered inconsequential. Otters need to guard against ignoring relevant issues that impact their world.

Know Thyself and Thy Team

As mentioned before, a person typically has a predominance of one or two of these types of traits that are part of who he or she is. A self-awareness of our strengths and weaknesses will go a long way in improving how we are able to contribute to the success of an improvement team. In addition, it will help us to recognize the various personality traits exhibited by team members. When all the team members have gained an understanding of the traits, then personality conflicts become less of a deterrent to team success.

If this is an issue for some of your teams, then help the team members to get a handle on what their personality characteristics are. The result will be meetings transformed from the wild jungle atmosphere to a peaceful animal kingdom.

The organizational structure of a team is key as well. Should someone be identified as the leader and be responsible for running the team? ABSC chose not to do that. Its Look Forward® teams are self-directed teams with no one designated as "the" leader. Normally, one or more people will naturally function in that manner just because of their personalities. However, ABSC thought that designating someone on the team as "the" leader was counterproductive due to the continuous nature of the teams and the prevalent functional organizational structure.

RECOGNIZING OPPORTUNITIES FOR IMPROVEMENT

Perhaps just as important to mention when discussing the successes that have been achieved with ABSC's continuous improvement approach is the opportunities for improvement. One of the key ingredients to any continuous improvement program is recognition that there will always be opportunities for improvement. This may sound somewhat cliché, but it is very true. The challenge is to identify which of those opportunities will add value to the company. Improvement opportunities are not always intuitively obvious, and in order to recognize them, you may have to improve your ability to "see" them. Even when improvement opportunities are obvious, they do not rise to the top due to prioritization of energies. Most companies have their share of both of these types of improvement opportunities.

The focus at ABSC has been on the establishment of an improvement culture that will continuously foster ongoing improvement. As we saw in Table 7-1, even though ABSC achieved world-class-level performance in reducing bad goods costs, there are certainly many additional opportunities for improvement that can make the company even stronger. Wil James, Toyota vice president of manufacturing, put it best during my interview with him at the Kentucky facility. He said that the low-hanging fruit is never gone. It is always there — you just have to improve your ability to see it.

At ABSC, there are loads of opportunities to improve the way the office processes are executed. The company is only in the initial stages of applying the Look Forward® management approach to this segment of the enterprise. Also, there are still opportunities to be capitalized upon within the manufacturing sector of the enterprise. All issues that relate to improving flow and motion in the factory are opportunities for improvement. ABSC currently has flow and motion improvement opportunities in the factory. No matter how much the existing identified opportunities are improved, there will always be new ones that arise. As James of Toyota stated in the previous paragraph, the Look Forward® structure will drive ABSC to come up with new says to "see" them.

You may be thinking at this point: "This sounds good, but how do I go about implementing it at my company? My company is much smaller (or larger) than ABSC, so can the Look Forward® approach still work?" Of course it can. It is a universal approach that is built upon the foundation of AS9100/ISO 9001:2000.

The first step is to formulate the management review team and make sure that this management team is focused on providing a consistent message to the team members that promotes the *FREE, EASY, ROAR,* and *UTOPIA* application tools. Second, you need to identify the product family or process that you want to target for a continuous improvement team. Once you have an idea of the areas you want to attack, select your team members. It is important to use some judgment in the team member selection process. Try to stack the deck in your favor by identifying key individuals who will be able to be change agents.

With your new teams in place, select a couple of key metrics that you want to use to monitor effectiveness, and challenge the teams to identify some goals to be measured against these metrics for the coming year. Then train them in the *FREE, EASY, ROAR,* and *UTOPIA* application tools.

This creates the framework for improvement; the rest is up to everyone involved. It is not easy, but it is definitely well worth it. The effort does not end after six months or a year. It is ongoing, continuous, self-sustaining, and eventually, when mature, churns along without the need for intervention.

LOOK FORWARD®: CASE STUDIES

The successful execution of any continuous improvement project is a challenge, and what constitutes success needs to be defined before you begin. In the world of AS9100/ISO 9001:2000, all activities within the corporation need to be subservient to the company's quality policy. The quality policy establishes the vision from which corporate objectives are established. These objectives act as guideposts for the direction your continual improvement efforts should be taking. Do your continual improvement efforts work toward achieving the realization of your corporate quality policy? If not, then you are wasting your time and should redirect your efforts.

Chances are your focus is on the right activity if the fruit of your labors is a savings of money for the company. Let's take a look at some of the activities that Look Forward® teams at Aircraft Braking Systems Corporation (ABSC) have undertaken over the years. Recall that these activities are a part of the team members' everyday responsibilities and not the result of being assigned to a particular project.

CASE STUDY 1:
CARBON PATTERN LOOK FORWARD® TEAM
FOCUS ON SCRAP REDUCTION

ABSC has been the world leader in carbon disks for many years, and much of that success can be attributed to the strength and depth of the company's R&D expertise and manufacturing execution. Traditionally, ABSC designed and developed the carbon it used and had it manufactured by a supplier. That all changed in 1998 when ABSC initiated making its own carbon with a new carbon manufacturing facility located in Akron, Ohio. ABSC was the world leader in carbon development, and now the challenge was to become the same in carbon manufacturing.

The inaugural year was a challenge, during which many opportunities for improvement surfaced. The carbon pattern bad goods cost for calendar year 1998 was $1.1 million, which happened to be 69% of the company's total bad goods cost during the previous year. It was during this inaugural year that the Carbon Pattern Look Forward® Team was initiated. Almost all of the $1.1 million was due to scrap costs. Typically, very little in the way of rework dollars is expended for this product line. Therefore, the primary objective of the team when it was formed became crystal clear. The team needed to focus on reducing the amount of carbon pattern scrap.

At the time, this newly formed team was getting a significant amount of visibility because its commodity type accounted for 69% of the overall bad goods dollars. Everyone wanted to see improvement as quickly as possible. The carbon facility is somewhat of a unique operation, compared to the rest of ABSC manufacturing, due to the nature of how carbon is manufactured (i.e., molding, heat treating, etc.). In addition, the personnel on this newly formed team had no prior exposure to the other Look Forward® teams and the methodologies used by them. As a result, the team had the double challenge of reducing the highest contributor to bad goods cost with the personnel least experienced in using the Look Forward® methodology in the company. Therefore, the team members needed to be coached on effective team-building skills concurrently with Look Forward® problem-solving methodology.

The team members accepted the challenge, and the result of their collective efforts after the first year was a 31% reduction in bad goods cost, down to $760,000. This was viewed as a success for this first-year team, but there still was a long way to go. The first year's savings were somewhat attributable to reaping the low-hanging fruit, and the trees still seemed populated with some easy pickings.

In the team's second year, team members rose to the challenge. They knocked their bad goods cost down to $486,000, a 36% reduction over the previous year and less than half of what it was when the team was formed a mere two years earlier.

Clearly, these were tremendous gains that benefited the company's bottom line. Everyone on the team was feeling pretty proud of themselves for achieving these savings and, as a result, momentarily took their eyes off of the ball. This was apparent in the following year's performance. The bad goods cost for carbon patterns in 2001 came in at $517,000, slightly higher than the previous year and well off of the team's projected goal.

The low-hanging fruit was gone, and the team's ability to make additional gains in bad goods cost reduction was diminishing as well. The team members had mixed emotions about their current state. On one hand, they perceived themselves as being in a much improved position over their inaugural year in which their bad goods cost was more than double. They rationalized that even though they showed no improvement in 2001, bad goods cost was still half of what it was two years earlier. That's not so bad. Right?

On the other hand, in their heart of hearts, they knew that they needed to be continuously improving. These conflicting mind-sets resulted in a sense of frustration among the team members. They were floundering and needed to be refocused.

This is where the Look Forward® management structure became an effective tool for the team to overcome this impasse. The ABSC management review team (MRT) has oversight responsibilities over all of the Look Forward® teams. The MRT meets with the Look Forward® teams throughout the year for dual-directional feedback on team performance and direction. The frequency of these meetings is dependent upon the needs of the particular Look Forward® team. If a team is achieving high performance and is effectively managing the world of its commodity, then it would require less intervention. If a team is struggling, then more frequent oversight would be appropriate.

The Carbon Pattern Team found itself in the latter position. Its improvement efforts had waned. As a result, the MRT scheduled more frequent meetings with the team in order to provide assistance with its plan going forward. As it turned out, the primary benefit of the MRT in this process was assistance with identifying areas for the team to focus on.

The team grabbed the ball and ran with it, and as a result, the MRT reduced the frequency of meeting. It was clear the team had a new focus and was headed in the right direction. This showed through loud and clear in the team's performance for 2002. The carbon pattern bad goods cost for 2002 was $273,000, which was nearly half of the previous year. What is even more impressive is that this benefit was achieved during the introduction of a new carbon material, called NUCARB®, into production. The introduction of a new material into the mix of this heavily process-oriented commodity opens many new opportunities for error. The team absorbed them and clearly overcame them. The team found its way and clearly had a breakthrough. It continued its winning ways with its performance in 2003. The carbon bad goods cost for 2003 was $98,465. This was 36% of the previous year's total and a mere 9% of the inaugural year's total, a short five years earlier.

This is phenomenal improvement, and the team aggressively continues to attack the causes that contribute to scrap. It is ongoing, ever-evolving, and — now — requires little intervention.

What follows is a synopsis of some of the activities that the team utilized to achieve its improvements.

Objectives

Some of the objectives for the Carbon Pattern Look Forward® Team for calendar year 2002 were:

1. Significantly reduce carbon pattern scrap by developing and implementing a strategic well-defined plan
2. Establish calculated scrap reduction goals

Strategic Plan

The following approach was taken for the structure of the strategic plan:

1. Develop a flowchart (path) to follow
2. Focus on the three largest scrap contributors
3. Define the top one to three causes for each main contributor
4. Develop and implement a problem-solving process for each cause

Problem-Solving Process

The problem-solving process utilized by the Look Forward® team was a typical Six Sigma DMAIC approach, where DMAIC stands for Define, Measure, Analyze, Improve, and Control. The team added to the DMAIC process slightly to address some additional issues and came up with the following problem-solving process:

1 Define the problem
2. Develop measuring techniques
3. Establish current baseline
4. Develop a corrective action plan
   ■ Establish commitment dates
5. Define expected results
6. Monitor results

To establish a starting point, the team created a process flowchart for the process of the creation of carbon pattern scrap (Figure 8-1). Notice on the

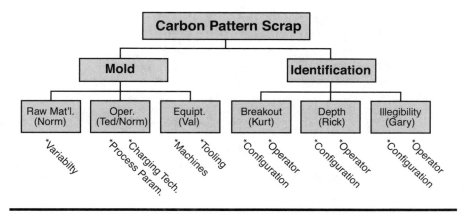

Figure 8-1.   Process flowchart. (Courtesy of Aircraft Braking Systems Corporation.)

process flowchart that the flow of carbon pattern scrap originated from eight primary sources:

1. Raw material variability
2. Operator charging technique
3. Operator process parameters
4. Tooling
5. Machines
6. Operator identification errors
7. Identification configuration
8. Identification character set

The two primary areas that these carbon pattern scrap sources affected were mold and identification. The team began its modified DMAIC problem-solving process in each of these areas.

Mold

The mold area was broken down into three key elements: raw material, operator, and equipment. The team's first look was into the raw material area.

Raw Material

The primary raw material analyzed in this effort was a resin-coated fiber that is used to charge the carbon molds. A particular test is performed on this fiber to evaluate how it will react when under the pressures and temperatures of the mold operation. The metric used to evaluate the results of this test is a percent-

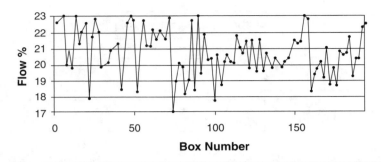

Figure 8-2. Control chart. (Courtesy of Aircraft Braking Systems Corporation.)

age of flow that exists when the material is subjected to the conditions of the test.

Norm Mack, the manufacturing process specialist on the team, took on the task of working with the supplier of this material in an effort to determine how the supplier's processes were performing in terms of the percentage of flow metric. The supplier instituted statistical process control (SPC) for this manufacturing process. Norm evaluated the SPC control charts for this feature, and it was determined that the process was out-of-control and not capable. Figure 8-2 depicts the SPC analysis of the percentage of flow.

Let's examine in detail each step of the Look Forward® team's problem-solving process.

Step 1. Define the Problem
For the raw material mold scrap, the problem was defined as follows:

Variability in the percentage of flow of the raw material

Step 2. Develop Measuring Technique
With the problem identified, the team then needed to determine, in addition to the visibility it would get from its supplier's SPC charts, what metrics needed to be used to drive improvement. The team began to take a closer look at the standard deviation values of the percentage of flow for the lots of raw material received from the supplier. Figure 8-3 illustrates an example of this review. It is apparent from the chart that a fluctuation in variability exists from lot to lot.

Lastly, a scatter plot was created to illustrate the relationship between the percentage of flow standard deviation and the associated percentage of scrap within the lot. A graph illustrating this relationship is shown in Figure 8-4. These metrics were selected to satisfy the second step of the team's problem-solving process.

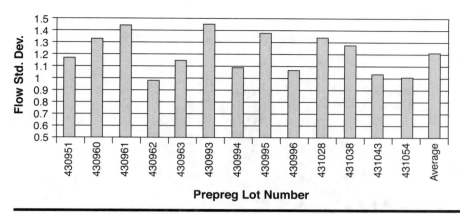

Figure 8-3. Standard deviation of flow. (Courtesy of Aircraft Braking Systems Corporation.)

Step 3. Establish Current Baseline
With step 2 under its belt, the team needed to determine a reference point to start from with these metrics in order to evaluate whether or not its efforts were effective. The baseline for the flow standard deviation was determined to be 1.21, and the percent of mold scrap baseline was 4%. This gave the team the information needed for the third step of the problem-solving process.

Step 4. Develop a Corrective Action Plan
With the problem identified and the baselined metrics in place, the team then set out to determine a corrective action plan. To gain further insight into the most significant problem areas in relation to carbon pattern scrap, the team

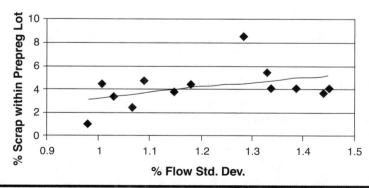

Figure 8-4. Percent scrap versus percent flow standard deviation. (Courtesy of Aircraft Braking Systems Corporation.)

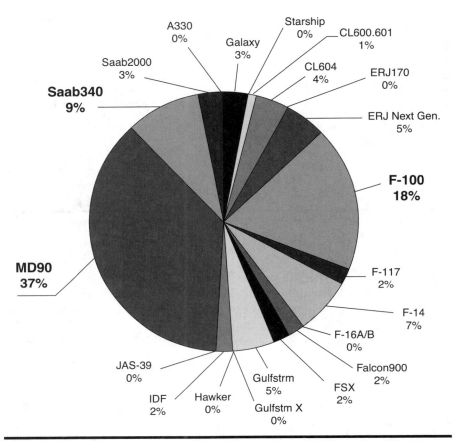

Figure 8-5. Breakdown of 2001 carbon scrap dollars. (Courtesy of Aircraft Braking Systems Corporation.)

created a pie chart (Figure 8-5) to illustrate the percentage of carbon scrap by aircraft program.

It was clear from this chart that the F-100 program and the MD90 were the biggest contributors to carbon pattern scrap in the previous year. The team decided to give special consideration to these programs, given that they represented the greatest opportunity for improvement.

The team incorporated a mistake-proofing technique by adding a presorting inspection of the raw material prior to charging the molds and only utilizing raw material that had a desired standard deviation of percentage flow. Concurrently, a corrective action plan was implemented at the supplier's facility. The supplier typically ran this raw material on two separate production lines. Analysis of the supplier's data indicated that one line performed much better than the other in terms of variability of the percentage of flow. It was mutually agreed that the product would be run on the high-performing line and that mutual efforts would be made to further optimize the performance of this line.

The commitment date for implementation of the mistake-proofing inspection operation and running the material on the supplier's high-performing line was immediately. Further optimization of the production line was ongoing. The team had now completed the fourth step of the problem-solving process.

Step 5. Define Expected Results
This plan was targeted and specific to the problem areas that contributed to carbon pattern raw material scrap. Through data analysis, it was estimated that these factors alone would contribute approximately $50,000 to total carbon scrap dollars, based on the previous year's performance. Therefore, the team used this amount as a reasonable representation of its expected savings in scrap cost reduction. This addressed the fifth step of the team's problem-solving process.

Step 6. Monitor Results
The visual factory is utilized by the team in order to monitor the progress and effectiveness of its expended efforts. Charts and graphs illustrating carbon mold performance (Figures 8-6 to 8-8) are provided to all team members and are on display in the mold manufacturing area. This addressed the sixth step and completes the problem-solving process for carbon mold scrap due to raw material.

Operator

The next area of focus for the team was carbon mold scrap that was attributed to the mold operator. The team went through the same problem-solving process as for raw material.

The first step was to define what the problem was in relation to the mold operator. After a review of the process, it became apparent that the problem was

The mold charging technique and the process parameters

The metric the team decided to utilize in order to evaluate operator performance was

Percent of scrap produced per operator

In order to establish a baseline to benchmark the success of its efforts, the team used a two-month rolling average from the previous two months. Figure 8-6 illustrates this performance metric.

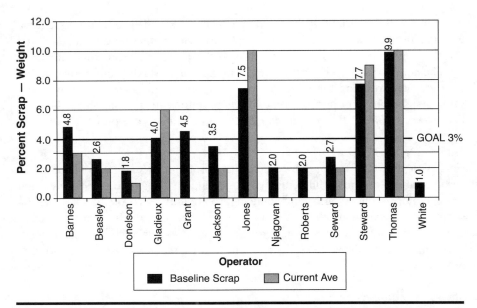

Figure 8-6. Percent scrap by operator for November 1, 2001 through January 1, 2002. (Courtesy of Aircraft Braking Systems Corporation.)

The corrective action plan for operator-influenced carbon pattern scrap was multifaceted, with a focus on the two programs with the greatest amount of carbon pattern scrap: the MD90 and F-100. The decision was made to select some of the most proficient operators and assign them exclusively to the two problem programs. At the same time, a cross-training program was instituted so that all mold operators would become equally proficient in the desired charging technique. A mistake-proofing action was also incorporated into the process. An audible timer was mounted on the mold presses to signal the operator when process changes were required.

After performing some data analysis, it was estimated that these efforts alone would result in a $30,000 annual savings of carbon mold scrap attributed to the operator. Therefore, the team used this amount as a reasonable representation of its expected savings in mold scrap attributed to the operator.

Equipment

The next area the team looked at was carbon pattern scrap caused by the equipment. The team defined two problems related to equipment issues: tooling and maintenance. The following is a summary of the problem-solving process for each of these problems:

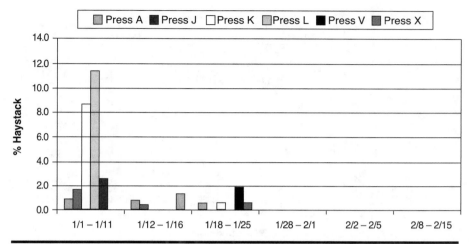

Figure 8-7. Haystacking by press by week. (Courtesy of Aircraft Braking Systems Corporation.)

- ■ **Problem**
  - □ Tooling and maintenance
- ■ **Metrics**
  - □ Subjective evaluation of scrap and monitor levels per press
  - □ Newly acquired data from production process
- ■ **Baseline**
  - □ Will be developed from newly acquired production process data
  - □ Strip damage history
  - □ Scrap report by press

Figures 8-7 and 8-8 provide two examples of the data tracking for press performance.

- ■ **Corrective action plan**
  - □ Develop scheduled preventive maintenance and adjust accordingly depending on the data

An analysis of the data indicated that an estimated $10,000 would be saved through the implementation of these activities.

Identification

The last, but most certainly not least, of the areas reviewed for carbon pattern scrap was identification. The same problem-solving process was applied:

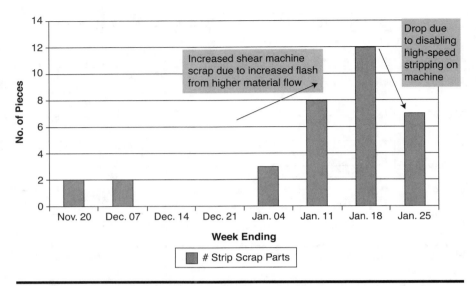

Figure 8-8. Scrap due to stripping damage. (Courtesy of Aircraft Braking Systems Corporation.)

- **Problem**
  - ☐ Operator
  - ☐ Configuration
  - ☐ Process variability
- **Metrics**
  - ☐ Subjective evaluation of scrap and monitor levels
  - ☐ Newly acquired data from production process
- **Baseline**
  - ☐ Scrap report
- **Corrective action plan**
  - ☐ Attack program with the highest scrap (S-340)
  - ☐ Develop accountability (log sheet/engrave program modifications)
  - ☐ Retrain engravers with problems
  - ☐ Implement inspection validation
  - ☐ Incorporate mistake proofing at the machining and stores build operations by requiring operators to perform in-process inspections
  - ☐ Evaluate the identification process for possible opportunities for improvement
- **Expected results**
  - ☐ A $60,000 annual reduction in carbon pattern scrap due to identification

Results

The total estimated annual savings from the activities associated with the corrective action plans was $50,000 + $30,000 + $10,000 + $60,000 = $150,000. Given that the total cost of carbon bad goods for the previous year was $507,425, these savings would bring the new goal down to $357,425, which would be a 29.5% improvement over the previous year.

So how did the team do? The team exceeded expectations for reducing carbon bad goods cost for calendar year 2002. The goal was $357,425, and the result was $273,239 at year end. This reflected a 46% reduction in total carbon bad goods cost from the previous year. Clearly, the efforts of the team were effective and expectations were exceeded by saving the company more money than anticipated. But the story doesn't stop there.

The team was energized by its success and continued down the same path in 2003, applying poka-yoke or mistake-proofing techniques throughout the process. As a result, the team was successful in reducing the carbon bad goods cost in calendar year 2003 even further. The total bad goods cost for 2003 was $98,465, which was a 64% reduction from the previous year's total and a mere 9% of the calendar year 1998 total cost of $1,091,904. This equates to a 91% improvement in a five-year period. Figures 8-9 to 8-11 reflect the progress of the Carbon Pattern Look Forward® Team over the past several years.

In summary, the team's efforts have been successful over the years and continue to be. Since it is a permanent team, there is no end to the improvement project. It is ongoing and continuous.

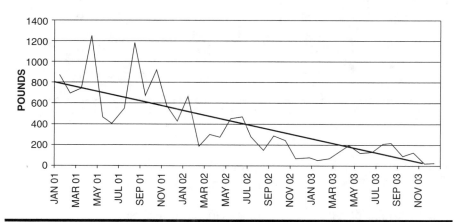

Figure 8-9. Monthly pounds of carbon scrapped. (Courtesy of Aircraft Braking Systems Corporation.)

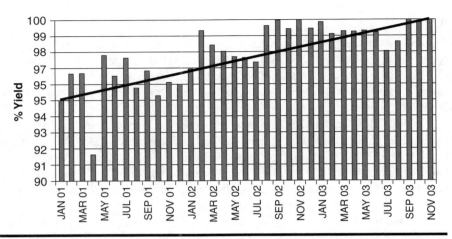

Figure 8-10. Percent yield. (Courtesy of Aircraft Braking Systems Corporation.)

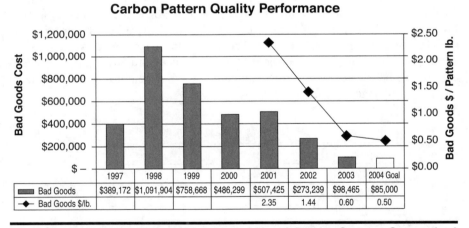

Figure 8-11. Bad goods costs. (Courtesy of Aircraft Braking Systems Corporation.)

The following Lean, Six Sigma, or Theory of Constraints tools were used by the Carbon Pattern Look Forward® Team:

- Brainstorming
- Pareto analysis
- Histogram analysis
- Scatter plot
- Graphical analysis
- Sampling
- DMAIC (modified)
- SPC

- Mistake proofing
- Visual factory
- Pie chart analysis
- Constraint management

This case study involved an effort across the supply chain. Figure 8-12 presents some thoughts from the supplier's perspective.

For more than 25 years, Cytec Engineered Materials (CEM) has worked closely with ABSC. Initially, ABSC had outsourced the molding portion of its manufacturing process and the company's relationship with CEM was based primarily on developmental activities. In the late 1990s, however, ABSC brought molding operations in-house. That move heightened the firm's focus on processing issues such as molding scrap reduction, as well as its relationship with CEM, from which it purchased molding compounds for friction materials.

CEM technologists respected ABSC's insightful approach to scrap reduction from the outset. Too often, such efforts focus on raw material alone — with few gains realized. ABSC, on the other hand, began its scrap reduction efforts with an in-depth analysis of its molding process. Only after it had a clear understanding of the potential of its process did ABSC initiate a scrap reduction partnership with CEM.

Two fundamental characteristics are vital to the ultimate quality of a finished part: composition and moldability. Both parameters are monitored and controlled during the production of the carbon-fiber-reinforced phenolic molding compound.

Composition is measured by percent fiber content, while moldability is measured by percent flow. The specification limits for these two properties were set years ago based on a combination of industry practice and process capability.

Throughout the composites industry it is understood that fiber content affects flow (i.e., flow cannot effectively improve while fiber content is variable). Given this process interaction, CEM first focused on enhancing its coating operation. Molding compound is produced by drawing carbon fibers through a bath of solvent-based phenolic resin. Previous methods of fiber content control included the manual addition of solvent, based on the specific gravity of the resin solution. In support of this effort, an automated closed-loop viscosity-control system was implemented. The implementation of the viscosity system involved tuning both the pumping system (resin and solvent delivery) and the viscosity control system. Because many fibers are coated in parallel, fiber-to-fiber variation also was monitored.

As a result of ABSC's thorough process analysis groundwork, the company determined that material produced at the extremes of the flow specification limits was problematic. Material with low flow was not fully consolidating, while material with high flow resulted in excess resin bleed (a cleanup nightmare for the press operators).

Once the fiber content variation was under control, the focus shifted to flow control. The flow of this material is controlled by a combination of oven temperature

Figure 8-12. Molding scrap reduction at ABSC from a supplier's perspective. (Courtesy of Cytec Engineered Materials, Winona, Minnesota. Reprinted with permission.)

and dwell time. Through planned experimentation, it was determined that better control is realized by processing fewer fibers at a faster speed. CEM was able to assist through tightly controlled variation.

Reducing the variation of the flow was only a part of the solution, however. Zeroing in on the best flow range involved very close communication between CEM and ABSC technologists. Collaboration occurred in a production environment involving a wide variety of ABSC's mold dies and across all of the company's mold presses. In order to minimize molding scrap during this phase, a number of small, incremental changes were made based on the outcome of the planned experimentation.

The result? The implementation of an efficient waste reduction process that has consistently yielded zero to near zero molding scrap for more than two years.

Figure 8-12 (continued).

CASE STUDY 2:
WHEEL DETAIL LOOK FORWARD® TEAM
ANODIZE PROCESS IMPROVEMENT

Over the span of the 75 years of its existence, ABSC has manufactured countless aircraft wheels and brakes serving both commercial and military aviation. In addition to these markets, the company has periodically supplemented its core wheel and brake business by producing a variety of products that would satisfy a need in the marketplace.

There was no greater need than that driven by World War II. Germany was having its way in Europe and Japan had just decimated the prize U.S. naval base at Pearl Harbor. President Roosevelt declared war and we were in it for the long haul. All of American industry was being called upon to do its share for the war effort. ABSC was no exception.

The manufacturing facilities at ABSC were long, wide buildings with huge doors at each end that could be elevated in the same fashion as an airport hanger. With ABSC's aviation experience and the characteristics of its manufacturing facilities, it soon became apparent that it would be an ideal location for manufacturing airplanes.

Thus ABSC was commissioned by the military to manufacture the famed Corsair aircraft that was key to the success of the U.S. Air Force in Europe. This effort required a significant amount of retooling and reorganizing manufacturing equipment. Making airplanes was going to be a challenge for this manufacturer of aircraft wheels and brakes. An evaluation of all the existing processes was required, and it needed to be done in an expeditious manner.

One process in particular that was evaluated was the anodize process. A part is anodized by immersing it into a bath of chemicals in order to cause a reaction with the surface of the material such that a protective coating is created on the surface of the part. Technically, anodize is an electrochemical process that converts the surface of aluminum into a form of its own oxide. Benefits of anodizing include:

- Increased corrosion resistance
- Increased abrasion resistance
- Excellent wear properties
- Improved base for paint adhesion
- Provides an electrically nonconductive surface
- Provides thermal insulation
- Protects polished and other mechanically finished surfaces
- Improves appearance of the substrate
- Adds color

There are various types of anodize processes:

- Type I: Conventional chromic acid anodize
- Type II: Conventional sulfuric acid anodize
  - Class 1: Nondyed coatings
  - Class 2: Dyed coatings
- Type III: Hard coatings
  - Class 1: Nondyed coatings
  - Class 2: Dyed coatings

The challenge in applying this anodic coating or anodize to the wings of the Corsair aircraft for a wheel and brake manufacturer was the availability of tanks big enough to dip the wings into. ABSC was up for the challenge and brought on line an anodic coating line suitable for Corsair aircraft manufacturing. Soon after the war ended, ABSC got out of the Corsair manufacturing business and went back to its core business of making aircraft wheels and brakes.

The long dip tanks which were suitable for dipping the Corsair wings were to be used for wheels and brakes. ABSC is continuously looking for opportunities to eliminate waste, and from a space utilization standpoint, these long tanks, which were excellent for Corsair wings, were not the optimal utilization of space for processing wheels and brakes. Thus, one opportunity to eliminate the waste was identified: utilization of anodic tank space. This alone was reason enough for a Look Forward® team improvement activity, but in this case there were additional reasons to justify an improvement effort.

The Wheel Detail Look Forward® Team is chartered with owning all issues that pertain to machined detail wheels. One step within the process of machining a typical wheel is the anodize finishing operation. The team continuously looks for ways to improve the process flow of its commodity. The anodize operation was identified as one such opportunity. The manner in which material flowed through this operation was inefficient, and because it was the last operation in the process, it had a direct impact on how soon product could be delivered to the customer. As Eli Goldratt would say, it was a bottleneck.

In addition, corrosion-related defects were increasing. The cause was attributed to the aging anodizing equipment, which although still effective required vigilant operator oversight in order to prevent errors.

Lastly, the team was chartered with making the anodize line more environmentally friendly. The government was looking to manufacturers to reduce the usage of chrome in their facilities. Recall that Type I anodize is a conventional chromic acid solution. ABSC saw this as an additional opportunity to take the lead instead of waiting for chrome removal to be mandated by the government.

The team's efforts were broad based, and the entire project from initial planning to implementation spanned a two-year period. The team redesigned the entire anodize line to make it a high-quality, efficient, and environmentally friendly operation. To achieve this, the team brought in anodize experts and visited state-of-the-art anodizers in order to learn how to optimize performance. All along the way, the management review team was kept abreast of activities and called upon for assistance when appropriate (i.e., capital allocations, etc.).

The project was a complete success and accomplished all of the objectives established by the team. Throughput was improved, and the required operator oversight was significantly reduced. There was a reduction of over 1000 operator hours in the first two years of operation, equating to over $30,000 in savings for 2001 and 2002. Quality was much improved, and chrome was eliminated from the new line, making it more environmentally friendly.

The following is a synopsis of how the team achieved these improvements. Although the team did not utilize a formal Six Sigma DMAIC approach, its problem-solving approach addressed most aspects of the Six Sigma method.

An additional aspect of the team's focus was elevation of the constraint that existed at the anodize operation. The objective was to improve the throughput of material through this bottleneck. Let's start by looking at the team's problem definition.

Define

The problem the team set out to overcome was threefold:

1. Throughput was compromised due to the restrictions of the antiquated equipment that was initially oriented toward processing Corsair wings.
2. The leeching of chrome was an environmental concern.
3. Corrosion defects were excessive.

Measure

With the problem statements identified, the team measured current process performance in relation to each of the problems defined. For the leeching of chrome, it was clear that the presence of any chrome at all would be deemed unacceptable from an environmental standpoint. Therefore, the metric was clear. For throughput and the corrosion defects, the team measured both rejections attributed to corrosion and lead time of wheel details through the manufacturing facility. Once the measuring was completed and a baseline established, the team went on to analyze and evaluate the data and determine an appropriate course of action.

Analyze and Evaluate

The internal objective of eliminating the use of chrome moved ahead of the anodize line improvements. The decision was made to no longer use Type I anodize, and the tanks containing the chromic acid were drained once and for all. As a result, several of the old tanks used for coating the Corsair wings laid empty. Wasted space.

Regarding possible causes of the corrosion defects, the following anodize process variables were analyzed to determine if a cause-and-effect relationship existed:

Temperature	Deoxidization
Agitation	Surface metals
Percent sulfuric acid	Contamination
Type of water (deionized)	Surface finish
Anode-cathode ratio	Seal temperature
Current density	Ramp time
Voltage	Dissolved metals
Contacts	Base material
Anodize time	Part handling/flow

It was determined that none of these process variables had a direct impact on corrosion, with the exception of part handling/flow. Parts were often degreased in the large "wing" tanks, put on carts, and rolled over to smaller anodize tanks for subsequent processing. Queue time varied, and if the parts were not properly drained/dried at the degrease operation, it was determined that water could pool, creating ripe conditions for corrosion. As a result, proper handling and drying techniques were implemented to eliminate water pooling.

A separate investigation uncovered the fact that a majority of parts recently rejected for corrosion had been sent to a supplier for liquid penetrant nondestructive testing (NDT). It was found that the supplier was not properly ringing off the dry (powder-like) developer that coats the parts during the NDT process before shipping the parts back to ABSC. The developer acted as a sponge, attracting atmospheric moisture prevalent during the humid Ohio summer to the unprotected aluminum surfaces of the parts. The result was spotty corrosion all over the parts, not just in areas where liquid had pooled. The NDT supplier was instructed in proper rinsing techniques, and deionized water was obtained for rinsing.

The team analyzed the current state of the process across the entire value stream in order to determine if there were any opportunities for improvement. One of the problem areas identified was throughput.

In order to get a clear understanding of the current-state flow throughout the process and its impact on throughput, the team created a map of the process flow (Figure 8-13). At first glance, it looked like there were many wasted movements and poor utilization of space. Of three problem areas initially identified, this appeared to be the team's biggest challenge. The challenge was how to redesign the entire anodic coating line that had initially been put in place to best serve the manufacture of Corsairs.

The team members knew quite a bit about the anodize process and had a good understanding of how to optimize flow, but their understanding of the anodize equipment that was currently available was limited. Therefore, the team hired an anodize equipment consultant, who basically joined the team temporarily as an adjunct member. The consultant brought to the table the much needed insight about the best anodize equipment and applied his expertise to ABSC's unique application. The team members were encouraged because the consultant confirmed the ideas they had arrived at through their prior investigation. They were now empowered to request some preliminary quotes for an entire new anodize line from several contractors. The process of weeding out the quotes consisted of site visits to some recent installations, which provided the team members with some additional insight and helped to validate many of their conclusions.

For the first time in 50 years, the process flow of material through the anodize line was not being fit into a process flow model developed for an entirely different commodity. The industrial engineering member on the Look

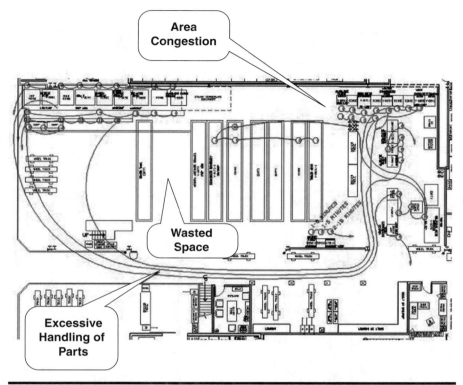

Figure 8-13. Current-state view of product flow. (Courtesy of Aircraft Braking Systems Corporation.)

Forward® team brought to the table his expertise and was able to specify the optimum tank size that should be used based on the size and quantity of parts that would be flowing through the area, thus optimizing flow and increasing throughput.

Figure 8-14 illustrates the future state of how the process flowed after the team revamped the anodize line. Clearly, it is much more streamlined, with an optimal utilization of space and motion. In addition, the new line is much more effective in utilizing chemicals that are less aggressive while achieving higher quality. The new setup also made the operator's task much easier. There are fewer tanks, which are easily accessible, and they come with built-in mistake-proofing controls like timers and the new "auto-ramping" rectifier control.

The quality of the finish of the anodized wheels has improved dramatically. Consistency and uniformity are commonplace and expected results. The icing

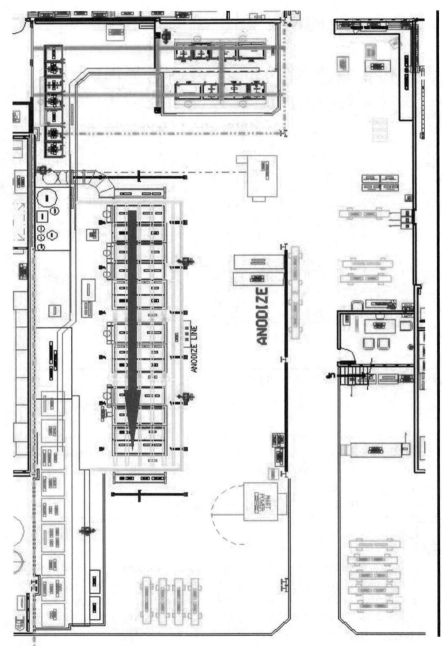

Figure 8-14.   Future-state view of product flow. (Courtesy of Aircraft Braking Systems Corporation.)

on the cake is that in addition to improving throughput and product quality, some significant environmental improvements were also made:

- Reduced chrome-containing process tanks from 13 to 3
- Removed old tanks and concrete from the anodize area
- Poured new concrete and applied chemical-resistant seal
- Improved ventilation
- Shut down a secondary plating area and combined all plating activity in the one new line

Figure 8-15 illustrates throughput before and after improvement.

The project was a success on all fronts. It resulted in a reduction of over 1000 operator hours in the first two years of operation, representing over $30,000 in savings in 2001 and 2002.

The following Lean, Six Sigma, or Theory of Constraints tools were used by the Wheel Detail Look Forward® Team:

- Brainstorming
- Mistake proofing
- Process flow map
- DMAIC (modified)

CASE STUDY 3:
BRAKE/TORQUE TUBE LOOK FORWARD® TEAM
DUCTILE IRON CONVERSION PROJECT

How often have you thought to yourself, "If I only had a dime for every time…, I would be a millionaire"? Fill in the blank however you want. Usually it is something like "that copier didn't work" or "it rained on the weekend" — typically things seemingly out of our control.

But what about those things that happen day in and day out that are in our control? Things that annoy us in some fashion or another, but for some reason just seem to be part of the way things are. Oftentimes, we become comfortable with the status quo, and it seems easier to accept things the way they are than to think about how to do them differently, even when the status quo causes us to do things we would rather not be doing.

Such is the case with some processes in manufacturing. Our challenge as change agents is to obtain the appropriate information that will provide us insight into how to be able to "see" opportunities for improvement, such as

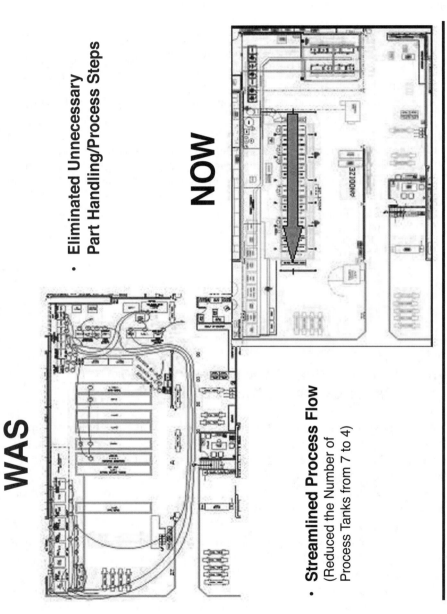

Figure 8-15. Contrasting the current and future states. (Courtesy of Aircraft Braking Systems Corporation.)

waste that exists in processes — those things that happen day in and day out which we accept as the status quo.

Pulling yourself out of your normal daily activity and looking at it with an objective eye with the intent of identifying what is wrong with it is not an easy task — especially if you had something to do with establishing the way things are currently done. Doing so requires you to put your pride on the back shelf and make the betterment of the process the primary objective. That has to be the mind-set of any permanent continuous improvement team.

It is much easier for a team that is assigned a six-month improvement project to walk away from it with demonstrated improvement. Then, after a couple of years, when everyone has gotten smarter about how to do things, another project team can come in for a six-month initiative to improve on the first team's efforts. It is easier, but not necessarily better. No one knows the value stream, the process variables, and the inputs and outputs better than a permanent team that has been living and breathing them day in and day out.

This is not an easy thing to do, and it should not be attempted by the faint of heart. A culture must exist in which egos are minimized and doing the right thing is prioritized. Improvement is not a project — it is ongoing and continuous. Until the culture of a company reaches the point where it is a natural activity for a team to question and improve upon its own big idea of yesterday, improvement may not be as continuous as we would like.

This mind-set was an essential element of the activity of the Brake/Torque Tube Look Forward® Team as it set out to overcome one of the annoying aspects of its commodity type that was in its control. This case study illustrates some of the initial efforts, which took place back in 1997 and resulted in marked improvement, followed by a continuous reevaluation of these improvements over the years with the purpose of improving upon them.

The Brake/Torque Tube Look Forward® Team is chartered with managing the business of brakes and torque tubes, from cradle to grave. This study focuses on one of the activities the team undertook in order to improve the torque tube commodity.

Torque tubes play a key role in the aircraft braking function. Inside of each wheel on an aircraft is a brake assembly that consists of primarily a brake housing, a stack of brake disks, and a torque tube (see Figure 8-16).

The torque tube looks like a flat plate with a fluted cylinder projecting out of the center of it. The disks slide over the torque tube and rest on the plate. The housing is mounted on top of the cylindrical portion of the torque tube opposite the plate (see Figure 8-17).

The torque tube is secure and does not rotate with the wheel that it is inside of. On the other hand, every other disk in the stack of disks rotates with the

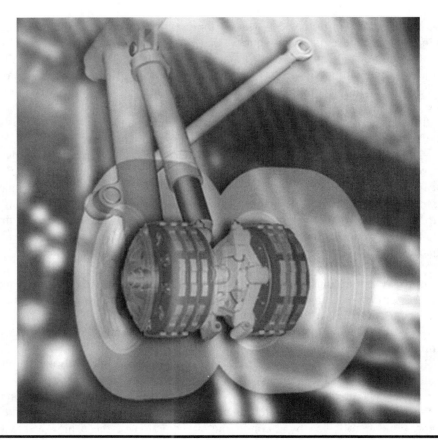

Figure 8-16. Landing gear and braking system. (Courtesy of Aircraft Braking Systems Corporation.)

wheel. The disks that do not rotate intermesh with the fluted projections on the torque tube and remain stationary.

In order to stop an aircraft, hydraulic fluid in the brake housing exerts pressure onto the stack of disks, causing them to rub against one another. The resulting friction between disks rotating with the wheel and disks held stationary with the torque tube causes the wheels to decrease their speed of rotation and thus stop the aircraft.

The torque tube is clearly critical to the execution of the aircraft braking process, and this criticality is what drives the objectives of the Brake/Torque Tube Look Forward® Team. Some of the team's objectives in 1997 were to

Figure 8-17. Torque tube and brake assembly. (Courtesy of Aircraft Braking Systems Corporation.)

reduce the amount of scrap dollars incurred and to reduce operating costs through cycle time reduction, setup time reduction, and standard work.

One of the ways the team set out to accomplish these objectives was to try to eliminate one of those annoyances that were part of the status quo for torque tubes at the time. A number of the legacy designs had not been created in a concurrent engineering fashion and thus may have been functional but not necessarily robust. Such was the case for those torque tubes that were designed to be made from ductile iron castings. Achieving the required engineering properties from a ductile iron casting is a difficult manufacturing challenge. However, as difficult as it was, it was attempted day in and day out.

One of the ductile iron casting challenges was trying to make a part that did not have excessive porosity or casting defects. At the time, casting defects were almost inevitable on any ductile iron casting. In fact, one part in particular, the C-130 torque tube, had a 60% rejection rate due to excessive porosity and other casting-related defects. This rejection rate was not reflective of the scrap rate, because there was a rework operation for some rejected parts that removed some of the defects, although that meant the obvious addition of rework costs, lost time, and interruption to product flow for those parts. This one example was somewhat the poster child for the greater issue of the robustness of ductile iron castings.

As the team gathered all of the data pertaining to the ductile iron casting issues, a number of concerns were identified as attributable to ductile iron castings:

- Long lead times for ductile iron castings had a significant impact on the team's ability to satisfy customer demand quickly.
- Excessive porosity and other casting defects resulted in scrapped parts or additional rework.
- The fluted areas on the cylindrical portion of the ductile iron cast torque tube required an induction hardening operation, which had a significant impact on throughput.
- The price of the castings was constantly rising because of the difficulties encountered in trying to produce them.
- The inconsistent microstructure created induction hardening problems.

In order to attack these issues, the team members held a brainstorming session to lay out their battle plan. All of the issues relating to ductile iron castings were discussed, and two possible alternatives to these castings came to the forefront: austempered ductile iron and steel tube stock.

Back in 1997, ductile iron castings comprised about one-third of all of the torque tubes ABSC manufactured. The other torque tubes were predominantly forgings, with some already made from tube stock. One factor to be considered in the decision to make a torque tube out of tube stock was its machinability. The configuration of some torque tubes made one wonder whether it would even be possible to machine and whether so much time would be spent doing so that it would not be cost effective.

Given that there were so many manufacturing and material issues to consider, the team members started with a form of visual control to help guide their activity. They created a matrix (Figure 8-18) that identified the aircraft model and a number of the key factors that would affect their decision-making process. Each material type was color-coded appropriately, so that any team member could understand the current status of the team's effort at a glance.

When the team cross-referenced the ductile iron casting concerns with the existing parts that were currently ductile iron castings, it was clear that this initiative would work toward achieving the objectives of reducing the amount of scrap dollars incurred and reducing operating costs.

To date, the team has successfully converted all current ductile iron casting production over to an alternative material. This study will focus on two pro-

Aircraft Model	T/T P/N	Assy No(s)	Brake Type	Outside Dia (in)	Inside Dia (in)	Length (in)	T/T Matl/ Spec	T/T Heat Treat	Key Heat Treat	Normal Stop Avg Torq	Str Torq Max Torq (ft-lbs)	Normal Stop Bearing	Coating Spec

Figure 8-18. Matrix of factors in decision-making process. (Courtesy of Aircraft Braking Systems Corporation.)

grams, the C-130 and Beech 1900, to provide a framework for reflecting the magnitude of the benefit from this Look Forward® effort.

Let's start by looking at the Beech 1900 torque tube. In 1997, it was one of the first torque tubes converted over to austempered ductile iron (ADI). ADI has some key benefits over a traditional ductile iron casting. With ADI, the work hardening and strength properties are such that it is not necessary to perform the induction hardening operation of the fluted areas of the torque tube. Therefore, it was possible to eliminate this operation entirely, which improved throughput. Also, when the induction hardening operation was performed, there was always the risk of distortion and cracking. ADI reduced the rejection percentage by eliminating this vulnerability.

The team went further than the obvious benefits attributed to the raw material change. The entire value stream of the Beech 1900 torque tube was evaluated to see if there was any nonvalued-added activity in the process given that the raw material was now ADI. Indeed, there was. ADI opened up some doors for redesigning the value stream to create a more robust manufacturing process. The team was now able to eliminate a significant amount of nonvalue-added activity. In fact, the team eliminated 65% of the operations. This was effective in reducing the run time of this particular torque tube by 62%.

In addition to this activity, the team instituted an analysis of the setup requirements for this part using a modified approach to the quick changeover method. As a result, the team was able to reduce the setup time by 63%. This was a tremendous improvement over the previous way of doing things and significantly drove down the rejection rate on this part as well.

This was only one of the parts on the matrix in Figure 8-18 that the team was evaluating for improvements. The lessons learned from the Beech 1900 activity served as valuable insight into possible solutions for improvements on similar torque tubes. This breeding ground of ideas and solutions served the team well in its quest to convert all ductile iron castings over to a more robust solution. In fact, a few years after the initial ADI effort in 1997, the team utilized some lessons learned on another solution to make even further improvements on the Beech 1900.

A permanent team, which the Brake/Torque Tube Look Forward® Team was, is continuously looking for ways to improve its commodity across the entire value stream. The effort is continuous and ongoing. Even after significant gains have been achieved, the team is always reevaluating how to do it better. Yesterday's gains are yesterday's news. In 2000, the Brake/Torque Tube Look Forward® Team took another step to eliminate nonvalue-added activity and improve the value stream throughput.

This time, the team focused in on the phosphate protective coating that was used on the Beech 1900 torque tube. The team again evaluated the value stream, and the processing steps required to apply the phosphate coating seemed like a new opportunity to eliminate waste. As with any improvement effort, the challenge is to be able to "see" the waste. What aided the team's vision in identifying this waste was the knowledge that the same protective properties could be obtained using a lubribond coating that would require less effort to apply. The team went through a similar analytical process as described for the material change and was successful in changing the processing on the Beech 1900 and all other torque tubes as well. This reprocessing saved the team $16,000 in the first year of production.

As a result of these combined efforts, the new torque tube is stronger, easier to manufacture, and more robust. The team is constantly focused on the value stream in an effort to identify improvement opportunities, even if those opportunities involve changing the raw material to improve throughput, quality, and setup time.

The second torque tube example for this improvement effort is the C-130. In 1997, the C-130 torque tube had a 60% reject rate due to excessive porosity and various other casting defects. The scrap and rework costs associated with this problem, in the neighborhood of $130,000 in a year's time for this part alone, were clearly unacceptable.

The team evaluated all factors for the C-130 and determined that the best solution at the time was to change the raw material from ductile iron casting to alloy steel bar stock. As a result, the raw material rejection rate went from 60% with the ductile iron casting down to 0% with the bar stock. This was a tremendous savings in scrap and rework costs.

In order to make such a drastic change in raw material, the team had to design a finished part that weighed less than or equal to the original ductile iron part and would perform better than the original. A huge obstacle the team faced was overcoming the considerable difference in density between ductile iron and the alloy steel. The density of the steel is approximately 9.7% heavier than the ductile iron, which meant that the steel part had to be made with almost 10% less material by volume than the original design. This problem was compounded by the fact that all of the interface dimensions had to be within the original design tolerances. This meant that the team could change only limited features to reduce the weight. The team members' knowledge of materials, processes, machining, and finite element analysis enabled them to design a part that was lighter and more robust, had virtually no raw material problems, and was cosmetically superior without increasing the cost. The U.S. military liked the new part so much that ABSC started taking orders for it away from the low-cost aftermarket competitor.

In 2003, the team made an additional improvement to the C-130 torque tube. This improvement had the net impact of eliminating one-and-one-half weeks off of the torque tube lead time — a significant reduction in time and improvement in throughput.

Finally, as a result of the team's global analysis of all of the torque tubes, it was possible to standardize the operations across the value streams for a majority of the torque tubes. This standardization ensures the incorporation of best practice approaches in the manufacturing processes and will aid the team in any future improvement efforts. This effort illustrates the ongoing improvement expectations of the Look Forward® team as measured by performance-driven metrics.

The following Lean, Six Sigma, or Theory of Constraints tools were used by the Brake/Torque Tube Look Forward® Team:

- Brainstorming
- Mistake proofing
- Process flow map

CASE STUDY 4:
STRUCTURAL PART LOOK FORWARD® TEAMS THROUGHPUT/STANDARD WORK PROJECT

In the aerospace industry, there is an enterprise-wide effort to standardize as many activities as possible. Engineering drawing standards reflect best practices from an engineering design standpoint. Standard procedures written by every functional area (i.e., marketing, procurement, etc.) describe how the processes that affect these areas are addressed by their respective personnel. Establishing a standard approach for performing a task or process is a valuable asset to an organization. Imai comments on standardization in his book entitled *Gemba Kaizen*.[1] He says that it is impossible to improve any process before it is standardized.

Clearly, when a task or process is standardized, a baseline has been established, which can be built upon or improved upon. Standardization is also beneficial in taking some of the guesswork out of a particular task for someone new on the job. There is an established way to perform the activity, instead of a best-guess approach.

When a task or activity is standardized, some up-front thought and analysis have been put into establishing the standard. The standard should reflect the optimum approach for performing the activity. This is not to say that a standard is set in stone and can never be changed. A standard is the present best practice and will remain so until additional insight justifies modifying it to reflect the improved method. Until then, the standard is viewed as the optimum approach for performing the task or process.

Standardization was the objective of the Brake/Torque Tube and Wheel Look Forward® teams when they evaluated their manufacturing processes. Special acknowledgment is given to Gary Svoboda of Industrial Engineering, who made this Look Forward® improvement effort possible.

The objective of this effort was to standardize the processing of the wheel details, torque tubes, and brakes in order to minimize the number of movements and travel distance for those parts.

Wheel Details

Prior to the processing standardization effort, the inspection area for wheels as well as brakes and torque tubes was in a central location surrounded by manufacturing cells. In an effort to streamline the process and more closely intertwine in-process inspection with manufacturing, three satellite inspection stations were established adjacent to the respective manufacturing cells. Moving the inspection operation to occur immediately after machining and debur incorporated immediate recognition and prevention of quality problems and avoidance of the extended cycles associated with the material review board and rework/repair process. Although the primary purpose of the satellite inspection stations was improved quality, there were plenty of logistics benefits as well. The yearly mileage of a wheel detail decreased from 968.5 to 891.2 miles, an 8.0% reduction. At the same time, the number of times a year the containers transporting the parts were moved decreased by 203 or 1.6%. In addition, the variable transports were reduced from 167 to 149. These numbers do not include the reduction in material review board traffic, which was significant due to the improved quality.

The processing standardization effort was performed on the wheel detail commodity type after the above improvements were implemented. The processing for wheel details was standardized by making the operations uniform, thus making the flow of material through the wheel cells consistent and easier to manage. The benefits realized from this effort are as follows:

- Reduced wheel detail yearly mileage an additional 27.7 miles or 2.9% while eliminating another 504 movements, representing 4.1%, made by the transportation containers
- Variable transports reduced from 149 to 107, where stronger relationships for process flow analysis have now been formed and better references for layout adjustment are given

In summary, the effort of the Wheel Detail Look Forward® Team resulted in the following benefits:

■ Yearly product miles reduced by 105 miles or 10.8%
■ Transportation container moves reduced by 706 or 5.7%
■ Variable transports reduced by 60 or 35.9%
■ Overall quality improvement

Torque Tubes and Brakes

Similar types of activities took place for the torque tube and brake commodities. The results of those activities for torque tubes are as follows:

■ Number of processes (51 torque tubes)
  □ *Strongly linked to product flow and process traceability*
  □ Before: 46 different processes
  □ After: 23 different processes
  □ 50.0% reduction
■ Variables (part traveling from/to)
  □ *Strongly linked to work center queuing and product management*
  □ Before: 117 variables
  □ After: 77 variables
  □ 35.3% reduction
■ Transportation container mileage
  □ Before: 858.2 yearly miles (1.83 miles per container)
  □ After: 749.7 yearly miles (1.60 miles per container)
  □ 12.7% reduction
■ Tow motor moves
  □ This was a direct result of moving torque tube identification into the cell either by etching on the machine or having the operator stamp parts within their run cycle, plus the removal of excess degrease operations
  □ Before: 9673 yearly moves
  □ After: 8952 yearly moves
  □ 7.5% reduction

The results of those activities for brakes are as follows:

■ Tow motor moves reduced by 21%
■ Material movement variables reduced from 97 to 68
■ Brake yearly mileage reduced by 33.2 miles or 14.5%

The following Lean, Six Sigma, or Theory of Constraints tools were used:

- Brainstorming
- Mistake proofing
- Process flow map

SUMMARY

The tools utilized in these improvement efforts were either one of the seven quality tools or from one of the three continuous improvement methodologies. The studies are not about the tools but rather about the permanent improvement teams that utilize them.

One objective of Toyota is to foster a climate in the workplace that supports employees working there for a long period of time. This is done for a variety of reasons. It is clear that the benefits derived from a stable workforce that has longevity are significant in terms of managing the value stream. Because ABSC is fortunate to have a labor turnover rate of 0.3%, the benefits of a stable workforce are reinforced even more so in the context of permanent Look Forward® teams. ABSC personnel have been empowered to manage and improve their value stream over the long haul. The result is ongoing, continuous improvement that requires minimal intervention on the part of management to maintain its momentum.

ENTERPRISE-LEVEL IMPROVEMENT INITIATIVES

It seems that everyone these days is in the process of trying to transfer the improvement methodologies they have used in manufacturing to the office environment. Aircraft Braking Systems Corporation (ABSC) is no exception. The low-hanging fruit of years gone by in the manufacturing sector seems plentiful in the white-collar environment. ABSC's efforts in the office thus far have been targeted and specific. The company is just at the beginning stages of expanding continuous improvement across the entire enterprise.

ABSC is rolling this out across the enterprise within the context of its Look Forward® management system. Undertaking enterprise-wide improvement without a holistic management system already in place seems nearly impossible to me. If you want to ingrain improvement into the culture such that it is a way of life and not a project, then you must institutionalize a holistic continuous improvement management method. Whether you do it first or follow up with it — just do it.

In this chapter, I will share with you a few examples of the white-collar improvement activities that ABSC has embarked upon to date. We will explore some activities that branched across the supply chain and examine some lessons learned that may be of benefit to you.

Three examples will be addressed in this chapter:

1. A Look Forward® effort to reduce or eliminate delinquencies of military shipments
2. A concurrent engineering effort to reduce the product development cycle
3. A Look Forward® effort that streamlined the supply chain interaction

CASE STUDY 1:
A LOOK FORWARD® EFFORT TO REDUCE OR ELIMINATE DELINQUENCIES OF MILITARY SHIPMENTS

In the aircraft braking business, there are two primary governing bodies that oversee the activities of manufacturers in order to assure that products being produced are airworthy. The Federal Aviation Administration (FAA) oversees the commercial aircraft side of the business. Its mandates originate from Washington, D.C., and the FAA enforces them through representatives in district offices throughout the country. The governing office for ABSC is in Cleveland, Ohio, and the company has frequent interaction with the assigned representatives. The nature of business with the FAA typically deals with the assurance of ABSC's ability to comply with the airworthiness regulations. Business-oriented issues such as on-time delivery are normally addressed by the final customer and not the FAA.

The Defense Contract Management Agency (DCMA) oversees the military aircraft side of the business. ABSC is one of the more significant defense contractors in its region and therefore has several defense contract administrators on-site at its facility. The DCMA's mandates also originate from Washington, D.C., and it enforces them through the resident defense contract administrators. The resident defense representative's role is slightly different than that of the FAA district representative. The defense representative not only oversees compliance to military regulations but also acts on behalf of the end customer. Hence, business-related issues such as on-time delivery are also of concern to the defense contract administrator.

Nowadays, ABSC works very closely with its defense contract administrators to quickly identify issues that impact the customer and to continuously improve them. However, back in 1999, it was evident that ABSC had taken its eye off the ball for a while in terms of military shipments. It was apparent in the percentage of military shipments that were delinquent. The percentage of military shipments that were delinquent in 1999 was 15.14%. At that time, there was no concerted effort to manage delinquent military shipments at ABSC. As a result, the 1999 figure of 15.14% grew to 17.5% by February 2000. This metric sounded a loud siren for help. As a result, the management review team chartered a Military Delivery Performance Look Forward® Team to focus on this process and its improvement.

The resident customer representatives were just as aware of the issues with delivery performance and became intimately involved with the activities of the Military Delivery Performance Look Forward® Team. It was an asset having them reside at the facility in order to facilitate acquiescence to the voice of the customer.

The team was comprised of individuals involved with military (and commercial) orders, and their focus was on issues and processes that impacted the delinquency of military deliveries. The team brought in other functional organizations whenever needed to address specific issues. Given the difficulty over the past couple of years of achieving even mediocre performance in military delivery performance, the asset of a cross-functional team directed by the company's management review team was invaluable. As with any Look Forward® team, the Military Delivery Performance Team established goals, milestones, and measurements to improve the unacceptable upward trend of military delinquency. The team members were from various functional areas:

- Packaging specialist
- Manager, contract management
- Production control planner
- Manager, receiving
- Contract administrator
- Manager, procurement

The DCMA representatives were not permanent team members, but since they were on-site and readily accessible, their input and comments flowed freely into the activities of the team. In order to further assure that the voice of the customer was being heard, monthly meetings were established between the resident DCMA representatives, the Military Delivery Performance Look Forward® Team, and the management review team. The agenda of these meetings was to review the activities of the Military Delivery Performance Look Forward® Team, which were focussed on the elimination of delinquencies.

The cross-functional Look Forward® team met and brainstormed issues that impacted the company's ability to meet customers' expectations of delivery performance. In addition, the team did an analysis of the entire value stream of the military sales order process. Based on the output of the brainstorming session and the evaluation of the military sales order value stream, the team broke down the dominant issues that impacted delivery performance into three primary categories:

1. Enterprise resource planning system issues
2. Communication issues that affect delivery performance
3. Voice of the customer issues that are not heard or acted upon

As a result of the brainstorming session, the following enterprise resource planning system issues were identified:

- There is an identified need to create a military delinquency backlog report showing actual contractual delinquency date, priority rating, and higher visibility.
- Reprogram the delivery creation procedure so that material is allocated to ship in the correct line item sequence.
- Change the order entry procedure so that product distribution has visibility into the quantity variance (e.g., ±10).
- Add the contractual due date from the sales order to the shipping instruction's text field for better visibility to product distribution.
- Update the MRP controller codes to identify the responsible planner.
- Have MIS create usable "action notices," which will serve as a visual factory application enabling all parties to react accordingly to overcome specific issues that impact delivery.

As a result of the brainstorming session, the following communication issues were identified:

- Contract administrators need to receive from planning early notification of delays on actual or potential delinquent orders.
- There needs to be improved communication between planners and contract administrators on identifying the reason for delinquency.
- The team needs to utilize the military backlog report along with weekly and monthly meetings to enable the systematic review of orders and proactive monitoring of them.
- Up-front quoting needs to be supported such that there is integration between contracts/operations/capacity and resource planning in order to assure adequate lead times.

As a result of the brainstorming session, the following voice of the customer issue was identified:

- Continuous communication with the DCMA on-site representatives to provide the needed information for delinquent-rated orders.

In addition to these primary categories of issues to be addressed, the team identified some general recommendations that would have a positive impact on military delivery performance:

- Continue a high level of interaction between the team and the resident DCMA representatives.

- Continue monthly planner/contract administrator meetings utilizing the monthly military delinquency backlog report.
- Each individual buyer needs to review the military delinquency backlog report and respond appropriately.
- Implement the "action notice" procedure in procurement to effectively eliminate delinquencies that are attributed to procured material.
- Develop a report that will provide greater visibility of delinquent issues that are associated with the receiving process.

The cross-functional Look Forward® team met weekly to focus on the previously mentioned issues (enterprise resource planning, communication, and voice of the customer). The team's direct association with the resident DCMA representatives was critical in the execution phase of the improvement project. With a partnering effort across the demand chain, the team was effective in achieving significant improvement in the delivery performance of military shipments. Figure 9-1 illustrates the progressive improvement that the team achieved after implementing the ideas that were mutually agreed upon between the team and the customer.

This demand chain Look Forward® effort was successful in driving a 17.5% delinquency rate in military shipments down to 0% delinquencies. It took the team a year to achieve this level of performance, but once the necessary process discipline was determined, this level of performance soon became the new status quo.

That really is the key to any improvement effort — being able to "see" those activities that are wasteful and eliminating them, such that exceptional performance becomes the expectation.

The following Lean, Six Sigma, or Theory of Constraints tools were used by the Military Delivery Performance Look Forward® Team:

- Brainstorming
- Mistake proofing
- Process flow map

CASE STUDY 2:
CONCURRENT ENGINEERING AND
THE PRODUCT DEVELOPMENT CYCLE

These days, much continuous improvement energy is focused on transforming the processes in the office environment. The same improvement tools that have been successful in the manufacturing sector are equally applicable to the office.

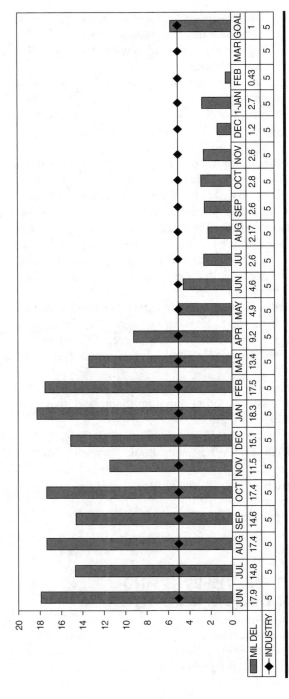

Figure 9-1. Delivery performance of military shipments. (Courtesy of Aircraft Braking Systems Corporation.)

One office process transformation that many companies have already adopted is concurrent engineering. ABSC is no exception. It implemented a concurrent engineering approach to product development in 1997. Since then, it has recognized significant reductions in the product development cycle, enabling the company to bring a new product into production faster than ever before. The time it takes to bring a new product on-line is a fraction of what it was before concurrent engineering was implemented.

The team members for the concurrent engineering effort represented various areas key to the process:

- Program operations
- Product support
- Research and technology
- Financial and price analysis
- Information technology
- Customer support
- Quality engineering
- Production administration
- Product design

Figure 9-2 illustrates the cellular arrangement that was created in the office environment in order to facilitate the interaction among all product development stakeholders.

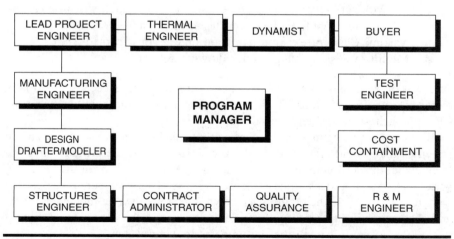

Figure 9-2.   Office cellular arrangement for Concurrent Engineering Product Development Team. (Courtesy of Aircraft Braking Systems Corporation.)

The team had a clear and concise mission with three primary areas of focus:

- Reduce time to market
- Minimize manufacturing and total life cycle costs
- Synchronize cross-functional area work efforts

The first activity that the team set out to accomplish was to map the current state of the product development process. The flow of the process was evaluated from the initial request for proposal all the way through the delivery of flight test hardware. During this evaluation, nonvalue-added activities were identified and opportunities for improvement were noted.

In an effort to empower the team members as much as possible with the skills to implement concurrent engineering, they all participated in a variety of learning exercises prior to implementation. These activities entailed reading the most recent literature on concurrent engineering, attending seminars on how to implement concurrent engineering, and visiting companies that were doing concurrent engineering to learn from existing best practices.

The corporate goals for the project of implementing concurrent engineering were defined at the very beginning of the project:

- Develop the team concept approach to the design process
- Improve communication between functional areas
- Eliminate process redundancies and nonvalue-added steps
- Develop up-front design strategy, objectives, and cost targets
- Obtain design input earlier in the design effort
  - □ More effective integration of manufacturing, quality assurance, and supplier input/involvement during the design process
- Maximize use of existing hardware and lessons learned
- Minimize design changes after drawing release

This was an aggressive set of goals for the team to achieve because it initially required some inroads to be made in changing the corporate culture from the silo approach to cross-functional design.

The team members met regularly as a group and brainstormed various kaizen activities that would contribute to the transformation of the product development cycle. In addition to these regular team meetings, portions of the team met periodically in subprocess-focused kaizen efforts. The three subprocesses that were focused on were the preliminary drawing system, the one-model approach, and cost/estimating integration. Let's look at some of the activities of each of the subteams, starting with the preliminary drawing system.

Preliminary Drawing System

A preliminary drawing release system was essential to eliminating a significant number of wasteful steps in the design process flow because it would enable much of the concurrent activity across engineering disciplines to take place. Thus, one of the first deliverables of this subprocess team was the implementation of a new drawing release system. Some of the issues that were addressed within this system are:

- Define the roles of each team member during the drawing process
- Provide all team members with visibility into the drawing release schedule
- Require all drawings to be approved by all team members and released prior to the start of production or the release of any supplier purchase orders
- Utilize the periodic team meeting to increase up-front communication and functional input
- Streamline the drawing release and drawing change notice procedure
  - □ Reduce required signatures to those on the team and minimize the time required to release drawings
  - □ Hold a meeting where all team members come together to sign off on drawings in a cell arrangement, as opposed to a serial handoff from one member to another
- Once the improvements to the process have been identified and agreed upon, change the standard work to reflect these changes (in this case, the standard work is the engineering operations procedure for the product development cycle)

One-Model Approach

CATIA models have literally had a breakthrough effect on the product development life cycle. They have added an aspect of portability to engineering design that facilitates expeditious transfer of knowledge and sharing of information. A specific ABSC application of modeling will be addressed in the next case study, but for now let's take a look at some of the general benefits generated from the 3D model:

- Design engineering uses the model to establish design features and required weights
- Structures uses the model to perform finite element modeling and thermal and vibration evaluations

- Procurement uses the model for supplier price quotations and the supplier selection process
- Manufacturing and quality assurance use the model for tooling and inspections

All of this contributes to reducing design time and analysis time while achieving a higher level of quality in the final design. These aspects of the modeling approach are documented in standard work in order to assure consistent application of the methodology. As with the preliminary design system, documentation of the modeling process is done in an engineering operations procedure. This standard work will also serve as a baseline for future improvements in the modeling approach.

Cost/Estimating Integration

In the old approach to product development, all of the design and manufacturing processing was determined in sequential order before cost management even got involved. In the concurrent engineering world, cost containment and management are integrated into every step of the new product development flow. This input is valuable in that it redirects a particular approach because of its impact on the overall cost.

This process flow permits an ongoing interaction to take place among all functional representatives so as to foster a sense of camaraderie while minimizing the amount of waste in the process. The bottom line is that it has resulted in an 80% reduction in product development cycle time and an overall reduction in project costs. The first program that went through the concurrent engineering approach came in at 20% below the target costs, and these savings are now expected outcomes for all programs.

The following Lean, Six Sigma, or Theory of Constraints tools were used by the Concurrent Engineering Product Development Team:

- Brainstorming
- Mistake proofing
- Process flow map
- Kaizen

CASE STUDY 3:
MODELING AND THE SUPPLY CHAIN

In 1990, ABSC started using modeling as an aide to the design process. At first, the tool was used specifically to help facilitate the drafting/design function.

Since then, it has evolved into a key tool for streamlining the supply chain process. The innovation of modeling software alone was responsible for process improvements in the drafting and design functions. It enabled processes to be done faster and better.

The impact that modeling had on the drafting process is similar to the impact the latest machinery would have on the production process. The analysis that was performed when considering utilization of modeling was no different as well. What impact will it have on throughput? What impact will it have on the quality of the output? What effect will it have on operating cost? I mention this to illustrate the point that a process is a process, whether it occurs on the factory floor or in the office environment. The challenge for all of us is to be able to see the office activities as processes with defined inputs and outputs that have perceived performance expectations.

One opportunity for process improvement that ABSC was able to "see" was in the supply chain, in particular, information transfer between ABSC and its two primary forging suppliers. A number of benefits resulted from modeling internally, including:

- Models enable higher quality parts because they are optimized for weight reduction and strength through finite element analysis.
- Models provide parts that are easier to manufacture. An NC programmer can study the finished model and provide feedback to the designer with changes that will allow more efficient techniques.
- With CATIA, drawing graphics are generated from and associated to the 3D model. When the model changes, the graphics of the drawing are updated automatically.
- In assemblies, models allow checking for fits and clearances between parts.
- Models provide accurate weight estimates.
- End customers require models in order to verify fit with mating components. Often, the entire aircraft is assembled in a virtual world.
- In the future, the tool paths on machine centers will be generated from a model.

All this benefited the company, but even greater gains were obtainable by having forging suppliers partner with ABSC in this information transfer process. In the days before modeling, ABSC would provide the forging supplier with a drawing and instructions to make the forging to the print. This kicked off the traditional activities in the supplier's facility in order to fabricate the desired forging. Once the supplier produced the part, it was inspected using traditional layout techniques and/or standard measuring equipment. All of this has changed in the modeling world.

In summary, modeling was a Look Forward® improvement effort that reduced lead time for the product development cycle and forging supplier manufacturing. It also eliminated numerous nonvalue-added activities and motions for ABSC and its suppliers.

The following Lean, Six Sigma, or Theory of Constraints tools were used in modeling:

- Brainstorming
- Mistake proofing
- Kaizen

CONCLUSION

This is one of the most exciting times to be involved in business — any business. The continuous improvement tools and the management philosophies being practiced these days are light-years ahead of their predecessors. Or are they? Recall the discussion in Chapter 2 when we reviewed the teachings of two of the quality pillars of this century, Dr. Deming and Dr. Juran. Their 14 principles espoused the need for management's direct involvement in the business of improvement instead of merely providing lip service.

Dr. Deming also preached that PDCA was a key element of any effective management system. Recall that in its early years, Toyota studied American manufacturers and thought leaders. It adopted Dr. Deming's philosophy on PDCA, and today PDCA is considered to be the DNA of the Toyota Production System.

While Toyota practices the Toyota Production System, many other companies follow the structure outlined in the 2000 version of the ISO 9000 international standard. The objective of any global management structure is to foster a culture that assures successful execution of the business objectives and enables a pursuit of continuous improvement. Many claim that ISO 9000:2000 can charter the path that enables a business to recognize this objective. I concur.

You do not have to look very far to see Dr. Deming's influence in the ISO 9000:2000 standard. In Chapter 2, we saw that PDCA is also a key proponent of ISO 9000:2000. When executed to the fullest intent of its authors, it promotes a culture that fosters ongoing continuous improvement. It seems to me that there is not much departure between the teachings of Dr. Deming, the Toyota Production System, and ISO 9000:2000. The silver bullet, then, is not something that is elusive and mystical, but rather is simplistic. It comes down to execution.

So what are the obstacles that prevent us from executing the tasks at hand? Why don't we all adopt the Nike slogan for every task we are chartered with and "Just Do It"? Larry Bossidy and Ram Charan wrote an entire book on execution.[1] It is an excellent read, and the following execution building blocks resonate from its pages: the essential behaviors needed in leadership, creating the framework for cultural change, and having the right people in the right places. To change a business culture from one that is nonexecuting to one that executes without even thinking about it takes hard work and emotional fortitude. Bossidy and Charan identify four core qualities that are necessary elements of emotional fortitude: authenticity, self-awareness, self-mastery, and humility. You will not be able to lead your people to excel as never before if you rely on smoke and mirrors. A leader needs to be the real deal.

Jim Collins echoes some of these same thoughts in his book entitled *Good to Great*,[2] which outlines some of the characteristics of companies that made the leap from being "good" to being "great." In terms of leadership, people, and culture, he has the following to say:

> We were surprised, shocked really, to discover the type of leadership required for turning a good company into a great one. Compared to high-profile leaders with big personalities who make headlines and become celebrities, the good-to-great leaders seem to have come from Mars. Self-effacing, quiet, reserved, even shy — these leaders are a paradoxical blend of personal humility and professional will. They are more like Lincoln and Socrates than Patton or Caesar.
>
> We expected that good-to-great leaders would begin by setting a new vision and strategy. We found instead that they *first* got the right people on the bus, the wrong people off the bus, and the right people in the right seats — and *then* they figured out where to drive it. The old adage "People are your most important asset" turns out to be wrong. People are *not* your most important asset. The *right* people are.
>
> All companies have a culture, some companies have discipline, but few companies have a *culture of discipline*. When you have disciplined people, you don't need hierarchy. When you have disciplined thought, you don't need bureaucracy. When you have disciplined action, you don't need excessive controls. When you combine a culture of discipline with an ethic of entrepreneurship, you get the magical alchemy of great performance.

All of these arguments about the necessary ingredients for achieving success support the need for a holistic management system. The Toyota Production

System does it for Toyota, and Look Forward® does it for Aircraft Braking Systems Corporation (ABSC). Management needs to lead, not merely manage. That entails establishing the vision for the company and practicing principled leadership to earn the trust and respect of those who should follow. One aspect of this vision must be the continuous fostering of a corporate culture that expects and promotes ongoing continuous improvement. Lastly, empower those on the front lines to unleash their creative capacities for achievement beyond their wildest expectations.

In my discussions with a number of representatives from Boeing, it was interesting to learn that it took the company 22 days to process a 737 through its final assembly process using the traditional way of assembling planes. When Boeing employees first started to brainstorm about what could be done to make the final assembly process faster, there were plenty of naysayers who in essence said that *there was no possible way to assemble a plane any quicker.* Thank goodness the naysayers did not prevail. The possibility thinkers knew there was a way; the only challenge was finding it. They did find a way at Boeing, and it came in the form of a totally different processing method. As we saw in Chapter 1, Boeing now assembles planes in a moving assembly line. As a result, it can now make a plane in 11 days instead of the previous 22 — half the time. That is what is possible with an empowered workforce that is driven to continuously improve.

The critical piece to this whole puzzle is the characteristics of your people. The analytical part is easy compared to figuring out how to optimize all of the unique traits that each person brings to the table. The vision of where to go is clear. Getting there most likely will require some change to occur, maybe in leadership traits or maybe in effective team execution. Change is definitely not easy.

Even though ABSC has been practicing Look Forward® for the last 10 years, there is still a long way to go to get to where the company would like to be. ABSC is confident that it will get there because it has the structure in place to support ongoing improvement. It is expected now and is part of the culture. ABSC's people make it happen with management's facilitation.

Look Forward® is the ABSC way. It flourishes in an ISO 9000 type of environment. It is results oriented and driven by the metrics that impact the business. Every company mentioned in this book that is a leader in its industry has found its own way to manage continuous improvement. A common theme from most is a holistic management approach that is driven by metrics that impact the business. Find your own way within the context of your own culture.

Hopefully, this book has given you some ideas about the ABSC Look Forward® approach or any other improvement method that may be of some benefit to you in your improvement journey. I wish you well!

RESOURCES

ORGANIZATIONS

Duggan & Associates Inc.
308 Cowesett Avenue, West Warwick, RI 02893
Phone: 401-826-2007, fax: 401-826-8684
http://www.dugganinc.com/home.htm

The Lean Aerospace Initiative
77 Massachusetts Avenue, Room 41-205, Cambridge, MA 02139
Phone: 617-253-7633, fax: 617-258-7845
http://lean.mit.edu/

Lean Construction Institute
Gregory A. Howell, P.E., Box 1003, Ketchum, ID 83340
Phone: 208-726-9989, fax: 707-248-1369
http://www.leanconstruction.org/

The Lean Enterprise Institute
P.O. Box 9, Brookline, MA 02446
Phone: 617-713-2900, fax: 617-713-2999
http://www.lean.org/

Lean Productivity Systems
Member TWI Network, A Division of Zero Loss Quality Systems
P.O. Box 73589, 509 St. Clair Avenue West, Toronto, ON M6C 1C0
Phone: 416-424-3056, fax: 416-424-2245
http://thedennisgroup.com/lean/

The Manufacturing Performance Institute
2835 Sedgewick Road, Shaker Heights, OH 44120
Phone: 216-991-8390, fax: 216-991-8205
http://www.mpi-group.net

Michigan Engineering Center for Professional Development
Professional Development Programs
2401 Plymouth Road, Suite A, Ann Arbor, MI 48105-2193
Phone: 734-647-7200, fax: 734-998-6127
http://cpd.engin.umich.edu/

National Institute of Standards and Technology
Manufacturing Extension Partnership
100 Bureau Drive, Stop 4800, Gaithersburg, MD 20899-3460
Phone: 301-975-5020
http://www.mep.nist.gov

Six Sigma Academy
Americas: 8876 East Pinnacle Peak Road, Suite 100, Scottsdale, AZ 85255
European headquarters: Ettore-Bugatti-Strasse 6-14, 51149 Koln, Germany
United Kingdom: The Coach House, Nowhurst Lane, Horsham, West Sussex
    RH12 3PJ, United Kingdom
France: 45 Allée des Ormes, E Space Batiment C, Parc de Sophia Antipolis,
    06250 MOUGINS, France
Phone: United States, Canada, Mexico 480-515-9501; Germany +49 2203 890
    3600; United Kingdom +44 1403 783456; France +33 4 93 74 91 34
Fax: United States, Canada, Mexico 480-515-9507; Germany +49 2203 890
    3605; United Kingdom +44 1403 218788; France +33 4 93 95 02 85
http://www.6-sigma.com/

SUGGESTED READING

Six Sigma

Six Sigma for Everyone by George Eckes
Good introductory book for people with no prior knowledge

The Six Sigma Way by Peter S. Pande
Good overview of what Six Sigma is and how large companies are using it

Implementing Six Sigma by Forest W. Breyfogle
Good detailed implementation book if you have a background in statistics

New Six Sigma by Matt Barney
Good management coverage of how Six Sigma is being used at Motorola

Six Sigma for Small and Mid-Sized Organizations by Terence Burton and Jeff Sams
Good scaleable implementation guide for any size organization

Six Sigma Producibility Analysis and Process Characterization by Mikel Harry
Good coverage of statistical process control

Vision of Six Sigma by Mikel Harry
Good project-based deployment

Lean Manufacturing

The Lean Manufacturing Pocket Handbook by Kenneth Dailey
Good primer for basic concepts

The Machine That Changed the World by James Womack, Daniel Jones, and Daniel Roos
Good historical coverage of Lean in the auto industry

Lean Thinking: Banish Waste and Create Wealth in Your Corporation by James Womack and Daniel Jones
Good conceptual and philosophy book

Lean Manufacturing Implementation: A Complete Execution Manual for Any Size Manufacturer by Dennis Hobbs
Good implementation guide

Becoming Lean: Inside Stories of U.S. Manufacturers by Jeffrey Liker
Good case study book

Dynamics of Profit-Focused Accounting: Attaining Sustained Value and Bottom-Line Improvement by C. Lynn Northrup
Good Lean accounting book that integrates Theory of Constraints, Lean, Six Sigma, and other methods

The Lean Extended Enterprise: Moving Beyond the Four Walls to Value Stream Excellence by Terence Burton and Steven Boeder
Good total value chain book that integrates other methods

The Toyota Way: 14 Management Principles from the World's Greatest Manufacturer by Jeffrey Liker
Good principles and Lean culture book

Lean Manufacturing That Works: Powerful Tools for Dramatically Reducing Waste and Maximizing Profits by Bill Carreira
Good Lean teams book

Quantum Leap: Next Generation by Dean Gilliam and Steve Taylor-Jones
Good real-time technology book that integrates Lean, Theory of Constraints, and Sales and Operations Planning

Theory of Constraints

The Goal by Eli Goldratt
Good introductory executive novel that makes a strong case for the value of Theory of Constraints

Theory of Constraints by Eli Goldratt
Good conceptual book

Viable Vision: Transforming Total Sales into Net Profits by Gerald Kendall
Fully evolved Theory of Constraints as a profitable business strategy with coverage of its various applications

Thinking for a Change: Putting the TOC Thinking Processes to Use by Lisa Schneikopf
Presents all the Theory of Constraints thinking tools

Management Dilemmas: The Theory of Constraints Approach to Problem Identification and Solutions by Eli Schragenheim
Good case study book

Securing the Future: Strategies for Exponential Growth Using the Theory of Constraints by Gerald Kendall
Presents a full set of Theory of Constraints logic trees

The Measurement Nightmare: How the Theory of Constraints Can Resolve Conflicting Strategies, Policies and Measures by Debra Smith
Good Theory of Constraints metrics book

Dynamics of Profit-Focused Accounting: Attaining Sustained Value and Bottom-Line Improvement by C. Lynn Northrup
Good throughput accounting book

Manufacturer's Guide to Implementing the Theory of Constraints by Mark Woeppel
Good implementation guide for manufacturing

Critical Chain by Eli Goldratt
Good Theory of Constraints/project management conceptual book

Project Management in the Fast Lane: Applying the Theory of Constraints by Robert Newbold
Good how-to book for Theory of Constraints/project management single project

Advanced Project Portfolio Management and the PMO: Multiplying ROI at Warp Speed by Gerald Kendall and Steven Rollins
Good application to full portfolio of projects and use with a project management office

Manufacturing at Warp Speed: Optimizing Supply Chain Financial Performance by Eli Schragenheim and William Dettmer
Good application to supply chain

Goldratt's Theory of Constraints: A Systems Approach to Continuous Improvement by William Dettmer
Good explanation of Theory of Constraints principles (drum-buffer-rope)

The World of the Theory of Constraints: A Review of the International Literature by Victoria Mabin and Steven Balderstone
Bibliography of international literature on Theory of Constraints, including books, white papers, and articles

WEBSITES OF INTEREST

www.rogo.com
www.toc-goldratt.com
www.tocinternational.com

BIBLIOGRAPHY

Chapter 1

1. Automotive News Data Center, *2004 Global Market Data Book,* Automotive News Europe, Automotive News Data Center, Auto Resources Asia Ltd. and Marketing Systems GmbH, Munich, Germany, 2004.
2. Ford, H., *Today and Tomorrow,* Doubleday, Page & Company, Garden City, NY, 1926.
3. Hill, M. and Gardner, G., *The Harbour Report North America 2004,* Harbour Consulting, 2004, pp. 28 and 35.
4. Park, A. and Burrows, P., What you don't know about Dell — A look at the management secrets of the best-run company in technology, *Business Week,* November 2003.

Chapter 2

1. Carden, P.D., Aft, L.S., and Dusharme, D., Rating the registrars. Third Annual registrar customer satisfaction survey, *Quality Digest,* July 2001.
2. Deming, W. Edwards, *Out of the Crisis,* The MIT Press, Cambridge, MA, 1982.
3. Fredenberger, W.B., Superville, C.R., and Dusharme, D., Does your registrar measure up? Second annual registrar customer satisfaction survey, *Quality Digest,* July 2000.
4. Juran, J., Leader success factors, excerpted from a 2004 speech given by Dr. Juran, Juran Institute, Southbury, CT, 2004.
5. Juran, J., *Quality Control Handbook,* McGraw-Hill, New York, 1951.
6. Shewhart, W., *Economic Control of Quality of Manufactured Product: 50th Anniversary Commemorative Reissue,* American Society for Quality Control, Milwaukee, 1980.

7. Society of Automotive Engineers, *AS9100 Aerospace Standard,* Society of Automotive Engineers, Warrendale, PA, 2001.

Chapter 3

1. Box, G. and Draper, N., *Evolutionary Operation: A Statistical Method for Process Improvement,* John Wiley & Sons, New York, 1969.
2. Byrne, D. et al., *Taguchi Methods and QFD: Hows and Whys for Management,* The American Supplier Institute, Dearborn, MI, 1988.
3. Cochran, W. and Cox, G., *Experimental Designs,* John Wiley & Sons, New York, 1957.
4. Draper, N. and Smith, H., *Applied Regression Analysis,* John Wiley & Sons, New York, 1981.
5. Eckes, G., *The Six Sigma Revolution,* John Wiley & Sons, New York, 2001.
6. Grant, E. and Leavenworth, R., *Statistical Quality Control,* McGraw-Hill, New York, 1980.
7. Harry, M. and Schroededer, R., *Six Sigma: The Breakthrough Management Strategy Revolutionizing the World's Top Corporations*, Currency, Doubleday, New York, 2000.
8. Kume, H., *Statistical Methods for Quality Improvement,* The Association for Overseas Technical Scholarship, Tokyo, 1985.
9. Lewis, J., *Fundamentals of Project Management: Developing Core Competencies to Help Outperform the Competition,* AMACOM, New York, 2000.
10. Moen, R., Nolan, T., and Provost, L., *Improving Quality through Planned Experimentation,* McGraw-Hill, New York, 1991.
11. Montgomery, D., *Introduction to Statistical Quality Control,* John Wiley & Sons, New York, 1985.
12. Oriel, Inc., *Guiding Successful Six Sigma Projects,* Oriel, Madison, WI, 2000.
13. Ott, E., *Process Quality Control: Troubleshooting and Interpretation of Data,* McGraw-Hill, New York, 1975.
14. Rath & Strong, *Rath & Strong's Six Sigma Pocket Guide,* Rath & Strong Management Consultants, Lexington, MA, 2000.
15. Small, B. et al., *Statistical Quality Control Handbook,* Western Electric Co., Indianapolis, 1956.
16. Snee, R.D., Why should statisticians pay attention to Six Sigma? *Quality Progress,* September 1999.
17. Taguchi, G., *Introduction to Quality Engineering: Designing Quality into Products and Processes,* Asian Productivity Organization, Minato-Ku, Japan, 1986.
18. Taguchi, G., *System of Experimental Design: Engineering Methods to Optimize Quality and Minimize Costs,* UNIPUB/Kraus International Publications, White Plains, NY, 1987.
19. Walpole, R. and Myers, R., *Probability and Statistics for Engineers and Scientists,* Macmillan, New York, 1985.

20. Wortman, B. et al., *The Certified Six Sigma Black Belt Primer,* Quality Council of Indiana, West Terre Haute, 2001.

Chapter 4

1. Burton, T. and Boeder, S., *The Lean Extended Enterprise: Moving Beyond the Four Walls to Value Stream Excellence,* J. Ross Publishing, Boca Raton, FL, 2003.
2. Deming, W. Edwards, *Out of the Crisis,* The MIT Press, Cambridge, MA, 1982.
3. Duggan & Associates, Inc., *Product Quoting Process — Current & Future State Maps,* Dugan & Associates, West Warwick, RI, 2004.
4. Ford, H., *Today and Tomorrow,* Doubleday, Page & Company, Garden City, NY, 1926.
5. Hobbs, D., *Lean Manufacturing Implementation: A Complete Execution Manual for Any Size Manufacturer,* J. Ross Publishing, Boca Raton, FL, 2004.
6. Imai, M., *Gemba Kaizen: A Commonsense, Low-Cost Approach to Management,* McGraw-Hill, New York, 1997.
7. Lean Enterprise Institute, *Value Stream Manager,* reviewed November 15, 2004 from http://www.lean.org.
8. Lean Productivity Systems, *Policy Deployment Process and Worksheet,* Lean Productivity Systems, Toronto, 2003.
9. Liker, J., *The Toyota Way: 14 Management Principles from the World's Greatest Manufacturer,* McGraw-Hill, New York, 2003.
10. MacInnes, R. et al., *The Lean Enterprise Memory Jogger: Create and Eliminate Waste Throughout Your Company,* GOAL/QPC, Salem, NH, 2002.
11. Murman, E. et al., *Lean Enterprise Value: Insights from MIT's Lean Aerospace Initiative,* Palgrave, New York, 2002.
12. Shingo, Shigeo, *Non-Stock Production: The Shingo System for Continuous Improvement,* Productivity Press, Cambridge, MA, 1988.
13. Suzaki, K., *The New Manufacturing Challenge: Techniques for Continuous Improvement,* The Free Press, New York, 1987.
14. The Five Man Electrical Band, *Signs,* Lionel Entertainment Corporation, New York, 1971.
15. Womack, J., *Lean Thinking: The Next Leap,* reviewed August 11, 2003 from http://www.lean.org, 2000.
16. Womack, J. and Jones, D., *Lean Thinking: Banish Waste and Create Wealth in Your Corporation,* Simon & Schuster, New York, 1996.
17. Womack, J. and Jones, D., *Lean Thinking: Banish Waste and Create Wealth in Your Corporation — Revised and Updated,* The Free Press, New York, 2003.
15. Womack, J., *Lean Thinking: The Next Leap,* reviewed August 11, 2003 from http://www.lean.org, 2000.
18. Womack, J., Jones, D., and Roos, D. *The Machine That Changed the World: The Story of Lean Production,* Harper Collins, New York, 1990.

Chapter 5

1. Corbett, T., *Throughput Accounting,* North River Press, Great Barrington, MA, 1998.
2. Dettmer, W.H., *Goldratt's Theory of Constraints: A Systems Approach to Continuous Improvement,* Quality Press, Milwaukee, 1997.
3. Goldratt, E.M., *The Goal,* North River Press, Great Barrington, MA, 1984.
4. Goldratt, E.M. and Fox, R.E., *The Race,* North River Press, Great Barrington, MA, 1986.
5. Goldratt Marketing Group, *Biography of Eli Goldratt,* http://toc-goldratt.com/index.php?cont=21.
6. Kendall, G., *Viable Vision: Transforming Total Sales into Net Profits,* J. Ross Publishing, Boca Raton, FL, 2005.
7. Mabin, V.J. and Balderstone, S.J., *The World of the Theory of Constraints: A Review of the International Literature,* St. Lucie Press, Boca Raton, FL, 2000.
8. Management Coaching & Training Services, *The Theory of Constraints Summary,* reviewed August 11, 2003 from http://www.mcts.com/Theory-of-Constraints.html.

Chapter 6

1. Covey, S., *The 7 Habits of Highly Effective People: Powerful Lessons in Personal Change,* Simon & Schuster, New York, 1989.
2. Johnson, S. and Blanchard, K., *The One Minute Manager,* Blanchard Family Partnership and Candle Communications Corporation, New York, 1981.
3. Johnson, S. and Blanchard, K., *Who Moved My Cheese? An Amazing Way to Deal With Change in Your Work and in Your Life,* Putnam Pub Group, New York, 1998.
4. Robustelli, Pete, Beyond Six Sigma: Exploring the boundaries of the popular change initiative, *Quality Digest,* September 2003.
5. Smalley, G. and Trent, J., *The Two Sides of Love,* Tindale House Publishing, Wheaton, IL, 1999.
6. Womack, J.P., Lean Thinking: The Next Leap, presented at the Association for Manufacturing Excellence, November 2000.
7. Womack, J. and Jones, D., *Lean Thinking: Banish Waste and Create Wealth in Your Corporation — Revised and Updated,* The Free Press, New York, 2003.

Chapter 7

1. Brassard, M. et al. *The Team Memory Jogger,* GOAL/QPC, Methuen, MA, 1995.
2. Champy, J., *Reengineering Management: The Mandate for New Leadership,* Harper Collins, New York, 1995.
3. Hammer, M and Champy, J., *Reengineering the Corporation: A Manifesto for Business Revolution,* Harper Collins, New York, 2001.
4. Harper, Ann and Harper, Bob, *Skill-Building for Self-Directed Team Members: A Complete Course,* MW Corporation, New York, 1992.

5. Smalley, G. and Trent, J., *The Two Sides of Love,* Tindale House Publishing, Wheaton, IL, 1999.
6. The Manufacturing Performance Institute, *MPI Industry Week Magazine 2003 Census of Manufacturers*, The MPI Group, Shaker Heights, OH, 2004.
7. Webster, Noah, *Webster's Third New International Dictionary,* G&C Merriam Company, Springfield, MA, 1971.

Chapter 8

1. Imai, M., *Gemba Kaizen: A Commonsense, Low-Cost Approach to Management,* McGraw-Hill, New York, 1997.

Chapter 10

1. Bossidy, L. and Charan, R., *Execution: The Discipline of Getting Things Done,* Crown Business, New York, 2002.
2. Collins, J., *Good to Great: Why Some Companies Make the Leap and Others Don't,* Harper Collins, New York, 2001.

INDEX